JOHN RUSKIN
and the Victorian Eye

JOHN RUSKIN
and the Victorian Eye

With Essays by Susan P. Casteras, Susan Phelps Gordon, Anthony Lacy Gully, Robert Hewison, George P. Landow, and Christopher Newall

Harry N. Abrams, Inc., Publishers, in association with the Phoenix Art Museum

EDITOR: *Harriet Whelchel*
DESIGNER: *Darilyn Lowe Carnes*

Library of Congress Cataloging-in-Publication Data

John Ruskin and the Victorian eye / with essays by Susan P. Casteras . . . [et al.].
    p.   cm.
  Publication commemorating the exhibition "The art of seeing: John Ruskin and
the Victorian eye," organized by the Phoenix Art Museum and presented at
Phoenix and at the Indianapolis Museum of Art in 1993.
  Includes bibliographical references and index.
  ISBN 0–8109–3766–2 (Abrams)—ISBN 0–910407–27–4 (museum pbk.)
  1. Ruskin, John, 1819–1900—Criticism and interpretation. 2. Perception.
3. Art criticism—England—History—19th century. I. Casteras, Susan P.
II. Phoenix Art Museum. III. Indianapolis Museum of Art.
N7483.R8J64 1993
709'.2—dc20   92–30289
                                          CIP

Published in 1993 by Harry N. Abrams, Incorporated, New York
A Times Mirror Company

Printed in Japan

Frontispiece:
Figure 1
JOHN RUSKIN (1819–1900)
Self-Portrait with Blue Neckcloth. 1873
Watercolor, 13⅞ × 20″
The Pierpont Morgan Library, New
York; Gift of the Fellows, 1959.23

CONTENTS

ACKNOWLEDGMENTS

This publication commemorates the exhibition *The Art of Seeing: John Ruskin and the Victorian Eye*, organized by the Phoenix Art Museum and supported with funds provided by the Flinn Foundation and the National Endowment for the Arts. The exhibition, presented at Phoenix and at the Indianapolis Museum of Art in 1993, involved innumerable individuals. It is impossible here to acknowledge all those who labored on its behalf, but a few must be named. Foremost, we thank James K. Ballinger, Director of the Phoenix Art Museum, whose enthusiasm and assistance never failed at crucial moments. The Flinn Foundation of Arizona, unique in these times of stress for nonprofit cultural organizations in its committment to new and large endeavors, gave the financial catalyst needed to progress from conception to realization.

Linda Marrie, Museum Intern and Research Assistant, and Rosalind Robinson of the Humanities faculty at Arizona State University devoted immense energy and effort to every aspect of the exhibit and publication. Anne Gully edited the diverse texts with speed and efficiency. Members of the Phoenix Art Museum staff who contributed mightily include Heather Northway, Registrar; Brenda Rayman, Assistant Registrar; Janet Hillson, Curatorial Secretary; David Restad, Exhibit Designer and Chief Preparator; Gerald Lindner, Chief of Security; Jan Krulick, Curator of Education; Gail Griffin, Director of Membership; and Margaret Fries, Publicity. We are grateful to those who felt Mr. Ruskin's dominating presence in their homes for several years: Anne and Emma Gully and Andrew, Max, and Elizabeth Gordon.

Valuable scholarly advice and assistance, as well as essays, were provided by Susan P. Casteras, Robert Hewison, George P. Landow, and Christopher Newall. Their interest and enthusiasm were both gratifying and helpful. Alan Staley, Columbia University, and David Stewart, University of Alabama, freely gave of their expertise. Appreciation is also due to Thaïs Morgan, English Department, and Julie Codell, Director of the School of Art, Arizona State University, Tempe.

The success of the exhibition was due to the extraordinary generosity of its lenders. The degree of support from British and American institutions and private lenders is indicated in the objects reproduced. All but twelve of the works of art illustrated were lent to the exhibition, and those twelve are indicated as reference photographs. Special mention must be made of those without whom the exhibition would have been impossible: J. J. L. Whiteley and Catherine Whistler, Ashmolean Museum; Andrew Wilton and Robin Hamlyn, Tate Gallery; Janet Barnes, The Ruskin Gallery, Sheffield; James Dearden, Ruskin Galleries, Bembridge School, and the Education Trust Ltd.; Jane Farrington and Elizabeth Smallwood, Birmingham Museums and Art Gallery; Bret Waller and Martin Krause, Indianapolis Museum of Art; Samuel Sachs and Nancy Shaw, The Detroit Institute of Arts. Altogether, forty-five lenders greeted our inquiries and

Figure 23
JOHN RUSKIN (1819–1900)
Study of Dawn (The First Scarlet in the Clouds). n.d.
Pencil, watercolor, and body color on blue-gray paper, 5½ × 7½"
Ashmolean Museum, Oxford;
Educational Series 3

7

requests kindly, patiently, and cooperatively, and we are deeply grateful to each of the following:

City of Aberdeen Art Gallery and Museum, Scotland
The Visitors of the Ashmolean Museum, Oxford
Birmingham Museum and Art Gallery, England
Museum of Fine Arts, Boston
Bury Art Gallery and Museum, England
Delaware Art Museum
The Detroit Institute of Arts
The Detroit Public Library Rare Books Collection
Education Trust Ltd., Brantwood, Coniston, England
The Syndics of the Fitzwilliam Museum, Cambridge, England
The Fogg Art Museum, Harvard University Art Museums,
        Cambridge, Massachusetts
The FORBES Magazine Collection, New York
Glasgow Art Gallery and Museum
Guildhall Art Gallery, Corporation of London
Harris Museum and Art Gallery, Preston, England
The Trustees, The Cecil Higgins Art Gallery, Bedford, England
Indianapolis Museum of Art
Leeds City Art Galleries
Maier Museum of Art, Randolph-Macon Woman's College, Lynchburg,
        Virginia
Manchester City Art Galleries, England
The Metropolitan Museum of Art, New York
The Minneapolis Institute of Arts
Museo de Arte de Ponce, Luis A. Ferré Foundation, Inc., Puerto Rico
National Gallery of Art, Washington, D. C.
Philadelphia Museum of Art
The Pierpont Morgan Library, New York
Mr. and Mrs. Brian Pilkington
The Art Museum, Princeton University
Ruskin Galleries, Bembridge School, Isle of Wight
The Ruskin Gallery, Sheffield—The Collection of the Guild
        of Saint George
Ruskin Museum, Coniston, England
Santa Barbara Museum of Art
Sheffield City Art Galleries, The Mappin Art Gallery
Spencer Museum of Art, University of Kansas, Lawrence
The Trustees of the Tate Gallery, London
The Toledo Museum of Art
The Trustees of the Victoria and Albert Museum, London
Walker Art Gallery, Liverpool
The Watts Gallery, Compton, England
Wellesley College Library, Special Collections
The Whitworth Art Gallery, University of Manchester, England
Yale Center for British Art
Three Private Collections

Susan Phelps Gordon and Anthony Lacy Gully

INTRODUCTION

Susan Phelps Gordon and Anthony Lacy Gully

In 1877 John Ruskin wrote, "The teaching of Art, as I understand it, is the teaching of all things." (29:86)* Ruskin, a dedicated educator, tirelessly absorbed and imparted vast amounts of information and voiced opinions on subjects as diverse as contemporary art, art history, museums, architecture, historic preservation, literature, mythology, geology, botany, economics, consumerism, labor, and politics in well over two hundred publications. This prolific writer of eloquent prose described the splendors of creation, natural forms and processes, and the achievements of humanity. He also spoke as a polemicist, arguing against the social havoc, vulgarity, and materialism wrought by the Industrial Revolution. Above all, he interpreted for his audience the significance of everything he witnessed, from the resplendent to the abhorrent.

Born in London in 1819, the same year as Queen Victoria, and dying in 1900, Ruskin embodied the Victorian age in his diverse interests, abundant energy, passion for reform, and strong ethical convictions. Those who have condemned the age have also characterized as typically "Victorian" various other aspects of his personality, such as his difficult relationships with women or his scathing remarks against avant-garde art, which resulted in a libel suit brought against him by American artist James Abbott McNeill Whistler in 1878. Although often derided or simply dismissed in the twentieth century, Ruskin was an enormously influential as well as controversial man during his lifetime. The imprint of his mind was felt by individuals as diverse as George Eliot, Charlotte Brontë, Oscar Wilde, William Morris, Leo Tolstoy, Marcel Proust, D. H. Lawrence, and Mahatma Gandhi. Over the last thirty years, Ruskin has become the subject of prodigious scholarship by those who regard him as a fascinating historical personality as well as a pursuasive and sensitive writer, an insightful prophet, and a warrior in artistic, social, and environmental battles that continue to rage.[1]

Daunting as it is in volume and complexity, the essence of Ruskin's thought on art was based on a fundamental premise that knowledge and understanding of nature and humankind's place in it is gained through the act—indeed, the art—of seeing. He believed that his visual exploration gave him an understanding of physical and moral truths that were unseen, forgotten, or simply ignored by all but a few intuitive minds. He hoped to encourage and enable others to behold, as he did, the sanctity of nature as the setting for meaningful human activity. The practice of art sharpened and trained the artist's perceptive ability, but the creation of true art depended on insight. He explained, "You do not see *with* the lens of the eye. You see *through* that, and by means of that, but you see with the soul of the

Figure 3
JOHN RUSKIN (1819–1900)
Study of a Velvet Crab. n.d.
Pencil, watercolor, and body color on blue-gray paper, 12¾ × 9⅝"
Ashmolean Museum, Oxford;
Educational Series 199

In his handbook for novice artists, *The Elements of Drawing* (1857), Ruskin included the following statement: "The whole technical power of painting depends on our recovery of what may be called the *innocence of the eye;* . . . as a blind man would see them if suddenly gifted with sight." (15:27 n.) He felt, however, that the finest art was much more than the mere transcription of physical reality. To him, it was the fullest expression of the relationship of humankind to nature and to God. In its shape, design, and color, a crab, or any natural form, revealed the innate beauty and harmony of creative power.

10

---

* All such citations refer to the *Library Edition of the Collected Works of John Ruskin*, eds. E. T. Cook and A. Wedderburn, 39 vols. (London, 1903–12).

Figure 4
J. M. W. TURNER (1775–1851)
The Devil's Bridge. c. 1804
Watercolor, white crayon, and
scraping, 41¾ × 30⅛"
Yale Center for British Art,
Paul Mellon Fund

Turner was moved by the sublimity of
the precipitous Saint Gotthard Pass,
between Altdorf, Switzerland, and
Bellinzona, Italy. The Devil's Bridge
was its most celebrated feature. He
emphasized its awe-inspiring heights
and sheer cliffs in several watercolors,
the medium in which Ruskin felt the
artist realized his greatest achievements. Turner used various techniques
with ease in this large watercolor:
layered washes, stopping out with a
cloth, a dry brush to achieve texture,
and scraping to emphasize light. The
depth of the abyss is emphasized by a
break in the clouds that reveals snow-
capped peaks in the distance.

eye." (22:194) Inspired vision, embodied in the work of art, informed and
enlightened an attentive, thoughtful audience. Ruskin recognized in the
processes of creation and communication a vital, redemptive power that he
believed to be crucial to human felicity and peace. The fate of any society
rested on its ability to see clearly its relation to nature and to divinity, and
the art of each society was in turn a key to its moral virtue. He insisted that
every nation at every moment in history, including his own, must be judged
by the art it produced.

Ruskin believed that Britain had been blessed with one great artist
in the nineteenth century, Joseph Mallord William Turner. Turner's works
portrayed simultaneously the incidental and the enduring aspects of nature
with truth, clarity, and beauty and, in Ruskin's mind, a nature infused with
human significance. Comparing Turner to popular Old Masters and to
contemporary artists, Ruskin maintained that these others nearly always

Figure 5
JOHN RUSKIN (1819–1900)
Morning in Spring, with Northeast Wind, at Vevay. 1849
Pencil, watercolor, and body color on pale gray paper, $7 \times 10\frac{3}{8}$″
Ashmolean Museum, Oxford;
Educational Series 298(2)

Matthew Arnold, professor of poetry at Oxford, met Ruskin in 1877. He remarked that this description of Vevay from Ruskin's diary, written on Sunday, June 8, 1849, was the finest example of Ruskin's genius as a prose writer: "Such grass, for strength, and height, and loveliness, I never saw—all blue too with masses of salvia, and flamed with gold, yet quiet and solemn in its own green depths; the air was full of the scent of the living grass and the new-mown hay, the sweet breathing of the honeysuckle and narcissus shed upon it at intervals, mixed with the sound of streams, and the clear thrill of birds' voices far away. The sun's rays (as it fell from behind a western cloud) rose gradually up...casting the shadows of the pines far across its avenue of turf—that indescribable turf, soft like some rich, smooth fur, running in bays and inlets and bright straits and shadowy creeks and gulphs [*sic*], in among the forest, calm, upright, unentangled forest, itself scattered in groups like a happy crowd—with isolated tufted trees here and there, and then two or three together, and then many; graceful as clouds in summer sky—no wildness, nor crowding; no withering; each serene in his place and quiet pride. I looked at the slope of distant grass on the hill; and then at the waving heads near me. What a gift of God that is, I thought. Who could have dreamed of such a soft, green, continual, tender clothing for the dark earth—the food of cattle, and of man. Think what poetry has come of its pastoral influence, what happiness from its everyday ministering, what life from its sustenance." (5:xviii)

fell short of Turner's heroic standards. Most perpetuated tired rules of composition and style derived from Renaissance and Baroque art, all too often uninspired and even trivial in theme and content. Ruskin believed that one source of renewal lay in the uniquely modern contribution to the history of art made by Turner and a group of watercolorists who also depicted natural beauty humbly, lovingly, and thoughtfully. Early in his career, he also would see hope in the honesty and seriousness of the Pre-Raphaelite style.

Without exception, Ruskin's literary works were autobiographical, and some understanding of his "brave, unhappy life" is necessary to appreciate his philosophy and his art.[2] Ruskin was born on February 8, 1819, the dutiful, fragile, and only child of prosperous, middle-class parents, John James and Margaret Ruskin. They formed an unusually close family until the deaths of the parents in 1864 and 1871, respectively. The family's wealth allowed Ruskin the independence to pursue his particular talents and interests and to publish his views. Ruskin recalled being adored, guarded, and educated by his father and mother without toys or playmates. Even at an early age, he found solitary comfort and entertainment in the quiet exploration of his surroundings. John James, a partner in a sherry business, read widely and collected watercolors. He encouraged his precocious son's facility with words, urging him to write, and fostered his talent for drawing by providing drawing masters and taking him to exhibitions. When he won the prestigious Newdigate Prize for poetry as a student at the University of Oxford in 1839, Ruskin was already a published author known for his sketches. Margaret, a steadfast Evangelical Anglican, saw her child's future in the Church of England and tutored him thoroughly in biblical text and exegesis. His adoption of the style and didactic message of evangelical sermons defined his moral stance and determined the tone and structure of his writing. Literature and religion remained vital influences in his life, though not exclusively in the ways intended by his parents.

The family traveled extensively in England and on the Continent. With his expectations aroused by books and poetry illustrated by Turner,

Figure 6
SAMUEL PROUT (1783–1852)
Ulm Cathedral, Würtemberg, View of West Front. n.d.
Pencil on cream wove paper with stump and rubbing, 11 × 16½"
By Courtesy of the Board of Trustees of the Victoria and Albert Museum, London

Prout made several drawings in Ulm in 1823, and he published views of that city in his *Views of Germany* (1826), *Facsimiles of Sketches Made in Flanders and Germany* (1833), *Sketches at Home and Abroad* (1844), and other publications. In this large drawing, the weight of dilapidated houses set before the delicate tracery of the cathedral displays Prout's skill at factual documentation. Both he and Ruskin observed another reality: the contrast between earlier splendor and contemporary drabness.

Figure 7
JOHN RUSKIN (1819–1900)
Study of Portal and Carved Pinnacles, Cathedral of Saint Lô, Normandy. 1848
Pencil, brown ink, and brown wash on cream paper, 17⅞ × 12⅞"
The Fogg Art Museum, Harvard University Art Museums; Gift of Samuel Sachs

In Ruskin's essay "The Lamp of Power," in *The Seven Lamps of Architecture*, he recorded his impressions of this late Gothic building with the same relish in its complexity and floral ornamentation that this drawing displays. He enjoyed the excessive flamboyant decoration of Saint Lô: "Granting it, however, to be ugly and wrong, I like sins of this kind, for the sake of the courage it requires to commit them." (8:211) The striving for verticality by the builders, Ruskin believed, was wonderfully realized in the carved stylized stalks of plants on the facade. Ruskin correctly observed that, "If there be any one feature which the flamboyant architect loved to decorate richly, it was the niche." (8:211)

14

Samuel Prout, and others, the young Ruskin visited and sketched celebrated sites as he pursued his avid interest in biology, mineralogy, and geology. These experiences deepened his understanding of the legacy of historical art and the need to preserve it. They also broadened his thoughts on the social value of art and the crucial role of the artisan whose craft ought to be wrought with joy and directed toward a common good. Finally, his exhaustive study of Venice convinced him that Gothic architecture offered a paradigm of organic, functional architecture and civic cooperation and harmony that could flourish only in a humanely ordered society. These ideas led to two of his most memorable publications, *The Seven Lamps of Architecture* (1849) and *The Stones of Venice* (1851–53), and later to several of his most radical proposals for reform. His memory of the intense joy felt on his earlier tours of France, Switzerland, and Italy, so pivotal in his development and education, remained with him always. In the later, sadder years of the 1870s and 1880s, he attempted to revive the youthful rapture of the 1830s and 1840s by returning to the same locations and drawing the same sites.

Ruskin actually began his professional literary career in 1843 with the publication of the first volume of his vast, five-volume study of art, *Modern Painters*. This monumental series expanded an earlier article de-

Figure 8
JOHN RUSKIN (1819–1900)
Bit Book (Venice Notebook).
1849–50
Pencil and pen and ink, 7¾ × 4¾″ (closed)
Ruskin Galleries, Bembridge School, Isle of Wight

In his study of Venetian architecture, Ruskin measured and diagramed every detail that met his eye. The resulting book, *The Stones of Venice*, is one of his most important and enduring contributions to art history.

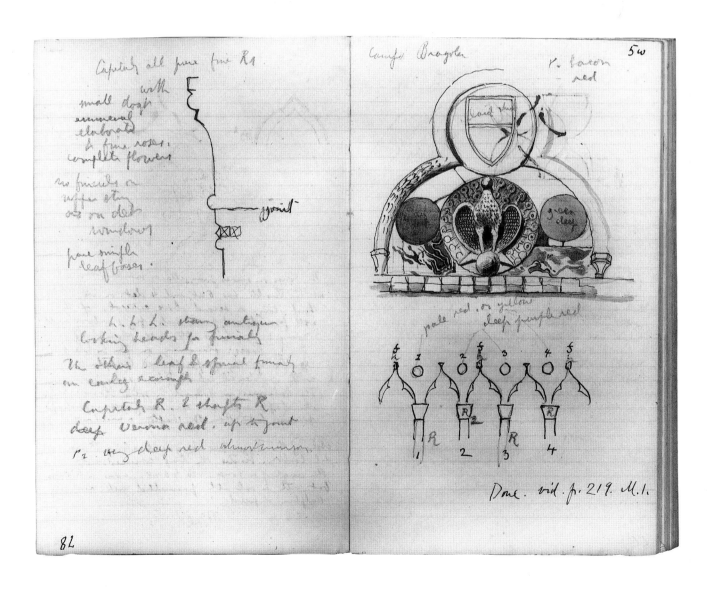

Figure 9
JOHN RUSKIN (1819–1900)
Lauffenburg on the Rhine. c. 1863
Watercolor, 8⅝ × 10⅝"
Birmingham Museum and Art
Gallery, England

Writing to his mother in the fall of
1863 from Baden, Ruskin extolled the
beauty of this picturesquely situated
town: "I am drawing as hard as I can at
Lauffenbourg and getting precious details of all sorts; it is the most wonderful place I ever saw." (17:xxxvi n.)

Figure 10
J. M. W. TURNER (1775–1851)
*Evening: Cloud on Mount Rigi Seen
from Zug.* 1841–42
Watercolor, 8⅝ × 10½"
Ashmolean Museum, Oxford

William Lake Price, a topographical
watercolorist, commented upon
Turner's constant sketching. Watch-
ing the artist on a Lake Como steamer
in 1843, Price described how Turner
held a tiny book in his hand, rapidly
noting the changing combinations of
mountains, water, and trees as the
ship's passage altered his view of the
scenery. Such sketches served as impressions for later use. This particular
drawing was made by Turner from the
window of the inn where he stayed, La
Cygne.

Several views of this region in
Switzerland were included in Turner's
bequest to the nation. Ruskin owned
this watercolor.

fending Turner against criticism that Ruskin judged to be ill informed and insensitive. Ruskin had met his champion in 1840, and, though the two were never truly close friends, Ruskin felt he knew Turner intimately through his drawings and watercolors. He collected them avidly, scrutinizing the small masterpieces as no one else had, and it was through their study that Ruskin conceived many of his ideas.

Ruskin's most direct involvement in the art of his own day was in the late 1840s and 1850s, when he wrote the last three volumes of *Modern Painters* as well as his handbook for beginning artists, *The Elements of Drawing*, and other essays. From 1855 to 1859 he also evaluated contemporary art in his series of reviews entitled *Academy Notes*, lent advice on the construction and Gothic-inspired decoration of the new Oxford Museum of Natural History, and lectured widely. For several years beginning in 1854, he lectured and taught drawing at the Working Men's College in London, which had been founded by Christian Socialist F. D. Maurice to feed both the intellects and spirits of workmen.

During the same period, the Pre-Raphaelite Brotherhood became the most vigorous and influential movement in British art. Their reading of

Figure 11
JAMES SMETHAM (1821–1889)
Christ at Emmaus. Exhibited 1852
Oil on panel, 19¾ × 15¾"
The FORBES Magazine Collection, New York

Smetham studied at the Working Men's College, where Ruskin and the Pre-Raphaelite artist Dante Gabriel Rossetti taught in hopes of bringing art and enlightenment to the masses. The son of a Wesleyan minister, the devout Smetham painted religious subjects in a realistic and historically accurate manner that Ruskin encouraged in *Modern Painters*. This painting, illustrating the Gospel of Saint Luke, tells of the miraculous appearance of Christ to two of his disciples after the Resurrection.

Figure 12
ALFRED WILLIAM HUNT
(1830–1896)
The Stillness of the Lake at Dawn.
1873
Watercolor, 9¾ × 13⅝″
Private Collection, England

An enduring friendship existed between Ruskin and A. W. Hunt, whom Ruskin praised as a landscape artist of quality and poetry. In May 1873 Ruskin invited Hunt, his wife, and their daughter to spend some weeks at his home, Brantwood, in Coniston. There the two men explored the countryside together. This drawing may be a product of that visit. It was exhibited the following spring at the Old Watercolour Society.

Modern Painters encouraged the Brotherhood's early penchant for detailed realism, brilliant color, symbolism, and moral subjects, and it was to Ruskin that they turned for defense from harsh criticism. Ruskin spoke publicly on their behalf, but his private support for a number of the artists involved with Pre-Raphaelitism was also important. He genuinely wished to nurture these promising young talents and to initiate a renaissance in British art and society.

His personal relationships with artists were often mutually frustrating and difficult, however, and he freely admonished friends about all matters from their painting techniques to their personal habits. Surely the most complicated was his alliance with John Everett Millais, a rising star of the Royal Academy whose daring Pre-Raphaelite paintings incensed those who supported more traditional art. Ruskin soon embraced Millais as a protégé and invited him to join Ruskin and his wife, Euphemia Chalmers Gray, or Effie, in Scotland for a working holiday in 1853. The Ruskins' six-year marriage was tense, due largely to their temperamental disparity, to Ruskin's problems with sexual intimacy, and to the intrusiveness of Ruskin's parents. Effie and Millais fell in love during the Scottish sojourn. The next year, the Ruskins' marriage was annulled on the grounds of nonconsumma-

tion and Effie wed Millais in 1855. This painful, humiliating episode labeled Ruskin impotent and later would impair his chances to marry Rose La Touche, to whom he remained devoted from 1858 until, and even after, her death in 1875. Ruskin continued to praise Millais's work after the shocking event until, in 1857, Ruskin sensed that Millais had abandoned the stringency of his earlier efforts and painted more for popularity than for artistic truth.

At the time of the annulment, Ruskin sought the friendship of others, including Dante Gabriel Rossetti, a Pre-Raphaelite painter and poet who shared Ruskin's love of Gothic art, and another young follower, Edward Burne-Jones. Just as Millais had done, these artists evolved in ways that Ruskin could not support wholeheartedly. Rossetti, obsessed with the beauty of his models, developed a style dedicated to the enigmatic portrayal of voluptuous, mysterious women that Ruskin found unsettling. Burne-Jones's mature work also dwelt upon an aloof feminine ideal. Their poetic images became associated with the growing Aesthetic Movement of Algernon Charles Swinburne, Albert Moore, and Whistler. Centered on the concept of art and sensual beauty for its own sake, Aestheticism denied the didactic, socially responsible program preached by Ruskin.

Figure 13
SIR JOHN EVERETT MILLAIS
(1829–1896)
A Highland Lassie. 1854
Oil on panel, 8½ × 6¼"
Delaware Art Museum; Samuel and Mary R. Bancroft Collection

Ruskin initially saw the promise of English art in Millais. Done shortly after the 1853 trip to Scotland with the Ruskins, this portrait was incorrectly thought to be a likeness of Effie Ruskin.

19

Figure 14
SIR EDWARD BURNE-JONES
(1833–1898)
Childe Roland. 1861
Pen and ink with gray wash,
17 × 9½″
The Trustees, The Cecil Higgins
Gallery, Bedford, England

Ruskin's writings and lectures first captivated Burne-Jones during his student years at Oxford in the mid-1850s. The young artist met his idol in 1859. Ruskin's friendship and influence brought patrons to Burne-Jones, and Ruskin's own commissions provided him with a measure of security and success in his early career. This drawing was in Ruskin's own collection. Rossetti's influence is evident in the tight linear style, crowded composition, and the literary theme, in this case Robert Browning's poem *Childe Roland to the Dark Tower Came.*

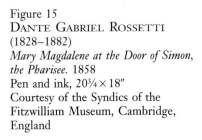

Figure 15
DANTE GABRIEL ROSSETTI
(1828–1882)
Mary Magdalene at the Door of Simon, the Pharisee. 1858
Pen and ink, 20¾ × 18″
Courtesy of the Syndics of the Fitzwilliam Museum, Cambridge, England

Sometimes described as a pendant to Rossetti's *Found* (Delaware Art Museum), this remarkable drawing was done for Ruskin, who thought it magnificent. The woman in *Found* rejects salvation, preferring to lead a sinful life. Mary Magdalene, however, forswears her worldly life, represented by the festivities on the left, to follow Christ. Pre-Raphelites often used friends as models, and several members of Rossetti's circle were included in this drawing. The head of Christ is a portrait of Burne-Jones and the man in the foreground is the poet Algernon C. Swinburne.

Figure 16
SIR EDWARD BURNE-JONES
(1833–1898)
The Sleeping Beauty, from The Briar
Rose Series. 1871
Oil on canvas, 24 × 46″
Museo de Arte de Ponce, Luis A.
Ferré Foundation, Inc., Ponce,
Puerto Rico

The Briar Rose series was inspired by
Tennyson's poetic version of *The Sleeping Beauty*. This panel is one of three in
the group that includes *The King and
His Court* and *The Prince Enters the Enchanted Wood*. Burne-Jones's paintings
gradually grew in size in the late 1860s;
his concern for pure beauty over narra-
tion increased as well. These changes
aligned him with the Aesthetic Movement. They are visible here, especially
in the sinuous lines of the sleeping figures, drapery, and rose branches, in
contrast to the tightness of the earlier
Childe Roland. After doing preliminary
studies for the project, Burne-Jones
visited Italy in 1870. There he renewed
a passion for Michelangelo's heroic
Sistine Chapel figures that remained
with him for the rest of his life. Ruskin
confronted Burne-Jones upon his return with a new Oxford lecture de-
nouncing Michelangelo and the High
Renaissance, blaming artists of the
early 1500s for debasing the piety and
innocence of earlier Italian art. The
encounter weakened the close relationship between Burne-Jones and
Ruskin, although they remained
friends.

Figure 17
DANTE GABRIEL ROSSETTI
(1828–1882)
Before the Battle. 1858
Watercolor on paper, mounted on
canvas, 16⅝ × 11″
Courtesy of the Museum of Fine
Arts, Boston; Special Picture Fund

The troubled correspondence over *Before the Battle* is indicative of the tug-of-war friendship between Ruskin and Rossetti. Done for Ruskin's dear friend Charles Eliot Norton of Harvard, in Rossetti's early medievalizing style, the scene depicts a lady affixing a pennon, or symbol of her favor, to the shaft of her knight's spear. Ruskin was certain its quality would disappoint Norton and ruin any reputation Rossetti might acquire in America. Having tenaciously assumed the role of Rossetti's critic as well as friend and protector, Ruskin pressed him to work harder on it. Finally, in January 1862, Ruskin wrote to Norton that he had triumphed: Rossetti had retouched the drawing and "he has modified in every respect so much advanced and bettered it that though not one of his first-rate works, and still painfully quaint and hard, it is nevertheless worthy of him, and will be to you an enjoyable possession." (36:404)

Figure 18
DAVID ROBERTS (1796–1864)
The Giudecca, Venice. 1854
Oil on canvas, 22 × 51″
Yale Center for British Art, Paul
Mellon Collection

Roberts, an eminent Royal Academician and one of Ruskin's early mentors, was reprimanded in *Academy Notes* for his Venetian pictures. Ruskin described one as an "energetic protest . . . against Turner's idea of Venetian Colour, and against all that I have endeavoured to urge or describe in support of that conception." (14:167) In a private note to Roberts, Ruskin explained that his duty as a critic was separate from personal affection. Roberts retorted that he would like to give Ruskin a "*sound thrashing*," and he hoped "that a broken head would not interfere with the sincere feeling of friendship that he [*sic*] hoped would always exist." (14:xxix)

Despite his dictatorial tone and frequently judgmental opinions on artistic probity, Ruskin's private and public criticisms were not meant to be malicious; rather, they were motivated by his real desire to encourage artists to do their utmost. Ruskin saw his duty, and that of every critic, "not so much to direct the multitude whom to go to, as what to ask for. . . . Their business is not to tell us which is our best painter, but to tell us whether we are making our best painter do his best." (3:618) The problem of modern criticism lay with the ill-suited individuals who wrote it—"persons altogether unversed in practice, and ignorant of truth." (3:619) Mere cleverness, or artistic sleight-of-hand, ought not to be mistaken for original expression, he insisted, nor indolence for well-earned confidence, nor melodrama for genuine sentiment.

Ruskin's critical opinions carried immense weight with a public eager to hear his views on all matters related to art. He was distinct from other critics and art journalists of his day in his ability to describe and interpret works of art in colorful and convincing language. He was also unique in his sweeping educational goals, which encompassed all segments of society, and in his notion of artistic responsibility. Significantly, he was among the first to consider art in its wider context as an indication of cultural and moral vitality and to detect social deterioration in the decay of art and its patronage.

Figure 19
JOHN BRETT (1830–1902)
Massa, Bay of Naples. 1864
Oil on canvas, 25⅛ × 40⅛"
Copyright 1992: Indianapolis
Museum of Art, James E. Roberts
Fund

Brett painted this work after an intense period under Ruskin's tutelage. Ruskin worked with Brett and another landscapist, John William Inchbold (1830–1888) in Switzerland between 1856 and 1858, attempting to impose his stylistic and thematic viewpoints upon them. Ruskin wrote to his father that Brett "wanted some lecturing like Inchbold. . . . He is much tougher and stronger than Inchbold, and takes more hammering, but I think he looks more miserable every day, and have good hope of making him completely wretched in a day or two more." (14:xxiii-xxiv) Painted six years later, this sweeping vista of the Bay of Naples still conformed to Ruskin's doctrine in its detail, faithful rendering of space, and brilliant color based on careful observation.

Ruskin's strong social conscience increasingly forced his attention from the immediate problems of art to others he found more pressing: the underlying social, economic, and political ills of England caused by industrialization and laissez-faire economics. In 1860 he not only completed *Modern Painters* but also published a series of articles collected under the title *Unto This Last.* The articles denounced systems that encouraged and perpetuated inhuman conditions, robbing all but the rich of hope and prosperity, and outlined themes that would occupy Ruskin for the rest of his life. Although his active involvement in contemporary art ebbed at that point, his expertise was still highly respected and, in 1869, he was appointed the first Slade Professor of Art at Oxford. He lectured and instituted a school of drawing there, and he donated important works from his own collection. Beginning in 1871, he also extended his educational efforts beyond the confines of the university through *Fors Clavigera*, a series of ninety-six letters addressed to the working men of England, in which his thoughts ranged from art to sights and sounds outside his window to his utopian society, the Guild of Saint George.

Both his attempts to direct the course of British art and his efforts to alter British society disappointed Ruskin, and he became increasingly despondent over the futility of his endeavors. The last twenty-five years of his life were personally tragic as well. In 1875 he was devastated by the death of the young Rose La Touche, for whom he had had an abiding and frustrated love, and by the loss of the notorious Whistler trial, an event that very publicly called into question all that he had advocated. He became convinced that, despite his efforts, irreverence, pride, and carelessness were darkening the world and rendering it more physically and spiritually destitute. He described this ominous, evil gloom in his 1884 lecture "The Storm-Cloud of the Nineteenth Century." He was plagued by periods of mental illness that grew in number and duration throughout the 1870s, until he became entirely helpless in 1889. After living a "posthumous existence"[3] under the care of his cousin for more than a decade, he died in his home at Brantwood, Coniston, on January 20, 1900.

The following six essays offer an introduction to Ruskin's multifarious opinions on art. They do not provide an encyclopedic study of his life and interests, a herculean task that only a few of his most dedicated biographers have attempted. Instead, each essay presents a different perspective on a single theme: Ruskin's particular art of seeing, and ways in which he practiced and preached this art. Robert Hewison describes pivotal moments in Ruskin's life when, in Ruskin's own mind, encounters with specific works by Renaissance masters dramatically and suddenly altered the course of his thinking. In the late 1850s, he ascribed to such an experience his loss of faith, or, more accurately, the loosening of the evangelical strictures that initially had determined his ideas. Related to this is George Landow's consideration of the powerful sermonizing language with which Ruskin shared his experiences and interpreted them for his audience, exhorting and instructing readers, artist and nonartist alike, to see for themselves.

For Ruskin, an accomplished draftsman, drawing was a means of gathering information and fulfilling emotional needs. Christopher Newall analyzes the role of drawing at various times in Ruskin's life as well as his

Figure 20
WILLIAM HENRY HUNT
(1790–1864)
Lobster, Crab, and Cucumber. c. 1827
Watercolor, 5⅞ × 10½"
Birmingham Museum and Art
Gallery, England

Both Ruskin and his father collected Hunt's watercolors, and he placed several of them in his drawing school at Oxford. Dead animals were usually not Ruskin's favorites among Hunt's subjects, but he did own this arrangement of shellfish and vegetables. Ruskin referred to Hunt's remarkable skill at reproducing the shapes, textures, and colors of objects as "uneducated," by which he meant unaffected by prevailing fashion or academic habits.

love of the very process of observation and delineation. Using Turner's work as a paradigm for modern artists and his own drawing as a practical guide, Ruskin prodded others to work first for accuracy, then for comprehension and expressiveness. Susan Gordon discusses Ruskin's aspirations for modern art and his critical assessment of it as he surveyed contemporary exhibitions.

Ruskin based his art of seeing on the pragmatism of direct experience and the spiritual associations thus revealed. The physical record of geology would at first reassure his faith in God and later frustrate it. Anthony Gully explores the symbolic importance of geology for Ruskin and his clashes with the scientific community. Finally, Susan Casteras describes one of Ruskin's last educational efforts, the creation of a museum for his utopian scheme, the Guild of Saint George, in which he attempted to put theory into practice.

The content of the exhibition coincident with this publication, entitled *The Art of Seeing: John Ruskin and the Victorian Eye*, depended upon Ruskin's public and private pronouncements. Thus, as much as possible, the artists and the specific works illustrated here and displayed at the Phoenix Art Museum and the Indianapolis Museum of Art correspond to his personal likes and dislikes. In many respects, his judgments reflected those of his age and must be understood and appreciated in their historical context. Yet, his attempts to define the proper attributes of fine art and to promote art education and art museums continue today, along with his anguish over historic preservation, environmental issues, and social chaos. They not only predict contemporary concerns; they are their antecedents.

NOTES

1. The literature on Ruskin is extensive. The reader is referred to the selected titles in the Bibliography, many of which include more extensive citations.

2. Tim Hilton, *John Ruskin: The Early Years* (New Haven and London, 1985), xi.

3. John D. Rosenberg, *The Darkening Glass* (London, 1963), 224.

Figure 21
WILLIAM GERSHOM
COLLINGWOOD (1854–1932)
*Ruskin in His Study at Brantwood with
a View of Coniston Old Man through
the Window.* 1882
Watercolor, 18⅞ × 29″
Ruskin Museum, Coniston

In his last Oxford lecture series, in December 1884, Ruskin described Collingwood as a "pupil-friend, an accomplished and amiable artist." (33:536) Collingwood's association with Ruskin began in 1872, and he served both as Ruskin's secretary and as his first biographer. Ruskin was sixty-two when Collingwood depicted him in his Brantwood study. Two years earlier, one visitor described Ruskin as "a very small, gentle looking, old man, who does not look like a fighter at all. He has clear blue eyes with shaggy eyebrows, and a nose with very wide nostrils. All the rest of him is coat."

John Ruskin and the Argument of the Eye

Robert Hewison

Throughout Ruskin's life and work, the visual informed the verbal. His subject was the visual world: the elements of nature framed by landscape, the human shaping of those elements into architecture, and human response to them expressed in sculpture and painting. With all aspects of the visible, Ruskin's analysis equally was visual, through the practice of drawing at which he excelled. Images of the external world also shaped the internal operation of his imagination and molded his prose. Many of his arguments were governed by images that relate to each other as much visually as poetically or logically. His intellectual and emotional life was formed by visual experiences in front of specific paintings.

Like the romantic artists who did so much to form his vision of the world, Ruskin had no inhibitions about placing himself, his own perceptions and experiences, at the center of his work and then generalizing from them. It is for this reason that what follows is centered on a fragment of autobiography, a sketch that can be used to stand for the whole.

In the same spirit as that of an artist trying to make visual experience concrete, this autobiographical fragment is derived from a specific literary text. It was written on March 4, 1877, in Venice, the city that was the source of so many of Ruskin's ideas about art, architecture, and their relation to the societies that produced them.

As usual, Ruskin was up early that day. He was in Venice on his first extended visit in twenty-five years. He had arrived in the previous September to spend a winter away from his responsibilities in England as Slade Professor of Art at the University of Oxford, where he had founded his own drawing school, and from his duties as a much-consulted public figure. He wished to recapture the delight of first knowing Venice, and he had hoped that the return would be one of "exalting and thrilling pensiveness, as of some glorious summer evening in purple light." (37:204) But it was autumn when he arrived, and all he had was the feeling that much time had been lost. He wrote to his mother, "To find all the places we had loved changed into railroad stations or dust-heaps—there are no words for the withering and disgusting pain." (37:204–5)

Ruskin had begun his winter at the Grand Hotel, not far from Saint Mark's Square on the Grand Canal, but in February 1877 he moved to less expensive rooms above a restaurant on the Zattere. The Zattere embankment, in the Dorsoduro *sestiere*, looks south across the wide sweep of water that lies between the main body of Venice and the island of the Giudecca, and his new lodgings had the advantage of enabling him to watch both the sunrise and the sunset.

The morning of March 4 was bright, with the moon still visible in a soft sky. Inside the room that he used as his study were piles of books and

Figure 22
J. M. W. TURNER (1775–1851)
The Dogana and Madonna della Salute, Venice. Exhibited 1843
Oil on canvas, 24⅜ × 36⅝″
National Gallery of Art, Washington D. C.; Given in Memory of Governor Alvan T. Fuller by The Fuller Foundation

Venice was the setting for some of Turner's most poetic paintings and drawings, and for many of Ruskin's most penetrating insights. In Ruskin's opinion, no artist captured the beauty, atmosphere, and life of Venice so completely as Turner. Certainly, no single mind concentrated on its history and inferred so many messages from its art, architecture, history, and plight as did John Ruskin.

papers: sheets of proofs for correction, letters to and from his many correspondents, rapid sketches scribbled during his trips by gondola, and the careful watercolor studies that he was making of Vittore Carpaccio's *The Dream of Saint Ursula*. There were plaster casts of sculptures on the Ducal Palace, histories and guidebooks to Venice, the thirteenth edition of John Murray's *Handbook for the Traveller in Northern Italy*, which quoted Ruskin's own words from *The Stones of Venice*. There was a copy, in Greek, of Plato's *Laws*, from which Ruskin tried to translate a passage each morning, using Jowett's translation as a crib. Also there were *Punch*, and English newspapers, and, to distract him from the serious work, a copy of the memoirs of Casanova. Sea horses swam in a glass bowl, a cockleshell from the Venetian island of Saint Helena lay beside a snail shell picked up during a rowing expedition to the Lido. There was an Italian missal, his mother's Bible, as well as a fourteenth-century illuminated version.

Ruskin liked the view from his study, though there was a lime kiln opposite that blew smoke in a white cloud across the water. Large steamers would pass within thirty yards of his window, and the scream of their whistles and the rattle of their steam cranes were a strain on his nerves when he wanted to work.

As usual, he had set aside the first days of the month in order to write the next issue of his pamphlet *Fors Clavigera*, the letters to the working men of England that served as a kind of personal newsletter, and as the most direct form of address he could find outside the public lecture. The letter due for April would contain important news of his plans for social reform. Before coming to Venice he had been approached by a group of working men from Sheffield who wanted to set up what they called a "communist" farming experiment. Ruskin agreed to help by providing the land rent free. A small farm near Abbeydale, just outside Sheffield, had been bought, and in announcing the purchase Ruskin proposed to give his Sheffield workers some advice on coming into their property. In spite of the noise from the steamer *Pachino* as it made ready for the Sunday run to Trieste, he was at work as the moon set.

There is a particular reason for describing the circumstances of March 4, 1877, in such detail. The minutiae of this particular morning do not just set the scene, for the nature of Ruskin was such that many things that to other people might seem insignificant were full of meaning to him. What the weather was like, what objects were immediately to hand could be very important for Ruskin's mood and his choice of subject. There is a useful academic discipline in establishing which books an author has beside him when he or she writes, but in Ruskin's case books are only one inspiration: That morning, when he looked up from his table because of the noise from the steamer *Pachino*, he was surprised to see that the cross of Saint George was painted on her bows. Saint George was the patron saint of his ideal society, the Guild of Saint George, and the steam cranes and Plato's *Laws* and Saint George all made their way into his work that day.

Ruskin wanted to position his advice to the Sheffield workers in the wider context of his plans for social reform. As Plato had prescribed laws for an ideal society, so Ruskin had his own ideas to put forward. For the past three mornings he had been trying to put on paper the basis of belief for the vehicle of his reforms, the Guild of Saint George. The cross of Saint

Figures 23 and 24
JOHN RUSKIN (1819–1900)
Studies of Dawn (The First Scarlet in the Clouds, White Clouds and Purple Clouds). n.d.
Pencil, watercolor, and body color on blue-gray paper, (above) 5½ × 7½", Educational Series 3, (below) 6 × 8¾", Educational Series 5, Ashmolean Museum, Oxford

Speaking in *Modern Painters* of the incomparable beauties to be seen in early morning skies, Ruskin wrote: "It is of all visible things the least material, the least finite, the farthest withdrawn from the earth prison-house, the most typical of the nature of God, the most suggestive of the glory of His dwelling place." (4:81) This drawing, reminiscent of Turner's celebrated color studies, captures the dual nature of Ruskin's understanding of the natural world: his abiding spiritual regard and his scientific curiosity about natural phenomena. This drawing is one of several included in Ruskin's Educational Series for his drawing students.

31

George on the bows of the steamer seemed to confirm that this should be his topic in *Fors Clavigera* for April. His intention was to "state unambiguously" the creed of the guild. (29:86)

To explain the guild's beliefs, he felt he should first explain his own religious attitude. That in turn involved saying something about the course of his personal life. As is often the case with Ruskin, he allowed himself to be diverted, and he did not manage to fulfill his intention that morning, or that month. Instead of solemn creed, he gave us the sketch of an autobiography—a sketch that is a revealing self-portrait.

He began to analyze the course of his spiritual life, but he did so in unusual terms. He began by saying: "All my first books, to the end of *The Stones of Venice*, were written in the simple belief I had been taught as a child; and especially the second volume of *Modern Painters* was an outcry of enthusiastic praise of religious painting, in which you will find me placing Fra Angelico (see the closing paragraph of the book) above all other painters." (29:87)

Ruskin was trying to explain the progress of his spiritual life through the development of his critical ideas on art. His justification was that the teaching of art was the teaching of all things—which may sound like a glib remark but it was an article of faith, of religious faith, throughout his life. But his belief that art was the expression of God's will had been founded long before he knew very much about Fra Angelico, indeed about any Italian art. It became the inspiration for *Modern Painters*, the book that had made his reputation as a young man.

The great work *Modern Painters*, which took seventeen years and five volumes to complete, had its seed in a juvenile essay in defense of J. M. W. Turner. In 1836 Turner's paintings shown at the Royal Academy—*Juliet and Her Nurse*, *Rome from Mount Aventine*, and *Mercury and Argus*—were attacked in *Blackwood's Magazine*, and the sixteen-year-old Ruskin was prompted to write a reply. Ruskin's father, a prosperous merchant in the sherry trade, was already a patron of Turner and thought it prudent to show the essay to the painter, who discouraged its submission for publication. A further attack on Turner in *Blackwood's Magazine* in 1842, in which Turner had shown, among other works, his vision of Napoleon, *War: The Exile and the Rock-Limpet*, stimulated Ruskin to undertake *Modern Painters* itself.

It is important to remember, however, that the Turner whom Ruskin knew as a young man was not the artist of the cloud studies, "color-beginnings," and semiabstract effects that have been celebrated in the twentieth century. He was the painter of large canvases that sought to gain for landscape painting the degree of respect afforded by contemporary Neoclassical taste to history painting. Part of his strategy depended on adopting classical subjects, such as *The Goddess of Discord Choosing the Apple of Contention in the Garden of the Hesperides*, shown at the Royal Academy in 1806. This picture held a particular fascination for Ruskin, and he devoted key pages in the final volume of *Modern Painters* to discussing it. But its original appeal to Ruskin was that the painting's grand treatment of landscape, the mountains, mist, and smoke—in Neoclassical terms, "the sublime"—formed a link with the contemporary romantic poetry, most especially that of William Wordsworth, that had such an important part in

Ruskin's literary formation. As Wordsworth wrote in his "Lines Composed a Few Miles above Tintern Abbey," this version of nature had

> *A presence that disturbs me with the joy*
> *Of elevated thoughts; a sense sublime*
> *Of something far more deeply interfused,*
> *Whose dwelling is the light of setting suns,*
> *And the round ocean and the living air,*
> *And the blue sky, and in the mind of man:*
> *A motion and a spirit, that impels*
> *All thinking things, all objects of all thought,*
> *And rolls through all things.*
>
> (lines 94–102)

For both Wordsworth and Ruskin the visible elements of the natural world provoked thoughts of the essential unity between humankind and nature, and, through nature, to God.

By the time Ruskin came to reconsider *The Goddess of Discord* for the last volume of *Modern Painters* in 1860, its mythological sources had become the subject of a lengthy analysis that in effect remythologizes the picture into Ruskin's own system of symbolic thought, governed by the visual polarities of lightness and dark. The nymphs of the Hesperides become beneficent expressions of the female principle of sweetness and

J. M. W. TURNER (1775–1851)
The Goddess of Discord Choosing the Apple of Contention in the Garden of Hesperides. Exhibited 1806
Oil on canvas, 61⅛ × 86″
The Turner Collection, Tate Gallery, London

33

Figure 25
JOHN RUSKIN (1819–1900)
*Quick Study of a Leaf Contour:
Bramble.* n.d.
Pencil and watercolor, 8⅝ × 6¼″
Ashmolean Museum, Oxford;
Rudimentary Series 280

Ruskin, who saw a divine vitalism in all of nature, equated the curves of brambles with "the expanding power of joyful vegetative youth . . . [an unassuming bramble] is of all simple forms the most exquisitely delightful to the human mind." (5:266) The bramble's curve is matched in great mountains, where it represents the "falling force" as opposed to the "vital force" in the roadside plant. This drawing was in Cabinet number 12 of Ruskin's Rudimentary Series at Oxford as an example of masterful "Tree Drawing," and it was reproduced during the artist's life in the July 1897 issue of *Artist*.

Figure 26
JOHN RUSKIN (1819–1900)
First Process of Sepia Sketch of Leafage.
n.d.
Pencil and sepia ink, 10¾ × 5½″
Ashmolean Museum, Oxford;
Rudimentary Series 290

Ruskin sometimes assigned rather fanciful, romantic meanings to natural forms. Leaves were no exception. In his *Fors Clavigera* letter of May 1871, he wrote: "But the pure one [the leaf] which loves the light has, above all things, the purpose of being married to another leaf, and having child-leaves, and children's children of leaves to make the earth fair for ever. And when the leaves marry, they put on wedding-robes, and are more glorious than Solomon in all his glory, and they have feasts of honey and we call them 'Flowers.'" (27:84)

light, the dragon a darkly menacing figure of pollution and greed. Yet, though developed by Ruskin far beyond its original purpose, this method of symbolic interpretation had as its source the system of biblical exegesis he had learned as the child of devout Evangelical Anglican parents. This system held that the events, people, and even places in the Bible were both real and symbolic; they were "types" that lost none of their physical reality for carrying their freight of symbolic meaning.

The significance of this for Ruskin was that his avid study of the natural world and his emotional response to it could be contained within both a religious and a scientific frame of reference. The accurate study of landscape was also a careful reading of the work of God. Ruskin had studied geology and mineralogy from a very early age; in fact he was making notes on rocks and stones long before he was making notes on paintings. Deep in his study of Turner's symbolic meanings in the last volume of *Modern Painters*, he used his authority as a geologist to compare Turner's representation of the dragon that guards the garden of the Hesperides to a glacier: "If I were merely to draw this dragon as white, instead of dark, and take his claws away, his body would become a representation of great glacier, so nearly perfect, that I know no published engraving of a glacier breaking over a rocky brow so like the truth as this dragon's shoulders would be." (7:402)

For Ruskin the literal truth achieved through close observation—in this case geological accuracy, or in 1851 the attention to nature of the Pre-Raphaelite Brotherhood—was the first step in the process of creation. But accurate perception led to imaginative penetration. Taught to believe both in the literal truth of the Bible and its existence as a symbol of the spiritual word of God, Ruskin was able to lift up his eyes to the hills both with the curiosity of a geologist and the understanding of one who also saw them as an expression of the Creator. And in the decay of the hills, he saw a symbol of the fall of humanity.

This "other meaning" of nature was also very convenient to Ruskin as a justification for his straightforward response to Turner. What he called in his autobiographical sketch "the simple belief I had been taught as a child" affirmed that nature was the work of God, so how could there be any harm in this pleasure in Turner, who portrayed nature so well? (29:87) When he published the first volume of *Modern Painters* in 1843, his purpose was to prove that Turner communicated both a literal and a spiritual truth.

Yet Ruskin's visual perception was far from innocent. It was structured very directly by the conventions of the times, as communicated by lessons from drawing masters, the first of whom, the almost unknown Charles Runciman, taught Ruskin an eighteenth-century gentleman-amateur's tricks. Later he was taught by two far better known and more advanced watercolor artists, Copley Fielding and J. D. Harding, but Ruskin began his career with a perception cast very much in the mold of the picturesque, the greatest exponent of which, in his view, was Samuel Prout.

Prout was a personal friend of Ruskin and his father's, and he had a profound influence on Ruskin's early drawing style, as can be seen in their two drawings of the same subject, the Casa Contarini Fasan on the Grand Canal in Venice (figures 27 and 28). Ruskin later claimed that Prout had borrowed his drawing—made in 1841 before *Modern Painters* was begun—

Figure 27
SAMUEL PROUT (1783–1852)
Venice, the Palazzo Contarini Fasan on the Grand Canal. n.d.
Pen and ink, watercolor, and body color, lights reserved with scratching-out, 17 × 12
By Courtesy of the Board of Trustees of the Victoria and Albert Museum, London

Ruskin admired the picturesque qualities of Prout's Italian subjects, dis-played in this view of the Palazzo Contarini Fasan. It is set at an angle like the *Arch of Constantine* (figure 100) and flooded in shadow at its base, with its remaining surface thrown into relief by the play of light. Costumed figures lend scale to the structure. In this case, the student provided the model for the master. Prout reportedly composed his version from Ruskin's earlier depiction of the same site (figure 28).

Figure 28
JOHN RUSKIN (1819–1900)
Casa Contarini Fasan (and Neighboring Palaces on the Grand Canal), Venice.
1841
Pencil, pen and ink, watercolor, and wash on blue-green paper,
16¾ × 12½″
Ashmolean Museum, Oxford;
Reference Series 65

This late Gothic city palace held Ruskin's admiration throughout his long association with Venice. For him it was "the most elaborate piece of architecture in Venice." (8:228) The richly decorated facade formed "one of the principal ornaments of the very noblest reach of the Grand Canal." (11:369) In his *Seven Lamps of Architecture*, Ruskin confessed his delight in the modest scale of the palazzo and "how much beauty and dignity may be bestowed on a very small and unimportant dwelling-house." (8:228)

to make his own. But whatever the order in which the drawings were made, it is evident that as a young man Ruskin drew like his mentor Prout rather than Prout like Ruskin.

Ruskin however was to abandon the picturesque perception typified by this drawing, with its delight in crumbling textures and broken lines and dots and dashes in the manner of Prout's lithographs. One reason for this was his much closer acquaintance with the work of Turner. In 1842 Turner showed to some of his patrons, including the Ruskins, a series of watercolor sketches from which he proposed to make more finished works, of which the Ruskins commissioned at least two. Ruskin's observation of these drawings—plus his own unsuccessful attempts to reproduce Turner's style—helped Ruskin in his search for the theory of the imagination that would show up the weaknesses of the superficial tricks of the picturesque. In his autobiography *Praeterita*, which he began to publish in 1885, he describes how at this period his own practice of drawing, as well as the sight of Turner's preliminary sketches, made him appreciate the inner laws of

37

Figures 29, 30, 31
J. M. W. TURNER (1775–1851)
Venice: Entrance to the Grand Canal.
n.d.
Watercolor, 8¾ × 12⅝″
The Turner Collection, Tate
Gallery, London

*Venice: Looking East from the
Giudecca, Sunrise.* 1819
Watercolor, 8¾ × 11⅜″
The Turner Collection, Tate
Gallery, London

Venice: Moonrise. 1840 (?)
Watercolor, 8¾ × 12½″
The Turner Collection, Tate
Gallery, London

Turner visited Venice over a fourteen-year period, from 1818 to 1832, and was captivated by the city's rare beauty, its light, and its color. He studied it at all times of the day, from sunrise to sunset, recording the city's ever-changing, form-dissolving atmosphere in washes of glowing tones that anticipate the French Impressionists some forty years later. Ruskin called Venice Turner's city: "She was the joy of his heart, no less than his great teacher. The Alps brought him always sadness, but Venice delight. (He died, happily, before he saw what modern Venetians and English would make of her.)" (13:497)

nature as opposed to those of external appearance, and that "no one had ever told me to draw what was really there!" (35:311) Nonetheless Ruskin did not rid himself of his picturesque leanings until after 1845, when he had already published the first volume of *Modern Painters*. It is important to remember that today we read *Modern Painters* in a revised edition. In the first edition he made a number of favorable comments about contemporary artists who were working in the picturesque tradition, comments he later revised or dropped entirely.

These revisions were the result of Ruskin's visit to Italy in 1845, a visit crucial to Ruskin's development, as evidenced in his autobiographical sketch of 1877. He had already been to Italy several times, but as the enthusiastic vision of the romantic traveler became refined by the critical insights of the art historian, he also discovered artists very different from Turner.

In Florence Ruskin began properly to appreciate for the first time Fra Angelico and the other painters who were truly pre-Raphaelite.

FRA ANGELICO (1387–1455)
The Annuciation. 1452–53
Tempera on panel, 15⅛ × 14½″
Museo di San Marco, Florence

TINTORETTO (JACOPO
ROBUSTI) (1518/19–1594)
The Crucifixion. c. 1565
Oil on canvas, 17′7″ × 40′2″
Scuola di San Rocco, Venice

This led him to decide that *Modern Painters* would have to be revised on his return. In spite of his Evangelical Anglican inhibitions about Catholic art, he decided to place Fra Angelico at the top of the list he was making of religious painters: Fra Angelico, he wrote in a letter home to his father, is "in a class by himself, he is not an artist, properly called, but an inspired saint."[1]

This was dangerous talk for an Anglican, but Ruskin had found in Fra Angelico's shapes of red and gold a religious glory that at least equaled the romantic glory of Turner. So volume 2 of *Modern Painters* became, as he says, "an outcry of enthusiastic praise" for the religious art of Italy. Fra Angelico, however, was not the only discovery of 1845. Ruskin later jokingly regretted that he had ever traveled on from Florence to Venice that year.

For a start he was shocked by the decay, and the so-called restorations—which he called destruction—of the buildings. He felt impelled to draw what he could of the city's Byzantine and Gothic architecture, which was doubly threatened by modernization and neglect. The year 1845 marks the beginning of a serious turn to architectural, as well as art-historical, study.

But other discoveries were in store also. The religious content of Fra Angelico's paintings was justification enough for the pleasure he felt in seeing them, but in Venice Ruskin's eye was seduced by Tintoretto, and Titian, and his Anglican conscience was troubled. Recalling his feelings, Ruskin wrote in 1877: "I discovered the gigantic power of Tintoret [*sic*], and found that there was quite a different spirit in that from the spirit of Angelico; and, analysing Venetian work carefully, I found,—and told fearlessly, in spite of my love for the masters,—that there was 'no religion whatever in any work of Titian's; and that Tintoret only occasionally forgot himself into religion.'" (29:87)

The effect of Tintoretto was indeed "gigantic." One day, having idled by the canals and sketched the market boats, Ruskin and his friend and

latest drawing master, J. D. Harding, wandered into the halls of the Scuola di San Rocco, encountering for the first time the magnificent sweep of paintings by Tintoretto that climaxes with the vast *Crucifixion*. They were overwhelmed by what they saw. Ruskin wrote home to his father: "We both sat down, and looked—not at it—but at each other,—literally the strength so taken out of us that we couldn't stand!" (4:354) And again later: "I have had such a draught of pictures today enough to drown me. I never was so utterly crushed to the earth before any human intellect as I was today, before Tintoret."[2]

Ruskin delayed his departure from Venice in order to make a study in black and white from the central section of the *Crucifixion*. The intensity of his response can be seen in the vigor of the drawing. In his list of painters Tintoretto was now "in the school of Art at the top, top, top of everything."[3]

The sensuous nature of the experience of seeing Tintoretto was a reminder to Ruskin of his own humanity. As a repressed only child of elderly religious parents, he felt a delight in the faculty of sight that helped to compensate for other pleasures that were unknown to him. The joy was none the less physical for that. Tintoretto, he wrote, "took it so entirely out of me today that I could do nothing at last but lie on a bench and laugh."[4]

The consequence of the experience in the Scuola di San Rocco was not simply a major revision of *Modern Painters*. In a sense the direction of the rest of Ruskin's life was set. He felt that there was a connection between

Figure 32
JOHN RUSKIN (1819–1900)
Central portion of the *Crucifixion*, after Tintoretto. 1845
Pencil, pen and ink, black chalk, and gray wash, 14½ × 21"
Ruskin Galleries, Bembridge School, Isle of Wight

Ruskin's admiration for Tintoretto knew no bounds. The *Crucifixion* was declared in *Modern Painters* to be the artist's "noblest work." (4:127) In Ruskin's guide to the wonders of Venice, *The Venetian Index*, he praised the titanic work, claiming that "it is beyond all analysis, and above all praise." (11:428) Ruskin sought to understand the ingenious skill in its painting as well as the spiritual truth it revealed. He was certain that Tintoretto had penetrated "into the root and deep places of his subject, despising all outward and bodily appearances of pain, and seeking for some means of expressing, not the rack of nerve or sinew, but the fainting of the deserted Son of God." (4:270)

41

Ruskin wrote his father on December 23, 1849, that, upon entering the Casa Bernardo, he was dismayed to find Count Bernardo living in only one room of this crumbling ruin. Such glimpses of poverty led him to the important conclusions reached in *The Stones of Venice*: "And the great cry that rises from all our manufacturing cities, louder than their furnace blast, is all in very deed for this, that we manufacture everything there except men, we blanch cotton, and strengthen steel and refine sugar, and shape pottery, but to brighten, to strengthen, to refine, or to form a single living spirit, never enters into our estimate of advantages." (10:196)

the art of Tintoretto and the city of Venice that seemed to be crumbling about him. A link was made in his mind between Art, Humankind, and Society. In 1885, in *Praeterita*, he recalled: "Tintoret swept me away at once into the 'mare maggiore' of the schools of painting which crowned the power and perished in the fall of Venice; so forcing me into the study of the history of Venice herself; and through that into what else I have traced or told of the laws of national strength and virtue." (35:372)

The effect of this conjunction of art and social questions can be seen in the more critical attitude that developed in Ruskin's drawings. While remaining sensitive to effects of light, texture, and atmosphere, he also became concerned with an architectural accuracy that led him to measure buildings as well as to draw them, and to write up his ideas in notebooks. His social conscience was also developing. In 1845 he wrote to his father that he could not understand how someone as privileged and wealthy as himself, who treated "all distress as more picturesque than as real," could expect to write good poetry.[5]

The decision to study architecture and Venetian cultural history led first to *The Seven Lamps of Architecture* in 1849 and then to *The Stones of Venice*, published in three volumes between 1851 and 1853. Ruskin quickly discovered that the literary evidence about the architectural history of Venice was confused, nonexistent, or contradictory, so he was forced to turn to the evidence of his own eyes. He made an intense study of the city, measuring and drawing in notebooks and worksheets that now form a priceless record of some of the city's key buildings. He positively delighted in the recent invention of the daguerreotype, and he built up a large collection of photographs taken by his servant John Hobbs. Ruskin may well have been the first art historian to use photography in this way, and he based a number of his own drawings on daguerreotype studies.

In *The Stones of Venice*, Ruskin had applied his argument that there was a direct connection between the condition of art and the health of a nation to the whole historical and architectural fabric of the city. Yet these human interests pulled against the spiritual for Ruskin; he found that although the religious painters depicted a spiritual vision that as a religious man he had to respect, their art seemed not as great and did not give him so much pleasure as that of more worldly artists. Inevitably, in 1858, a crisis occurred as he studied Veronese's *Solomon and the Queen of Sheba* in Turin.

Ruskin gave two accounts of the spiritual change that overtook him in 1858, one written on that morning of March 4 in 1877, another later in *Praeterita*. The accounts differ, although the result is the same: Ruskin shed the Evangelical Anglicanism that had held him since childhood. In the first version, he leaves his work in the gallery in Turin and goes to hear a Protestant service in an evangelical chapel:

> *Under quite overwhelmed sense of his [Veronese's] God-given power, I went away to a Waldensian chapel, where a little squeaking idiot was preaching to an audience of seventeen old women and three louts, that they were the only children of God in Turin; and that all the people in Turin outside the chapel, and all the people in the world out of sight of*

VERONESE (PAOLO CALIARI)
(1528–1588)
Solomon and the Queen of Sheba.
c. 1560
Oil on canvas, 11′5⅜″ × 18′
Pinoteca, Turin

43

Monte Viso, would be damned. I came out of the chapel, in sum of twenty
years of thought, a conclusively un-*converted man. (29:89)*

In the later version the moment of decision was not so sudden. After the
service he returned to the gallery, and it is there that the essential change
took place:

> *Paul Veronese's* Solomon and the Queen of Sheba *glowed in full*
> *afternoon light. The gallery windows being open, there came in with the*
> *warm air, floating swells and falls of military music, from the courtyard*
> *before the palace, which seemed to me more devotional, in their perfect*
> *art, tune, and discipline, than anything I remembered of evangelical*
> *hymns. And as the perfect colour and sound gradually asserted their power*
> *on me, they seemed finally to fasten me in the old article of Jewish faith,*
> *that things done delightfully and rightly were always done by the help and*
> *in the Spirit of God. (35:495–6)*

This second version tells us more clearly what happened to Ruskin.
He had been suffering religious doubts for years, but it took a picture, the
argument of the eye, to decide him finally. It was in fact a synaesthetic
moment, for there was not only the sensual beauty of Veronese, but
also music, so that "perfect colour and sound" combined to ease him of
the problem that had troubled him for so long. The change was not the
outcome of a carefully argued debate between one set of religious principles
and another; it was a choice of images, between the negative sterility of a
Protestant chapel and the jewels and colors of Veronese. His own prose
conveys the emotions that he felt. Turner, Fra Angelico, Tintoretto, and
now Veronese marked the milestones in his life.

One effect of the moment in the gallery in Turin, however, was that
Ruskin moved away from the study of paintings for a while. His religion, as
he explained in his account in 1877, was now "the religion of Humanity." (29:90) And that meant engaging in human problems. The 1860s were
years of social criticism during which he found that, however popular he
might be as an art critic, his attack on the economic philosophy of the day
was considered ridiculous. Contact with art was not lost, for his argument
was still that the quality of art was an index of the health of a nation, but he
now believed that the medicine of reform—in his case a return to a
preindustrial system of social values—should be applied directly to society
if art were to thrive. Thus he said of a portrait of Doge Andrea Gritti, which
he bought in 1864 believing it to be by Titian (though it is now attributed to
Catena), that it "tells you everything essential to be known about the power
of Venice in his day—the breed of her race, their self-command, their
subtlety, their courage, their refinement of sensitive faculty, and their noble
methods of work." (19:250) And, to make a point about the political
leadership of his own day, he prefaced this by saying that it "should be
especially interesting to us English, for it is the portrait of a Merchant
King." (19:248)

Free of the constraint of a religious dogma, Ruskin was able to take
a wider view of art, and he began to create for himself a system that could
apply to all arts of all times. Building on the system of typological analysis he
had learned as a child, and adding to it the wide range of iconographic

reference he had acquired as a student of art and literature, he sought to show that art made sense of the world through images and symbols — if one knew how to look. The search for significance took Ruskin back to the religious painters, and again a turning point was reached in front of a picture.

In 1874 Ruskin went to Assisi and studied a fresco in the lower church that was believed to be by Giotto, *The Marriage of Poverty and Saint Francis*. In spite of the experience at Turin, Ruskin was still nagged by the apparent conflict between the ability to paint well — that is to render the truth of appearance — and the ability to convey religious truth. At Assisi the problem was solved as he drew from the fresco. He wrote in 1877:

> *While making this drawing, I discovered the fallacy under which I had been tormented for sixteen years, — the fallacy that Religious artists were weaker than Irreligious. I found that all Giotto's "weaknesses" (so called) were merely absences of material science. He did not know, and could not, in his day, so much of perspective as Titian, — or so much of the laws of light and shade, so much of technical composition. But I found he was in the make of him, and contents, a very much stronger and greater man*

45

Figure 34
JOHN RUSKIN (1819–1900)
Spray of Dead Oak Leaves. 1879
Watercolor and body color,
4¾ × 6¾″
The Ruskin Gallery, Sheffield—The
Collection of the Guild of Saint
George

Ruskin equated vegetation with the vitality he perceived in ancient buildings, often commenting on the parallels between the structure of leaves and architectural form. He pointed in particular to the abstracted tendrils and leaves carved into architectural supports. Such "ornaments" bound architecture to nature: "A single leaf laid upon an angle of a stone, or the mere form or framework of a leaf drawn upon it, or the mere shadow and ghost of a leaf, . . . possesses a charm nothing else can replace, a charm not exciting, nor demanding laborious thought or sympathy, but perfectly simple, peaceful and satisfying." (9:279)

than Titian; that the things I had fancied easy in his work, because they were so unpretending and simple, were nevertheless entirely inimitable; that the Religion in him, instead of weakening, had solemnized and developed every faculty of his heart and hand; and finally that his work, in all the innocence of it, was yet a human achievement and possession, quite above everything that Titian had ever done! (29:91)

This reconciliation with religious painting helped to reconcile Ruskin with religion itself. Veronese had helped him out of the narrow Protestantism of his youth, but he had found that living without any hope of an afterlife was as difficult as living in fear of eternal Hell. The return to belief was not a step back into earlier attitudes; rather, it was an expansion, as he saw first that Protestantism and then agnosticism were too narrow to permit a full comprehension of the world. He was, as he said himself, becoming "Catholic" in the true sense of the word. (29:92)

The problem for Ruskin's audience was that his expanded vision seemed to be becoming more and more mystical. Because he wanted to bring all things to unity, in his public writing he would jump from subject to subject in a confusing manner, and, although discussing quite simple things, he would give them a deep significance. The fresco at Assisi has simple shapes and colors, but iconographically it is very complicated, and in tracing the reticulated connections of mythological, literary, and religious reference Ruskin added layers of complexity that strains the coherence of his prose to the breaking point.

There is another reason for the stress that much of his later writing reveals. The public iconography also carried a private symbolism as the contradictions in Ruskin's private life became increasingly unbearable. His marriage to Effie Gray had been annulled in 1854 on the grounds that it had never been consummated because Ruskin was incurably impotent. While there is no reason to suppose that Ruskin did not die a virgin, like a number of other men of his education, class, and period he was undeniably attracted to young girls, whose innocence and purity had, paradoxically, an erotic appeal.

In 1858 he had given drawing lessons to a nine-year-old girl, Rose La Touche. In 1866, when she was seventeen and he forty-seven, he had proposed to her. She did not say no, but asked him to wait three years. Ruskin's age, the scandal of his annulment, and the fact that he no longer professed the Evangelical Anglicanism of Rose and her parents did not make the likelihood of marriage great. In addition, Rose was a strange, sick girl who suffered at times from religious mania. The result was an agoniz-

Figure 35
JOHN RUSKIN (1819–1900)
Oak Spray in Winter Seen in Front.
1867
Watercolor and body color on blue paper, 8⅝ × 10½″
Ashmolean Museum, Oxford;
Educational Series 266

Seeking a poetic mythological parallel, Ruskin called this delicate rendering of an oak stem "The Dryad's Waywardness." He also saw in the tangled and twisted, "poverty-striken, hunger-pinched and tempest-tossed" (7:94) fragment of the great English oak a symbol for moral persistence and the will to survive.

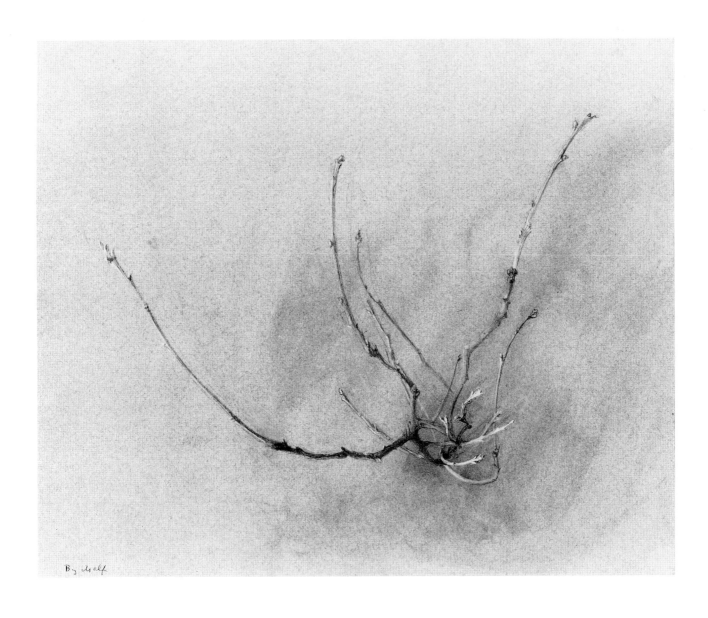

By myself

MASTER OF THE VEILS (active late thirteenth century)
The Marriage of Poverty and Saint Francis. c. 1296
Fresco
Lower Church, Basilica of San Francesco, Assisi

ing relationship for both of them, punctuated by brief, ecstatic encounters that were followed by long periods of mutual misunderstanding.

Rose died, insane, in May 1875. One of the sources of the "withering and disgusting pain" he felt when he arrived in Venice in September 1877 was undoubtedly Ruskin's private grief. But his obsession with Rose went beyond the grave. He had already begun to dabble in spiritualism in the 1860s, and he allowed mediums to persuade him that he could get in touch with his now-dead love. He also saw symbolic significance in the paintings he studied. Thus at Assisi he identified himself with Saint Francis because, like Saint Francis, he was in the process of giving away much of the fortune he had inherited from his father.

This mystical strain had become even more apparent during his stay in Venice in 1876 and 1877. Since September he had been making a study of Carpaccio's *The Dream of Saint Ursula* (figure 36). He had had the painting taken down from the walls of the Accademia Gallery so that he could examine it more closely in a private room, and almost every day he worked on the series of careful watercolor copies that he was making.

He found the work extremely difficult and, as he struggled with his studies, the painting took on an intensely personal meaning. Saint Ursula, like Rose, had died a virgin, prevented by martyrdom from consummating her marriage to a pagan English prince. Increasingly, Ruskin identified Carpaccio's sleeping saint with his dead love. At Christmas a friend sent him a pot of carnations very like the flowers that stand on Saint Ursula's windowsill, and art and life came together in a particularly painful way. He believed that the flowers were a sign that Rose La Touche was trying to communicate through the picture of Saint Ursula, and under the emotional stress he came near to insanity. In 1878 he was to break down completely for the first time.

Although he had hinted at the experience caused by Carpaccio's Saint Ursula in earlier issues of *Fors Clavigera* from Venice, Ruskin did not mention it again in the April issue, though Carpaccio, as the painter of a cycle depicting the life of Saint George, also had a more permissibly public significance for the master of the Guild of Saint George. Ruskin had already revealed a great deal of himself through Tintoretto, Veronese, and Giotto. A discussion of *The Dream of Saint Ursula* might have revealed too much. Instead, he abruptly cut short his account with a challenge from the Sheffield workers he was supposed to be addressing. "'But what is all this about Titian and Angelico to you,'" are you thinking? "'We belong to cotton mills—iron mills; —what is Titian to *us*!—and to all men. Heirs only of simial life, what Angelico?'" (29:91)

Belatedly, he tried to return to his original intention, but now there was no time to explain the creed of the Guild of Saint George. All he could offer was partial advice and the promise that, if his Sheffield workers persevered, the significance of Fra Angelico and Titian for iron workers eventually would become clear.

Neither the creed of Saint George nor Ruskin's autobiography was ever finished. Like so many of his drawings, the little sketch of his life was left incomplete. A finished description of Ruskin's work would be immense, but a rapid sketch can suggest a great deal. It is clear that he did not have the sort of mind that went directly forward on a single thread of argument. He worked less by a process of analysis, in which ideas are separated from each other and broken down, than by one of synthesis, gradually drawing ideas together into a whole.

His was the method of the painter as opposed to that of the scientist, and the crucial changes in his life that took place in front of paintings show that the faculty of sight was essential to him. His whole method as a critic depended on visual observation. But though Ruskin's imagination was visual, his public medium was words, and that has created a tension between image and idea. Ironically, for a time he was appreciated as only a great word painter, without it being realized how much his most profound insights depended on visual sensations. Ruskin himself did realize, however. He wrote in *Modern Painters*: "The greatest thing a human soul ever does in this world is to *see* something, and tell what it *saw* in a plain way. Hundreds of people can talk for one who can think, but thousands can think for one who can see. To see clearly is poetry, prophecy, and religion,—all in one." (5:333)

VITTORE CARPACCIO (c. 1465–1525/6)
The Dream of Saint Ursula. 1495
Oil on canvas, 8′11⅞″ × 8′9⅛″
Accademia, Venice

On Good Friday, 1877, Ruskin sent off to his printers in England the completed text for the first part of his guide to Venice, *Saint Mark's Rest*, which was intended to complete the work on the stones of Venice that he had begun twenty-six years before. In his preface he wrote: "Great nations write their autobiographies in three manuscripts;—the book of their deeds, the book of their words, and the book of their art. Not one of these books can be understood unless we read the two others; but of the three, the only quite trustworthy one is the last." (24:203)

The same can be said of the three aspects of Ruskin's biography: his life, his books, and art, both his own and the art that he made his own through the art of seeing. Of these three, it is the visual dimension, the evidence of his eyes, that will tell us most about him.

NOTES

1. John Ruskin, *Ruskin in Italy: Letters to His Parents, 1845,* ed. Harold I. Shapiro (Oxford, 1972), 144.
2. *Ibid.*, 211.
3. *Ibid.*, 212.
4. *Ibid.*
5. *Ibid.*, 142.

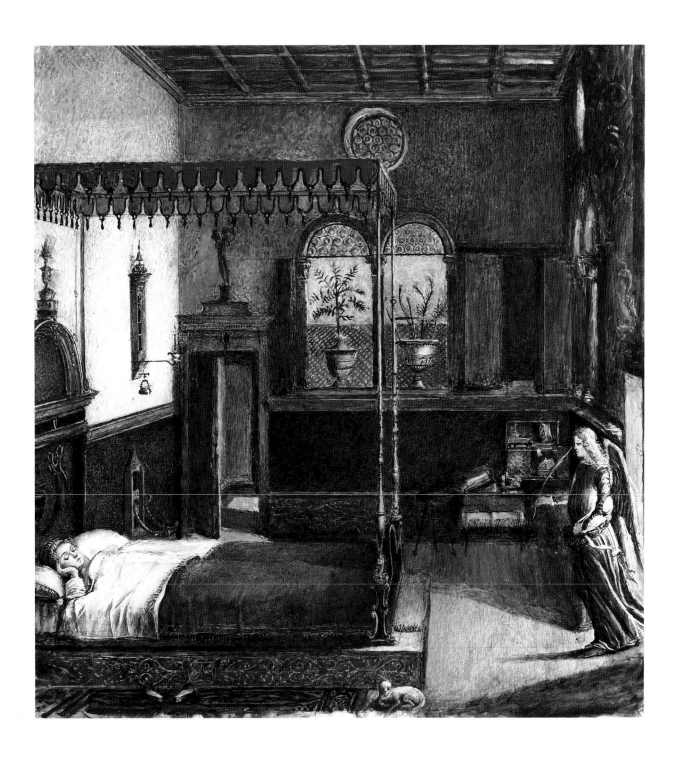

Figure 36
JOHN RUSKIN (1819–1900)
The Dream of Saint Ursula, after
Carpaccio. 1867
Watercolor and body color,
11½ × 10⅞″
Ashmolean Museum, Oxford

At first, Ruskin set about copying Carpaccio's eight paintings of the legend of Saint Ursula for the benefit of his Oxford students. (13:525 n.) He gained permission to have *The Dream of Saint Ursula* removed from the upper reaches of the Accademia's walls and lowered for him to see. Ruskin recalled in his diary on September 19, 1877: "Fancy having St. Ursula right down on the floor in a good light and leave to lock myself in with her. . . . There she lies, so real, that when the room's quite quiet, I get afraid of waking her!" (24:xxxvii) Carpaccio's work became an obsession for him as, more and more, he saw Saint Ursula as his lost, beloved Rose La Touche.

How to Read Ruskin: The Art Critic as Victorian Sage

George P. Landow

Figure 37
WILLIAM HOLMAN HUNT
(1827–1910)
The Shadow of Death. 1870–73
Oil on canvas, 36½ × 28¾"
Leeds City Art Galleries, England

Hunt worked on this and a larger version of *The Shadow of Death* (Manchester City Art Gallery) while in Bethlehem and Jerusalem from 1869 to 1872; he finally finished the two in London in 1873. Attempting rigorous exactitude, he actually studied carpenters' shops in Bethlehem and searched tirelessly for models, traditional tools, authentic textiles, and furnishings. His efforts epitomized Ruskin's definition of the Pre-Raphaelite's "one principle . . . uncompromising truth . . . obtained by working everything, down to the most minute detail, from nature, and from nature only." (12:157) As in *The Light of the World*, the overt realism holds deeper meaning: The startled Virgin turns to see a shadow cast on the wall, prefiguring His Crucifixion, the tools suggest the implements used to torture Him, His simple dress recalls the loincloth, the shadow of the saw becomes the spear that wounded His side. The fruit, scrolls, architecture, and other details also expand the sacred content.

John Ruskin, Victorian England's most brilliant and influential critic of the arts, gained much of his authority with contemporaries because he wrote in ways that his Victorian audience found compelling. Drawing upon the time, vocabulary, and techniques of sermon and biblical prophecy, satire, and romantic poetry, he created arguments for the arts and interpretations of individual works that had particular appeal for his readers then but which today often strikes us as, however brilliantly crafted, couched in an idiom foreign to our expectations for criticism. In other words, while looking at the works illustrated here, we would do well to make ourselves aware of his expectations and those of his readers; or to put this another way, we need to know how to read Ruskin.

In the following pages I propose, therefore, to point out some of the means that Ruskin employed to present himself as a Victorian sage, as one, that is, who saw and understood more intensely than his readers. Looking at *Modern Painters, Academy Notes*, and works of social criticism like *Unto This Last* and "A Joy For Ever." His approach to convincing his audience, which connects these very different works, provides us with a way to read this great critic of art and society. Understanding how Ruskin wrote as a secular prophet promises to give us a window into the mind, heart, and eye of both the Victorian age and its greatest guide to the arts.

Part of Ruskin's difficulty for readers in this last decade of the twentieth century lies precisely in the fact that he was preeminently Victorian. True, today Ruskin can still teach us to see the natural world and the art of Turner and the Pre-Raphaelites with new eyes. True, his advocacy of what has become the modern approach to social welfare still strikes us as immediately relevant. Aspects of his art criticism, such as his elaborate iconological readings of Turner and Hunt, also strike us as inherently modern, so much so that art historians have only recently begun to catch up to them. Nonetheless, however much Ruskin seems at times so essentially modern, so much our contemporary, he was a Victorian who embodied much of his age's extraordinary complexity.

For much of this century, the term Victorian, which literally describes things and events in the reign of Queen Victoria (1837–1901), has meant prudish, repressed, and old-fashioned. Although such associations have a basis in fact, they fail to convey the nature of this incredibly energetic, paradoxical age, which was a second English Renaissance. Like Elizabethan England, Victorian England saw a great expansion of wealth, power, and culture, and with this expansion came a consequent shift of the cultural center lower on the social and economic scale.

Figure 38
J. M. W. TURNER (1775–1851)
Study of an Industrial Town at Sunset.
c. 1830
Watercolor, 13⅝ × 19″
The Turner Collection, Tate Gallery,
London

This watercolor, made for Turner's series *Picturesque Views in England and Wales*, depicts smokey haze lying over one of the numerous industrial towns that Turner visited in England's Midland. Ruskin became increasingly horrified by the polluting effects of industry. In *Modern Painters* 5, he worried that "England should become the furnace of the world . . . and every kind of sordid, foul or venomous work which, in other countries, men dreaded or disdained, it should become England's duty to do." (7:425) He was certain that Turner shared his feeling of impending tragedy, and this affected his interpretation of Turner's works in that last volume of the monumental *Modern Painters.*

Ruskin had such enormous, indeed unrivaled, influence because he was the right man at the right time; this was due not only to his valuable knowledge and feeling for art, but also to his conception of the art critic as a combination of sage, satirist, and prophet exactly suited the needs of a new middle- and working-class audience. To his audience, many of whom were evangelicals both within and without the established church, Ruskin's use of argument, method, and tone derived from the Puritan tradition of preaching and scriptural interpretation made a great deal of sense; such procedure justified the importance of art in a manner that Ruskin's public valued, and it also made paintings and buildings seem very much a part of its overall conception of things. Ruskin, in other words, was the great master of Victorian relevance.[1] In particular, his defiance of tradition and recognized authority, which so infuriated conservative critics, struck just the right note for an audience in the midst of asserting its own power and place in Victorian society.

In science and technology, the Victorians invented the modern idea of invention—the notion, essentially, that one can create solutions to problems, that people can create new means of bettering themselves. Within this context, Ruskin's writings on art convey the characteristic Victorian drive for self-improvement and general reform. But such change also brought insecurity, for this Age of Change called into question notions of God, humanity, and the world. New understanding of biology, geology, and the origin and development of language undermined long-held assumptions about nature and the Bible. Paradoxically, this age in which religion seems to have permeated so many aspects of the intellectual and social fabric—something apparent in Ruskin's abundant citation of Scripture and adoption of prophetic genre—was also a great age of doubt, the first that called into question institutional Christianity on such a large scale.[2] Here, as in many aspects of his life, Ruskin appears a representative Victorian; he began his career as a devout Evangelical Anglican, abandoned his belief in 1858 under the pressure of geological discovery and rationalism, went through an agnostic and even atheist phase, and finally returned to a personal form of Christianity in the 1870s.[3] The Oxford Movement, the power of Evangelicalism, the spread of the Broad Church, and the rise of Utilitarianism, socialism, Darwinism, and scientific agnosticism were all in their own ways characteristically Victorian, as were the prophetic writings of Ruskin and Thomas Carlyle, the criticism of Matthew Arnold, and the empirical prose of Charles Darwin and Thomas Huxley.

This age of paradox and power created astonishing innovation and change, as reflected in the advent of democracy, feminism, unionization, socialism, Marxism, and other modern movements. In fact, this age of Darwin, Karl Marx, and Sigmund Freud appears to be not only the first that experienced modern problems but also the first that attempted modern solutions. Victorian can be taken to mean parent of the modern and, like most powerful parents, the age provoked a powerful reaction against itself.

More than any other quality, what made Victorians Victorian was their central emphasis upon social responsibility, a basic attitude that differentiates them from their immediate predecessors, the Romantics. In terms of the arts, the Victorians defined themselves by combining Augustan emphasis upon the general accessibility of art and its social effects with romantic emphasis upon the artist's feeling and imagination.[4] Furthermore, in contrast to the great figures of literary modernism, the Victorians assumed that artist and writer had central roles to play in society. From the point of view of the far less confident twentieth century, whose writers and artists often assume their own elitism and necessary alienation from their fellow citizens, the Victorians strike us as magnificent overreachers, completely unwilling to relinquish either personal or political, subjective or objective.[5] The major Victorians, Carlyle, Alfred, Lord Tennyson, Charles Dickens, and Ruskin, for example, sought to meet the potentially opposed needs of both the artist and the public by finding public use for personal experience.

This Victorian synthesis of Neoclassical and Romantic attitudes appears with striking clarity in *sage-writing*, a literary form uniquely characteristic of the age. Ruskin's social criticism, which exemplifies sage-writing at its finest, employs all the genre's chief devices.[6] These include a characteristic alternation of satire and positive, even visionary, statement, accompanied by a parallel alternation of attacks upon the audience and attempts to reassure or inspire it. The sage's tools for mocking accepted opinion include grotesque analogy and idiosyncratic definition of key terms. In addition, Ruskin's sage-writing, like that of Carlyle and Arnold, frequently directs the reader's attention to ostensibly trivial phenomena, which, only after an act of virtuoso interpretation, turn out to be indices of

Figure 39
DANIEL MACLISE (1806–1870)
The Play Scene in Hamlet. c. 1842
Watercolor, body color, and varnish
on paper, 14¼ × 25½″
The FORBES Magazine Collection,
New York

Maclise was a celebrated painter of literary and historical subjects, such as this scene from act 3, scene 2 of Shakespeare's play. Ruskin castigated Maclise's Shakespearean paintings and the popularity they enjoyed by saying, "Nothing can more completely demonstrate the total ignorance of the public of all that is great or valuable in Shakespeare than their universal admiration of Maclise's 'Hamlet.'" (3:82 n.) Ruskin found Maclise's interpretation shallow rather than emotionally or morally deep, a "grinning and glittering fantasy" that diminished rather than enhanced the theme. (3:619 n.)

the moral and spiritual Condition of England. Like the sage's acts of interpretation, a reliance upon grotesque contemporary phenomena (such as the murder of children), or upon grotesque metaphor, parable, and analogy, tends to associate with, or even produce, sage-writing's characteristic episodic or discontinuous literary structure, which depends upon analogical relation for unity and coherence. All these techniques produce the Victorian sage's defining ethos—the appeal to credibility—created not only by citing personal experience and even by admitting weakness but also by successfully establishing the writer as a virtuoso interpreter of the real.

Several of these devices in particular have special importance when Ruskin the art critic writes as a Victorian sage. Ruskin's comments upon contemporary art in *Modern Painters* and *The Stones of Venice*, for example, employ the sage's often aggressive attitude toward his audience, his positioning himself in opposition to society, his alternation of satire and vision, and his use of discontinuous literary structure. In addition, as we shall see, Ruskin also continually dramatized his dual roles as Master of Interpretation and Master of Experience—this latter role a characteristically Ruskinian use of autobiographical fact to create credibility for the advocation of unusual or eccentric views.

Ruskin always wrote as a polemicist, defining his position in relation to that he wished to refute. Such a manner of proceeding, which derives in part from both his evangelical upbringing and his thorough acquaintance with Alexander Pope, Jonathan Swift, and Samuel Johnson, requires a public voice, for it always implies a public performance. His

Figure 40
WILLIAM HOLMAN HUNT
(1827–1910)
Finished study for *Claudio and Isabella.* 1850
Pencil, pen, and india ink with wash, 12½ × 7½"
Courtesy of the Syndics of the Fitzwilliam Museum, Cambridge, England

In an 1853 Edinburgh lecture on Pre-Raphaelitism, Ruskin spoke of the painting (Tate Gallery) for which this study was made: "With all their faults, [Pre-Raphaelite] pictures are, since Turner's death, the best—incomparably the best—on the walls of the Royal Academy, and such works as Mr. Hunt's *Claudio and Isabella* have never been rivalled, in some respects never approached, at any other period of art." (12:159–60) Hunt was the Pre-Raphaelite most dedicated to moral and sacred subjects. In his "problem pictures," Hunt dramatized moments of moral conflict, such as the one in act 3, scene 1 of Shakespeare's *Measure for Measure*, when Claudio asks his sister Isabella, a novice, to yield herself to Angelo so that he, Claudio, may be saved from execution.

57

essentially polemical approach to art criticism appears with particular savagery in the masterful by satiric description in *Modern Painters* of Claude Lorrain's *La Riccia* (3:278–80); elsewhere he contrasts works valued by the art establishment with either the work of Turner or with nature itself. Such polemical criticism similarly characterizes the entire section he devoted to Abraham Cooper's *The Fusee* in the 1859 *Academy Notes*: "The sublime of English art, truly! A lake, with ingenious white touches at the edges, to mark it from the mountains; some rocks of leather; sky-blue heather; wooden-headed people, displaying themselves in the athletic exercise of smoking; and a pool of water, with vertical reflections of sloping lines! A superb art lesson for the line of the Academy—heroic and optical at once. It is interesting, especially, to see that, in the present state of British science, one may write R. A. after one's name, yet not be able to paint a gutter." (14:219–20) Ruskinian harshness also appears in his famous characterization in *The Art of England* of the "general effect" of Sir Lawrence Alma-Tadema's *Pyrrhic Dance* (figure 42) as "exactly like a microscopic view of a small detachment of black-beetles, in search of a dead rat." (33:321)

Figure 41
JAMES COLLINSON (1825–1887)
To Let. Exhibited 1857
Oil on canvas, 23 × 18″ oval
The FORBES Magazine Collection, New York

Collinson was one of the original seven members of the Pre-Raphaelite Brotherhood, but he resigned in 1850, just two years after its founding. His conversion to Catholicism and his ill-fated engagement to Rossetti's sister, Christina, perhaps contributed to his departure. He painted few rigorously Pre-Raphaelite works. *To Let*, depicting a woman showing an apartment to a prospective renter, is typical of the widely popular scenes of contemporary life that Ruskin often found well painted and generally interesting as social documentation. Yet, insisting on noble and inspirational art, Ruskin placed such incidental subjects below those that dealt with "deep thoughts and sorrows, as, for instance, Hunt, in his *Claudio and Isabella*." (5:49)

Ruskin's severity, which has more in common than he would have liked to admit with that of the periodical viewers who had originally attacked his idol Turner, derives in part from his need to create authority for his public pronouncements. Accustomed to evangelical rhetoric in sermons and tracts, many in his audience expected such forthright assignment of values from anyone who assumed a public role. In his writings on both art and society, Ruskin's harshness often appears directed at industrial civilization's destruction of the natural world. In the 1875 *Academy Notes*, for example, he turns from a picture of a highland glen to comment sarcastically: "Our manufacturers have still left, in some parts of England and Scotland, streams of what may be advertised in the bills of Natural Scenery as 'real water'; and I myself know several so free from pollution that one can sit near them with perfect safety, even when they are not in flood." (14:305) As this bitter Swiftian criticism of society indicates, Ruskin often took, late and early in his career, an artistic phenomenon and then easily moved to the social, political, and economic conditions that provided its context and for which it, in turn, provided a magnifying, clarifying lens.

Ruskin, who created much of his credibility when arguing for the importance of art by showing its essential relation to the society that made it, frequently directed a satirical glance at the connections between Victorian art and Victorian society. For an example of this kind of satire, the reader of *Academy Notes* does not have to do more than turn to the page containing his attack on the way his contemporaries destroy the environment. Discussing paintings of what he terms "policy," that is, paintings with explicitly political subjects, Ruskin points out how vastly Victorian art differs from Renaissance art. "In old times," he reminds us, "all great artistic nations were pictorially talkative" on the two subjects of religion and government. In fact, claims Ruskin, the art of "Venice, Florence, and Siena did little else than expound, in figures and mythic types, the nature of civic dignity, statesmanly duty, and senatorial or soldierly honour." (14:306) British art, in contrast, ignored all such matters of public policy, or, as Ruskin characteristically put it: "The verdict of existing British art on existing British Policy is therefore, if I understand it rightly, that we have none; but, in the battle of life, have arrived at declaration of an universal *sauve qui peut*—or explicitly, to all men, Do as you like, and get what you can." (14:307) Several things about this passage from Ruskin's art criticism demand comment. First of all, this serious, high-minded tone, which came so naturally to Ruskin, perfectly suited the needs and expectations of many in his audience. The author of *Modern Painters*, *The Stones of Venice*, and the *Academy Notes* fully understood the importance of being earnest. Second, Ruskin's placement of contemporary works in the wider contexts provided by political questions and art history simultaneously demonstrated his grasp of important issues and showed his competence in handling such issues. Such a manner of proceeding, in other words, showed his audience that art and architecture, like questions of poverty, unemployment, and religious doubt, validly belonged to the Condition of England. These matters, in other words, fell within the purview of the Victorian sage, within the compass of a secular prophet who told his contemporaries things that they might not want to hear but which they needed to know if the nation were to survive, much less flourish, in civil peace and prosperity.

Figure 42
SIR LAWRENCE ALMA-TADEMA
(1836–1912)
Pyrrhic Dance. 1869
Oil on panel 16 × 32"
Guildhall Art Gallery, Corporation
of London

Ruskin named Alma-Tadema as a leading exponent of the "Classic Schools of
Painting" in his 1883 Oxford lecture,
part of *The Art of England* series. Enormously successful and popular, Alma-
Tadema specialized in subjects depicting life in the ancient world, such as
this portrayal of a warlike Greek dance
named for its inventor, Pyrrichus. Ruskin admired Alma-Tadema's technique
but disliked certain elements of his
work, including its "universal twilight
. . . also universal crouching or lolling
posture,—either in fear or laziness.
And the most gloomy, the most
crouching, the most dastardly of all
these representations of classic life,
was the little picture called the Pyrrhic
Dance." (33:320–21)

As conceived by Ruskin, Carlyle, and Arnold, the role of secular prophet
consists of far more than simply pronouncing earnest readings of the
Condition of England in a mocking, satirical tone. Ruskin's criticism of art
and society alternated satire and positive recommendations, criticism and
encouragement. In his writings on art these passages of positive statement
that alternate with his satire take three forms, all of which relate closely to
the pleasures of vision. First of all, he creates detailed descriptions of
visual fact, particularly as it relates to landscape and to artistic representation of the natural world; second, Ruskin combines description with
narrative to create parables of exemplary visual experience; and third,
particularly in his social criticism, he offers explicitly visionary consolation
and encouragement.

In the first kind of positive passage, Ruskin assumes the role of
teacher, explaining general principles. For example, in his brief mention of
two of William Holman Hunt's pictures he remarks: "The gleam of the
Dead Sea in the distance of [the *View from the Mount of Offense* is] quite
marvellous, and the drawing of the Sphinx [figure 45] is an invaluable
record. Probably the reader who has never studied natural facts will think
the colouring extraordinary, as Turner's used to be thought. It is, nevertheless, precisely true—touch for touch. I have given the reasons of its apparent want of truth in *Modern Painters*." (14:70–71)

Far more typical are passages, such as that in the *Academy Notes* on
Frederick Goodall's *Felice Ballarin Reciting "Tasso" to the People of Chioggia*,
in which Ruskin makes a point that ties directly to one of his central
emphases—on nature's infinite variety or his belief that a realistic style
serves to educate the eye and hand of the beginning artist. In this case
Ruskin uses a work in the Royal Academy exhibition as an excuse for
expounding once again his theory that the visual arts do not—indeed,

cannot—imitate nature directly but require a syntax of proportionate relationships, or what Gombrich has taught us to call schemata.[7] After praising Goodall's picture, Ruskin remarks that it fails at a point that "involves an important principle[:] . . . It is wholly impossible to paint the effect of sunlight truly. It has never been done, and never will be." As he explains, repeating crucial points he made in the first and fourth volumes of *Modern Painters*:

> *Sunshine is brighter than any mortal can paint, and all resemblances to it must be obtained by sacrifice. In order to obtain a popularly effective sunlight, colour must be sacrificed. De Hoogh, Cuyp, Claude, Both, Richard Wilson, and all other masters of sunshine, invariably reach their most telling effects by harmonies of gold with grey, giving up the blues, rubies, and freshest greens. Turner did the same in his earlier work. Modern Pre-Raphaelites, and Turner in his later work, reached magnificent effects of sunshine colour, but of a kind necessarily unintelligible to the ordinary observer (as true sunshine colour will always be, since it is impossible to paint it of the pitch of light which has true relation to its*

Figure 43
THOMAS SEDDON (1821–1856)
Léhon from Mont Parnasse, Brittany.
Exhibited 1853
Oil on canvas, 22⅝ × 29½″
Museo de Arte de Ponce, Luis A. Ferré Foundation, Inc. Ponce, Puerto Rico

Seddon painted in the "prosaic" Pre-Raphaelite style that Ruskin preferred to the "poetic" style, for he felt it more forcefully contributed to the health of the nation. (14:468) Seddon said he attempted to represent "specimens of every tree in the universe" in this vista. Facing the onslaught of industrialism, Ruskin argued that unspoiled nature recorded in paintings such as this would be the only surviving tokens of a lost pastoral beauty.

Figure 44
J. M. W. TURNER (1775–1851)
Devonport and Dockyard, Devonshire.
c. 1828
Watercolor, 10⅝ × 17″
Fogg Art Museum, Harvard
University Art Museums; Gift of
Charles Fairfax Murray (in Memory
of W. J. Stillman)

Ruskin verbally painted the sky in this scene: "The breaking up of the warm rain-clouds of summer, thunder passing away in the west, the golden light and melting blue mingled with yet falling rain, which troubles the water surface, making it misty altogether." (13:439) The weather here very clearly relates to the subject. Naval crews are being paid off at the end of a war as distant storm clouds disappear to reveal a peaceful sky beyond. The gambrel-roofed buildings are dry-dock sheds in which the warships were built, the openings through which the ships were launched can be seen at the ends of the sheds. Ruskin owned this work, and although he extolled Turner's skilled drawing of the ships, he deplored the vulgarity with which the artist portrayed the figures.

Opposite, above:
Figure 45
WILLIAM HOLMAN HUNT
(1827–1910)
The Sphinx, Gizeh, Looking toward the Pyramids of Sakhara. 1854
Watercolor and body color, 10 × 14″
Harris Museum and Art Gallery,
Preston, England

Hunt visited Egypt and the Holy Land several times in the pursuit of absolute fidelity in his religious paintings. His topographical views of various sites proved to be accurate *aide-mémoire* and remarkable works of art in their own rights, combining a personal outlook with symbolic allusions. In the *Saturday Review* of July 4, 1857, a critic wrote that Hunt's "'Great Sphynx' represents the back of the colossal head, and seems somewhat wilful in the point of view taken, until we discern that the desert is the true subject, over which we are desired to look with the sphynx, who has been regarding the same for thirty centuries." Ruskin was not enthusiastic about Hunt's journeys, but he praised the extraordinary color in this and other watercolors in his 1856 *Academy Notes*.

Opposite, below:
Figure 46
WILLIAM HOLMAN HUNT
(1827–1910)
The Mosque at Sakrah, Jerusalem, During Ramazan, 1854. 1854–
c. 1860
Watercolor heightened with body color, 8¾ × 14½″
The Whitworth Art Gallery,
University of Manchester, England

Hunt's watercolor was exhibited with *The Sphinx, Gizeh* in 1856 at the Royal Academy under the title *Jerusalem by Moonlight—Looking over the Site of the Temple to the Mount of Olives.* This view from his house was described in a letter to Millais dated June 25, 1854, "I have the most lovely prospect from my window[;] to the right I look over the mosque of Homar which occupies the site of the Temple, towards the Mount of Olives which rises above everything in the town." Referring to this piece, *The Sphinx*, and one other work in *Academy Notes*, Ruskin wrote that all were "intensely faithful studies in the East." (14:70)

shadows). And thus the "Sun of Venice," and the "Slave Ship," with Hunt's "Two Gentlemen of Verona," "Stray Sheep," and such others, failed of almost all their due effect on the popular mind. (14:225–26)

Under these circumstances, the artist must make a choice between two mutually exclusive effects—tonality or color. "Give up your sunlight, and you may get Titian's twilight. Give up your Titianesque depth, and you may, by thorough study from Nature, get some approximation to noonday flame. But you cannot have both." (14:226)

Ruskin points to Goodall's inattention to the effects of light, citing as example the figure of a woman who sits with her "lap in sunshine, her head in shade. Whatever light touches the head would be reflected light, and it would be reflected from the ground, shining strongly under her brows and on the lower part of her face; instead of which there is a shadow under the brow, exactly as if she were sitting in a room with ordinary daylight entering from above through a window. The picture," Ruskin concludes, "is full of grammatical error of the same kind—the kind of error which in these days of earnest effort and accurate science, artists should get quit of with their long-clothes and spelling-books." (14:226–27)

In contrast to this kind of visual instruction that emphasizes an essentially intellectual comprehension of visual fact and the principles that underlie it, Ruskin also describes natural fact with a kind of visionary

J. M. W. TURNER (1775–1851)
Slavers Throwing Overboard the Dead and Dying—Typhoon Coming On (The Slave Ship). Exhibited 1840
Oil on canvas, 35¾ × 48″
Courtesy, Museum of Fine Arts, Boston; Henry Lillie Pierce Fund

intensity that imposes on the reader's senses the potential joy of nature, the art that represents it, and the critic who captures the pleasures of both. The *Academy Notes* for 1855 provides a fine example of such a passage of visionary beauty, which Ruskin often introduces unexpectedly. In this case Ruskin pauses in the midst of an argument with a writer from *The Globe*, who had disagreed with his valuation of David Roberts's *Rome* (14:28), and quotes a passage from the first volume of *Modern Painters* that the critic had taken out of context: "'I have seen the pale fresh green of spring vegetation in the gardens of Venice turned pure russet, or between that and crimson, by a vivid sunset of this kind, *every particle of green colour being absolutely annihilated*.'" Ruskin then points out that he never stated that sunset makes everything appear the same color. Rather, he explains, "the light which will turn green to brownish russet turns blue to purple, white to pale rose, scarlet to a burning-flame colour, far above all possible imitation, and brown to scarlet,—every colour retaining its due relation, in paleness or darkness, to every other; while all the shadows, down to the minutest angle of a stone, retaining the local colours unaltered by the light, and doubly brought out by opposition, fill the intervals and interstices of the warm effect with the most marvellous pieces of the purest blue, green or grey." (14:34–35) Reading such passages, one encounters the combination of a preternatural visual sensitivity with an astonishing ability to record what he has seen in a prose that permits others to share, for a few brief moments, Ruskin's prophetic intensity. These passages convince us that,

Figure 47
WILLIAM HENRY HUNT
(1790–1864)
Apple Blossom and Bird's Nest. n.d.
Watercolor and body color, 7⅝ × 11″
Harris Museum and Art Gallery,
Preston, England

Ruskin deplored paintings of hothouse flowers and fruit in "polite symmetry"; he contrasted the tradition of seventeenth-century still life with that of Hunt, whom he felt was a consummate still-life painter. Ruskin praised the humility of Hunt's common flowers and herbage, set down on mossy English banks and described with joy and love. (14:378) Though sometimes concerned by Hunt's overfidelity in foliage, Ruskin remained in awe of his abilities, saying "Hunt is the only man we have who can paint the real leaf-green under sunlight, and in this respect his trees are delicious, summer itself." (3:603–4) Hunt's frequent use of birds' nests as subject matter resulted in his nicknames "Bird's Nest Hunt" and "Hedgerow Hunt."

JOHN BRETT (1830–1902)
The Val d'Aosta. 1858
Oil on canvas, 34½ × 26⅞"
Private Collection

however odd some of his views might seem, Ruskin has seen more than most people ever have and that, furthermore, that he can teach *us* to see with at least some of his perceptiveness and intensity.

In *Modern Painters*, the essay entitled "Traffic," and works that combine art and social criticism, Ruskinian lessons in vision take other forms, one of the most important of which is the parable of experience, or word-painting. Drawing upon the writings of Ann Radcliffe and William Wordsworth, Ruskin frequently created quasi-cinematic prose that transforms description, most often of landscape, into narrative.[8] Thus, in his discussion of John Brett's *The Val d'Aosta* in the 1859 *Academy Notes*, he characteristically begins by situating the spectator in "a Piedmontese valley . . . in July," after which he directs the spectator's eye as if it were a movie camera. (In the following passages emphases have been added to show Ruskin's "camera directions.") "If you look," he tells us, "you will find it is jewelled and set with stars in a stately way. White poplars by the roadside, shaking silvery in the wind: I regret to say the wind is apt to come up the Val d'Aosta in an ill-tempered and rude manner, turning leaves thus the wrong side out; but it will be over in a moment." At this point, like the cinematographer using a zoom lens, he moves us deeper into the scene and then immediately pauses to explain its history and significance: *"Beyond the poplars you may see* the slopes of arable and vineyard ground, such as give the wealth and life to Italy which she idly trusts in — ground laid ages ago in wreaths, like new cut hay by the mountain streams, now terraced and trimmed into all gentle service." Similarly, when he wishes to focus our attention on specific details of the landscape that Brett has captured in his painting, he presents them as part of a narrative sequence. Thus, he tells us that if we want to know what Italian vines look like:

> *That is the look of them — the dark spots and irregular cavities,* seen through *the broken green of their square-set ranks, distinguishing them at any distance from the continuous pale fields of low-set staff and leaf, divided by no gaps of gloom, which clothe a true vine country.* There, *down in the mid-valley,* you see *what pasture and meadow land we have, we Piedmontese, with our hamlet and cottage life, and groups of glorious wood.* Just beyond *the rock are two splendid sweet chestnut trees, with forming fruit, good for making bread of, no less than maize;* lower down, far to the left, *a furlong or two of the main stream with its white shore and alders: not beautiful, for it has come down into all this fair*

Figure 48
JOHN RUSKIN (1819–1900)
Thunder Clouds, Val d'Aosta. 1858
Watercolor and body color, $5 \times 6\frac{7}{8}''$
Education Trust Ltd., Brantwood, Coniston

Ruskin made this drawing in the summer of 1858 to "show the height of clouds in the sky." He had his assistant and follower Arthur Severn enlarge the sketch for his lecture "The Storm-Cloud of the Nineteenth Century," delivered on February 4, 1884, in which Ruskin described an ominous and threatening darkness that he perceived growing over England.

country from the Courmayeur glaciers, and is yet untamed, cold, and furious, incapable of rest. But above, *there is rest, where the sunshine* streams into *iridescence through branches of pine, and turns the pastures into strange golden clouds, half grass, half dew; for the shadows of the great hills have kept the dew there since morning. Rest also, calm enough, among the ridges of rock and forest that heap themselves into that purple pyramid* high on the right. *(14:235)*

As Ruskin moves us through this scene, he transforms the visual into something close to the visionary. Part of his power of doing so comes from the way he doubly energizes the landscape: first by the movement of the spectator's eye and then, in the last sentences of the passage, by the movement of light that "streams" through the pine branches and "turns" the land below into "strange golden clouds"—by transfiguring, in other words, the visual into the visionary and the quotidian earth into the earthly paradise.

Whereas Ruskin's art criticism alternates satire with descriptions—or rather dramatizations—of great visual beauty, his social criticism tends to alternate prophetic attack with explicitly visionary encouragement. Ruskin thus characteristically closes "A Joy For Ever" with a promise of coming good:

A time will come—I do not think even now it is far from us—when this golden net of the world's wealth will be spread abroad as the flaming meshes of morning cloud are over the sky; bearing with them the joy of light and the dew of the morning, as well as the summons to honourable and peaceful toil. What less can we hope from your wealth than this, rich men of England, when once you feel fully how . . . you can . . . command the energies—inform the ignorance—prolong the existence, of the whole human race; and how, even of worldly wisdom, which man employs faithfully, it is true, not only that her ways are pleasantness, but that her paths are peace; and that, for all the children of men, as well as for those to whom she is given, Length of days is in her right hand, as in her left hand Riches and Honour?[9]

Like his scriptural allusion throughout his career, Ruskin's reference to Proverbs 3:16–17 creates moral and spiritual authority for his arguments. It also fulfills the needs of many in his audience, particularly Evangelicals, who wished to be reassured that the arts served God and not the devil. Ruskin's use of a visionary tone to inspire his readers' efforts places them within the world of the Bible. Even for readers with little knowledge of or feeling for that world, Ruskin's magisterial control of sentence rhythm and poetic imagery by themselves communicate his visionary rewards.

At times these visionary passages are very brief, like that in "A Joy For Ever," which asserts, "Nearly every great and intellectual race of the world has produced, at every period of its career, an art with some peculiar and precious character about it, wholly unattainable by any other race, and at any other time; and the intention of Providence concerning that art, is evidently that it should all grow together into one mighty temple; the rough stones and the smooth all finding their place, and rising, day by day, in

Figure 49
GEORGE FREDERIC WATTS
(1817–1904)
Peace and Goodwill. 1888–1901
Oil on canvas, 28 × 18″
The Watts Gallery, Compton, England

Ruskin stated that Watts, a good friend, was one of five geniuses—along with Turner, Millais, Rossetti, and Elizabeth Siddal—he had known during his life. (36:217) *Peace and Goodwill* exemplifies Watt's work. Universal concepts are embodied in human forms, infused with personal meaning, and rendered in a classical, Renaissance-inspired style. Watts explained that, here, "Peace was to be a queen, though she is a wanderer and outcast from her kingdom. She will turn wearily towards a streak of light which may mean the dawn of better things. The son, her heir, is still only a young child upon her knee." Ruskin appreciated Watts's lofty themes, but he continually lectured Watts for being too visionary and detached from the facts of reality.

Figure 50
RICHARD REDGRAVE (1804–1888)
The Valleys Also Stand Thick with Corn. 1864
Oil on canvas, 28 × 38″
Birmingham Museum and Art Gallery, England

Redgrave was a major artist, educator, and museum official whose career paralleled Ruskin's. Initially known for his genre scenes, he did landscapes in the latter part of his life. In his *Academy Notes*, Ruskin judged the merits of several Redgrave landscapes according to a Pre-Raphaelite standard, presuming that to be Redgrave's aim. Works such as this were not intentionally Pre-Raphaelite, but they shared many Ruskinian qualities in their celebration of nature's bounty, communal cooperation, and reference to biblical text. When exhibited in 1865, this painting was accompanied by an excerpt from Psalm 65: "The pastures are clothed with flocks; the valleys also are covered over with corn, they shout for joy, they also sing."

richer and higher pinnacles to heaven." (16:64) As this example shows, Ruskin's passages of visionary consolation and encouragement tend to share certain qualities and effects. They often begin with a stately, almost Johnsonian prose and build to a rhetorical climax, they provide effective closure for sections, chapters, or entire works; and they employ related congeries of images—light, sunrise, new life or spirituality, and heaven or the Promised Land.

Ruskin's elaborate biblical rhetoric, allusions to prophetic texts of Scripture, and his formal, ornate diction all struck particular notes in the minds of contemporaries that many of us are unlikely to hear today. In fact, like Carlyle, Thoreau, and Arnold, Ruskin self-consciously assumed the mantle of the Old Testament prophet. Ruskin's acts of interpretation therefore form one of his most powerful means of gaining the attention and allegiance of his audience. His Victorian readers, many of whom regularly attended two-hour sermons emphasizing detailed readings of Scripture, might have been surprised when he applied the commonplace methods of interpreting the Bible to the arts, but many of them would also have found his interpretative skills both entertaining as well as reassuring. Like the great preachers of his day, Ruskin employed elaborate interpretive set pieces as a means of simultaneously making his point and establishing his credibility.

One of the most influential of such Ruskinian acts of interpretation occurs in the second volume of *Modern Painters* when Ruskin sets out to show the reader how to see, experience, and understand Tintoretto's *Annunciation* in the Scuola di San Rocco, Venice. Ruskin begins his reading by dramatizing a spectator's experience of the painting's realism. Ruskin be-

TINTORETTO (JACOPO ROBUSTI) (1518/19–1594)
The Annuciation. 1583–87
Oil on canvas, 17′6″ × 40′2″
Scuolo di San Rocco, Venice

gins his guided tour by pointing out that one first notices the Virgin sitting "houseless, under the shelter of a palace vestibule ruined and abandoned," (4:264) surrounded by desolation. The next step Ruskin takes in leading us through this painting makes clear that he conducts such an act of interpretation as a form of narrative, for he emphasizes not simply what one sees but how one goes about seeing it. He tells us, therefore, that the spectator "turns away at first, revolted, from the central object of the picture forced painfully and coarsely forward, a mass of shattered brickwork, with the plaster mildewed away from it." (4:264) This method of presentation, we realize, places equal weight upon the perceiver and the perceived object, the ideal spectator and what he or she sees.

Then, having described the painting's genre details and the spectator's first reaction to them, Ruskin next points out that such might strike a spectator as merely the kind of scene the artist "could but too easily obtain among the ruins of his own Venice, chosen to give a coarse explanation of the calling and the condition of the husband of Mary." (4:264) In other words, Ruskin begins his presentation of this painting by dramatizing the paths the spectator's eye takes as it comprehends first major and then minor visual details. But because he believes that visible form inextricably relates to meaning, he then immediately presents us with an imagined spectator's

71

first conclusions about the meaning of these details: They appear, it seems, to reflect both the painter's contemporary surroundings in a ruined Venice and his modern fascination with the picturesque, that aesthetic mode that delights in ruin.

At this point, Ruskin takes us deeper into the picture's meaning, but he does so by first intensifying our visual experience of it. According to him, if the spectator examines the "composition of the picture, he will find the whole symmetry of it depending on a narrow line of light, the edge of a carpenter's square, which connects these unused tools with an object at the top of the brickwork, a white stone, four square, the corner-stone of the old edifice, the base of its supporting column." (4:265) Citing Psalm 118, Ruskin explains that these details reveal that the entire painting—and all its coarsely realistic details—bear a typological meaning, for, according to standard readings of this psalm, it prefigures Christ.[10] In Tintoretto's *Annunciation*, therefore, the "ruined house is the Jewish dispensation; that obscurely arising in the dawning of the sky is the Christian; but the corner-stone of the old building remains, though the builders' tools lie idle beside it, and the stone which the builders refused is become the Headstone of the Corner." (4:265)

Ruskin's guide through Tintoretto's *Annunciation* provides his reader with a lesson in a particular kind of perception. Using his gifts for word-painting, iconographical interpretation, and compositional analysis, Ruskin does not simply tell us what the painting in question means. Instead, he provides us with a fable or parable of ideal perception that dramatizes the experience of a spectator who gradually perceives the meaning of a painting and thus fully experiences the work of art. Ruskin understood his role as art critic as necessarily involving an imaginative demonstration of the experience of meaning. Just as *Modern Painters* 1 teaches his readers how to perceive the worlds of nature and art, later volumes teach them how to interpret those works as well, and in both projects, which Ruskin clearly saw completely intertwined, he concentrates on providing the reader with models of experience.

This passage from *Modern Painters* 2 took the form of a characteristically Ruskinian fable or parable of experience in which the sage tested on his own nerves and pulse the experience of encountering a particular work of art. This procedure served the dual rhetorical purpose of convincing the reader of Ruskin's interpretation of a work by dramatizing his experience of it, hence making it more creditable, and also teaching the reader to experience other works of art in the manner that Ruskin has demonstrated.

The aforementioned passage provided a major stimulus to the formation of the Pre-Raphaelite Brotherhood; according to William Holman Hunt (Millais agreed with his account), Ruskin's reading of Tintoretto's painting inspired him in at least two ways.[11] First, this experience convinced him that the artist could be a prophet, and, second, it inspired the Pre-Raphaelite Brotherhood's program of symbolic realism, a program based on the biblical symbolism that informs many of the early works of Holman Hunt, Millais, Rossetti, and others—and one of whose most successful embodiments appears in Holman Hunt's *The Shadow of Death* (figure 37).[12] The Pre-Raphaelite Brotherhood, in other words, has its genesis in a *reading* of another painting, and, as one might expect, that

Figure 51
DANTE GABRIEL ROSSETTI
(1828–1882)
Saint Catherine. 1857
Oil on canvas, 13½ × 9½″
Tate Gallery, London; Presented by Mrs. Emily Toms in Memory of Her Father, Joseph Kershaw, 1931

Rossetti and Ruskin shared a love for all Gothic arts, including illuminated manuscripts, which Ruskin collected passionately. *Saint Catherine*, a Ruskin commission, relates to several manuscripts, including one in Ruskin's collection. Rossetti's subject here is the art of painting rather than the saint's martyrdom. She poses for Saint Luke, the patron saint of painters, while holding the traditional attributes of the wheel and palm. Elizabeth Siddal modeled for the saint.

Figure 52
SIR EDWARD BURNE-JONES
(1833–1898)
Presentation in the Temple, after
Tintoretto. 1862
Watercolor with some scratching-
out, 7⅛ × 9½"
Ashmolean Museum, Oxford

By 1862 Burne-Jones and Ruskin were
close friends, and the artist, along with
his wife, Georgiana, accompanied
Ruskin to France, Switzerland, and
Italy. They separated at Milan. Ruskin
left Burne-Jones with a list of works to
be copied, including Tintoretto's *Presentation in the Temple*. Although anx-
ious to return to his own work, Burne-
Jones found the exercise of copying
"good" nonetheless. In 1870 Ruskin
copied this Tintoretto as well.

Figure 53
JOHN RUSKIN (1819–1900)
Presentation in the Temple, after
Tintoretto. 1870
Pencil and wash heightened with
white, touches of ink, 14 × 15½"
Ashmolean Museum, Oxford

Working from a scaffolding he had
constructed, Ruskin focused on the
central portion of Tintoretto's large
painting in the Scuola de San Rocco,
Venice. In a diary entry from 1846,
Ruskin contrasted Tintoretto and Titian, specifically their depictions of this
subject: "Tintoretto is grey, grand and
useful, no picturesqueness admitted,
Titian is brown and mean, and with all
the evil of picturesqueness." (11:396 n.)

relationship influenced the way the Pre-Raphaelites expected the spectator to receive their works.

Such elaborate interpretative set pieces, which appear throughout Ruskin's art criticism, appear at their most complex and detailed in his readings of Turner's work in the last volume of *Modern Painters* and in his readings of Pre-Raphaelite paintings. Like his word-painting, Ruskin's acts of interpretation, as we have seen, often take the form of narratives. The very act of interpretation, which in Ruskin's hands often presents a contemporary phenomenon or event as a setpiece, a discrete section of his text, also transforms it into an often grotesque, mocking emblem of what he finds wrong with art and society. Using his own term for elaborate allegorical imagery, I call these characteristic Ruskinian set pieces Symbolic Grotesques. Ruskin found much of his material for these pieces in contemporary phenomena.[13] For example, when complaining that the Academy hanging committee rejected a portrait by his friend George Richmond, he transforms this injustice into an emblem of modern treatment of important work. Asserting that "the French use their best old pictures, the treasures of Europe, in the same way [as the English], and hang Titian's and Rubens's portraits to balance each other, forty feet above the eye," Ruskin charged:

> Such treatment of great pictures is simply, and in the full sense of the word, 'savage'; such things cannot be done, whether by us here, or by the French in the Louvre, but in a clownish ignorance of the meaning of the work 'picture,' and of the entire value and purpose of painting. And, indeed, when the pictures are wholly precious and perfect, like the Titian with the red-capped Saint Joseph, which the French have hung high out of

Figure 54
SIR JOHN EVERETT MILLAIS
(1829–1896)
Study for *Christ in the House of His Parents*. c. 1849
Pencil and pen and ink with wash,
7½ × 11⅜″
Tate Gallery, London; Presented by
Sir Hickman Bacon, 1935

Inspired by Rossetti's early biblical subjects, Millais painted one of the most famous and provocative of all Pre-Raphaelite religious paintings, *Christ in the House of His Parents* (Tate Gallery). This study captures those qualities the *Times* described as "plainly revolting." The awkward poses and plain features conscientiously avoid artificial grace and beauty. His study of early Italian paintings and, perhaps, his knowledge of Ruskin's *Modern Painters* 2 through Holman Hunt also inspired his use of symbols: The sheep, well, nails, and hand wound refer to crucial moments in the Passion of Christ.

In this bit of curmudgeonly Ruskiniana, we observe him begin by apparently doing little more than express a pet peeve—that favorite works have been hung in such a way that he (and others) cannot adequately see them. He then proceeds to make this point an occasion for definition and interpretation, turning it, finally, into a Symbolic Grotesque that provides, in this case, a window into the mind and soul of two supposedly great and powerful nations.

Another such "found" Grotesque appears when he takes the supposed decline of Millais's early genius as the embodiment of British failings—hard work in the service of Mammon. Citing in his discussion of Millais's *Deserted Garden* the journal the *Spectator's* assertion, "If we must choose between a Titian and a Lancashire cotton-mill, give us the cotton-mill," Ruskin reaches back, draws the prophet's mantle around his shoulders, and condemns the spiritual and artistic Condition of England:

Figure 55
ELIZABETH SIDDAL (1829–1862)
Holy Family. c. 1856
Watercolor, 7¾ × 6″
Delaware Art Museum; Samuel and
Mary R. Bancroft Collection

Siddal occupied a unique position in the Pre-Raphaelite movement as model, muse, and artist. The wistful, delicate figures and melancholy mood of this vision are common to her style. She produced several religious works, focusing on the image of the Virgin and Child. Along with Holman Hunt, she differed from the majority of the Pre-Raphaelite artists who elected not to concentrate on religious themes as much as might be expected given the Brotherhood's early attention to Christian, even Catholic, subjects. Ruskin encouraged artists to portray the legends of the noble heroes and heroines found in the Bible, thus supporting in this one way, at least, the academic hierarchy of subject matter that placed great importance on virtuous subjects.

Literally, here you have your cotton-mill employed in its own special Art-produce. Here you have, what was once the bone and sinew of a great painter, ground and carded down into black-podded broom-twigs. . . . Threshed under the mammon flail into threads and dust, and shoddy-fodder for fools; making mainfest yet, with what ragged remnant of painter's life is in him, the results of mechanical English labour on English land. Not here the garden of the sluggard, green with rank weeds; not here the garden of the Deserted Village, overgrown with ungathered balm; not here the noble secrecy of a virgin country, where the falcon floats and the wild goat plays; —but here the withering pleasance of a fallen race, who have sold their hearths for money, and their glory for a morsel of bread. (14:302–3)

As Carlyle had done more than four decades earlier, Ruskin condemns England for allowing the mechanical to dominate and distort the human. Drawing once again on biblical language, imagery, and rhetoric, he also condemns the most talented British artist since Turner for having sold out—for having dribbled away his potential greatness in exchange for worldly success. Most of all, Ruskin condemns his age and nation for creating conditions of artistic production that make such artistic and spiritual failure all but inevitable. Of course, this passage in part simply

Figure 56
WILLIAM DYCE (1806–1864)
George Herbert at Bemerton. 1860
Oil on canvas, 34 × 44"
Guildhall Art Gallery, Corporation of London

An early-seventeenth-century poet and cleric, George Herbert was vicar of Bemerton. A love of nature and a deep spirituality pervaded his life and his poetry. Dyce captured these qualities in the serenely beautiful and meaningful landscape in which he placed Herbert: the lute refers to his love of music, the fishing equipment to his priestly calling as a fisher of men, and the spire of Salisbury Cathedral, to which he walked twice weekly, represents the kingdom of God. Dyce's work, infused with religiosity, is at once a portrait, a history painting, and a symbolic landscape. In it he incorporated ideas that Ruskin advocated early in *Modern Painters.*

77

Figure 57
J. M. W. TURNER (1775–1851)
Venice: The Accademia. c. 1840
Watercolor over pencil, pen and ink,
8½ × 12½"
Ashmolean Museum, Oxford

The Academy of Fine Arts was one of many structures in Venice that suffered from modernization of the city. By the time Ruskin described the location in 1877, the view differed considerably from that recorded by Turner around 1840. In his *Guide to the Principal Pictures in the Academy of Fine Arts in Venice*, Ruskin mourned, "If any of my readers care for either Turner or me, they should look at it with some moment's pause, for I have given Turner's lovely sketch of it to Oxford, painted as he saw it fifty years ago, with bright golden sails grouped in front of it where now is the ghastly iron bridge." (24:172)

expresses Ruskin's bitter resentment at what he took to be Millais's personal and artistic betrayal of him—Millais did, after all, side with Ruskin's ex-wife and marry her. At the same time, Ruskin expresses his more justifiable resentment at Millais's descent into the role of society painter within the context of long-standing ideas about the relation of art to society that he had expressed in "A Joy For Ever" and many other works. The difficulty of unraveling the personal and public and the valid and invalid components of this particular Symbolic Grotesque stands as the perfect emblem of Ruskin's flawed greatness as critic of art and society.

In contrast to such discovered Symbolic Grotesques, which Ruskin's interpretive acts derived from contemporary phenomena, are his created or invented ones, which take the form of elaborate analogies that he often combined with brief narratives. For example, in "A Joy For Ever," which argues that art constitutes an important part of a nation's wealth, he composed such a satiric emblem to mock his listeners for neglecting to preserve the great art of Venice and other places in which it faced ruin: "You conduct yourselves precisely as a manufacturer would, who attended to his looms, but left his warehouse without a roof. The rain floods your warehouse, the rats frolic in it, the spiders spin in it, the choughs build in it, the wall-plague frets and festers in it; and still you keep weave, weave, weaving at your wretched webs, and thinking you are growing rich, while more is gnawed out of your warehouse in an hour than you can weave in a twelvemonth."(16:76–77) At the time Ruskin wrote, he seemed to many in his audience particularly eccentric, haranguing them to save the art of Venice, which was fast decaying and in danger from military action. From the vantage point of our belief in the need to preserve our cultural heritage—a belief due in large part to Ruskin's efforts—his points strike us as obvious and proper. Making ourselves aware of Ruskin's literary methods makes us also better able to benefit from this great Victorian master of seeing and understanding.

NOTES

1. For a more detailed discussion of Ruskin within the context of contemporary art criticism, see George P. Landow, "There Began to Be a Great Talking About the Fine Arts," in *The Mind and Art of Victorian England*, ed. Josef L. Altholz (Minneapolis, 1976), 124–45.

2. Walter E. Houghton's *The Victorian Frame of Mind, 1830–1870* (New Haven, 1957) is the classic introduction to these issues.

3. George P. Landow, *The Aesthetic and Critical Theories of John Ruskin* (Princeton, 1971), 243–404; Timothy Hilton, *John Ruskin: The Early Years* (New Haven, 1985).

4. M. H. Abrams, *The Mirror and the Lamp: Romantic Poetry and the Critical Tradition* (New York, 1953).

5. E.D.H. Johnson, *The Alien Vision of Victorian Poetry: Sources of the Poetic Imagination in Tennyson, Browning, and Arnold* (Princeton, 1952), ix–xvi.

6. For discussion of the Victorian sage, see John Holloway, *The Victorian Sage: Studies in Argument* (London, 1953); George P, Landow, *Elegant Jeremiahs: The Sage from Carlyle to Mailer* (Ithaca, 1986); and Camille R. La Bossière, *The Victorian "Fol Sage": Comparative Readings on Carlyle, Emerson, Melville, and Conrad* (Lewisburg, 1989).

7. See George P. Landow, "J. D. Harding and John Ruskin on Nature's Infinite Variety," *Journal of Aesthetics and Art Criticism* 28 (1970), 369–80, and E. H. Gombrich, *Art and Illusion: A Study in the Psychology of Pictorial Representation*, 2nd ed. (New York, 1961).

8. For Ruskinian word-painting, see George P. Landow, *The Aesthetic and Critical Theories of John Ruskin* (Princeton, 1971), and Elizabeth K. Helsinger, *Ruskin and the Art of the Beholder* (Cambridge, 1982). Rhoda L. Flaxman's *Victorian Word Painting and Narrative: Toward the Blending of Genres* (Ann Arbor, 1987) is a fine introduction to the general subject indicated by its title.

9. (16:103). This closing passage recapitulates his earlier vision of a just and wealthy England, a nation in which, he tells his listeners whom he here treats as brothers and equals, they will "establish such laws and authorities as may at once direct us in our occupations, protect us against our follies, and visit us in our distresses: a government which shall repress dishonesty, as now it punishes theft; which shall show how the discipline of the masses may be brought to aid the toils of peace, as discipline of the masses has hitherto knit the sinews of battle; a government which shall have its soldiers of the plowshare as well as its soldiers of the sword, and which shall distribute more proudly its golden crosses of industry—golden as the glow of the harvest, than now it grants its bronze crosses of honour—bronzed with the crimson of blood." (16:26)

10. For traditional readings of this commonplace type, which Hunt employed in *The Finding of the Saviour in the Temple*, upon which he worked from 1854 to 1860, see Landow, *William Holman Hunt and Topological Symbolism* (New Haven and London, 1979), 100.

11. See Landow, *William Holman Hunt*, 2–7, and "Your Good Influence on Me: The Correspondence of John Ruskin and William Holman Hunt," *Bulletin of the John Rylands University Library of Manchester* 59 (1976–1977), 96–126, 367–96. See also Herbert L. Sussman, *Fact into Figure: Typology in Carlyle, Ruskin, and the Pre-Raphaelite Brotherhood* (Columbus, 1979).

12. Landow, *William Holman Hunt*, 116–25; *The Pre-Raphaelites* (London, 1984), 221–23.

13. Landow, *Elegant Jeremiahs*, 73–101.

RUSKIN AND THE ART OF DRAWING

Christopher Newall

F or John Ruskin the very act of observing his physical surroundings was a stimulus to thought and a source of inspiration. To meditate upon the elements of nature or the works of man with a frank enjoyment of beauty, but also to understand intellectually the spiritual associations of landscape or architecture was, Ruskin came to believe, the highest form of appreciation. In *Modern Painters* 2 Ruskin distinguished between "the mere animal consciousness of the pleasantness [which he called] Aesthesis; [and] the exulting, reverent, and grateful perception of it [called] Theoria. For this, and this only, is the full comprehension and contemplation of the Beautiful as a gift of God." (4:47) He had, as he said, "a sensual faculty of pleasure in sight." (35:619) He believed that "the first vital principle [of drawing] is that man is intended to *observe* with his eyes, and mind." (25:xxx) Ultimately, the action of seeing was more valuable than the process of replication, for, as Ruskin wrote in his preface to *The Elements of Drawing*, "I believe that the sight is a more important thing than the drawing; and I would rather teach drawing that my pupils may learn to love Nature, than teach the looking at Nature that they may learn to draw." (15:13)

Ruskin's prose reveals the clarity of his sight and the intensity with which he looked; on countless occasions he described the beauties of the physical world in passages that reverberate with emotion. Ruskin was prolific both as a writer and as a draftsman, and in both capacities he took great pleasure in recording the appearance of things, as he said in a letter to his father: "There is the strong instinct in me, which I cannot analyse, to draw and describe the things I love — not for reputation, nor for the good of others, nor for my own advantage, but a sort of instinct like that for eating or drinking."[1] The drawings he made have the same quality of delight and excitement in the very act of seeing as his writings, but with one fundamental difference: Ruskin wrote to impress his ideas upon others, to edify, to uplift, and to mortify, whereas when he drew, he sought to test his faculties of perception, to further his understanding of the structure and characteristics as well as to rejoice in the beauty of the physical world, and to abase himself through the self-chastisement of painstaking delineation.

In the course of his career Ruskin devised a variety of drawing styles quite unlike those of most of his contemporaries. He drew to satisfy his own intellectual and emotional temperament rather than to please others, and the style and subject of his draftsmanship evolved and adapted to suit different purposes. In analyzing how Ruskin used drawing at different periods, and by considering why the art meant so much to him, we may try to comprehend the complexities of his thoughts.

Figure 58
JOHN RUSKIN (1819–1900)
Stone Pines at Sestri, Gulf of Genoa.
1845
Pencil, pen and ink, washes, and
body color, 17⅜ × 13¼"
Ashmolean Museum, Oxford;
Educational Series 22

Ruskin placed this drawing in his Educational Series for his Oxford students to study. In discussing Sestri, Ruskin mystically advised: "Try always, whenever you look at a form, to see the lines in it which have had power over its past fate and will have power over its futurity." (15:91) He had described Sestri during a visit some five years before he made this drawing. Capturing its dramatic effects, he wrote: "The sun suddenly catching the near woods at their base, already coloured exquisitely by the autumn with such a burst of robing, penetrating glow as Turner only could even imagine." (35:282)

Figures 59 (above) and 60 (below)
J. M. W. TURNER (1775–1851)
Villa Madama for Samuel Rogers's
Italy. c. 1827
Watercolor, 9½ × 11¾″
The Turner Collection, Tate
Gallery, London

*Paduan Villa on the Night of the Festa
di Ballo* for Samuel Rogers's *Italy.*
c. 1827
Watercolor, 10 × 12⅛″
The Turner Collection, Tate
Gallery, London

These two studies are part of a group
of Turner's illustrations for Samuel
Rogers's volume of poetry entitled
Italy, published in 1830. Ruskin received a copy as a thirteenth birthday
gift from one of his father's business
partners. The words and especially the
vignettes served as poetic guides to the
sights and moods of Italy during Ruskin's first visit there with his parents.
He continued to treasure them
throughout his life as examples of
Turner's capabilities at the height of
his technical and expressive power:
"The vignettes to Rogers's *Italy* are of
Turner's best time and contain some of
his very best work, the more interesting because with very few exceptions
they are quickly and even slightly executed. (13:375–76) Others shared
Ruskin's enthusiasm. The *Atheneum*
rhapsodized, "This is such a volume
that we fear never to look on its like
again.... Poetry, wealth, taste, are
here blended beautifully, and the result
is the most splendid piece of illustrated
topography it has ever been our fortune to look on."

Since the Renaissance, instruction in drawing had been recognized
as a valuable form of education, in the practice of which the young might
learn better to appreciate beauty in art and nature. That an ability to draw
should be regarded as the necessary accomplishment of any educated
gentleman, as stated for example in Baldassare Castiglione's *Book of the
Courtier* of 1528, was an idea heartily endorsed by Ruskin's father, John
James Ruskin, who himself drew landscape subjects and who encouraged
his young son in his artistic experiments. In 1831 Charles Runciman was
employed to give the eleven-year-old Ruskin weekly drawing lessons. After
exercises in perspective, which Ruskin recalled in his autobiography,
Praeterita, as "an invaluable bit of teaching," Runciman went on to attempt
to instill in his pupil "a swiftness and facility of hand" (35:76–77) at odds
with the laborious delineation that was his first instinctive style. Furthermore, one of the distinguishing traits of Ruskin's draftsmanship—his ten-
dency to focus on specific parts of a composition while leaving peripheral
areas blank or incomplete—was something he learned from Runciman:
"He cultivated in me,—indeed founded,—the habit of looking for the
essential points in the things drawn, so as to abstract them de-
cisively." (35:77) Runciman went on to encourage Ruskin to compose
landscape subjects from his imagination, according to the conventions of
the Picturesque movement—which provided rules about how the elements
of landscape should stand in relation to one another and dictated to what
degree they should be generalized and harmonized. Always loath to invent,
Ruskin swiftly learned how to lift parts from existing landscape drawings
and to patch them together into credible compositions "with extreme
industry, and an independence of mind, quite distinct from originality—
that is to say, I borrowed or imitated just what pleased myself." (35:621)

Significant events in the development of Ruskin's drawing were his
acquisition of two books illustrated by principal artists of the day. Samuel
Prout's *Picturesque Sketches in Flanders and on the Rhine* inspired the Ruskin
family's first long Continental journey in 1833, in the course of which
Ruskin drew architectural subjects in Prout's style, delighting in the crusted
and decrepit surfaces of roofs and masonry and emphasizing heavily ornamented outlines. At about the same time he was given Samuel Rogers's
collection of verse tales, *Italy*, illustrated with vignettes by J. M. W. Turner.
Ruskin copied and imitated the plates of the book, and by analyzing the
qualities of their textures he came to understand how an animated and
densely patterned surface serves to suggest to the eye the appearance of
minute detail.

From about 1830 Ruskin and his father frequented the Society of
Painters in Water-Colours, making friends with artists, studying the drawings on display, and occasionally buying works for the growing collection in
the Ruskin family home at Herne Hill in London. Anthony Vandyke
Copley Fielding had become president of the society in 1831, and father
and son were gratified when in 1834 Fielding agreed to give a series of
drawing lessons. When the first volume of *Modern Painters* appeared in
1843 Ruskin praised Fielding's "faithful and simple rendering of nature."
(3:196) However, enthusiastic comments of this kind were expunged from
later editions, and by the time he wrote *Praeterita* Ruskin was cynical about
the tuition he had received: "Copley Fielding taught me to wash colour

Figure 61
JOHN RUSKIN (1819–1900)
Venice: The Piazzetta, Saint Mark's and the Entrance to the Ducal Palace.
1835
Pencil and pen and ink, 9½ × 13½"
Education Trust Ltd., Brantwood, Coniston

Ruskin was proud that, while Venetian antiquarians searched the archives for documents, he was the first to examine the masonry and the changes in sculptural style in his effort to date the Piazzetta. From the beginning of his career, Ruskin read the moral integrity of a culture through the history of its buildings. He wrote of the Piazzetta: "Beginning with the great shafts of the Piazzetta, you may look upon all the pillars of Saint Mark's, and of Venice rising round it, as upon so many stolen sticks and straws, plundered from the harried nests of unbelieving Birds [the Moslem Turks]." (24:434)

smoothly in successive tints, to shade cobalt through pink madder into yellow ochre for skies, to use a broken scraggy touch for the tops of mountains, to represent calm lakes by broad strips of shade with lines of light between them . . . to produce dark clouds and rain with twelve or twenty successive washes, and to crumble burnt umber with a dry brush for foliage and foreground." (35:215)

Ruskin came to realize the shortcomings of this technique: "I saw that my washes, however careful or multitudinous, did not in the end look as smooth as Fielding's, and that my crumblings of burnt umber became uninteresting after a certain number of repetitions. With still greater discouragement, I perceived the Fielding processes to be inapplicable to the Alps. My scraggy touches did not to my satisfaction represent aiguilles, nor my ruled lines of shade, the Lake of Geneva." (35:216)

In 1837 Ruskin's attention was drawn to the watercolors and drawings that David Roberts was sending back from Spain. Roberts struck Ruskin as a more modern artist than those whose works he was used to seeing at the Water-Colour Society. He was less dependent upon convention, and from him Ruskin learned "of absolute good, the use of the fine point instead of the blunt one; attention and indefatigable correctness in detail; and the simplest means of expressing ordinary light and shade on grey ground." (35:262) Under the influence of Robert's work Ruskin entered upon "a phase of grey washed work with lights of lemon yellow, which lasted till the winter of 1841." (13:507)

Ruskin reminisced on his progress as a draftsman: "The pencil drawings from nature of the year 1835 were really meritorious and of value. But their technical virtue was an acicular precison of sharp black line ending with a dot which, now at eighteen, I began to feel were inconsistent with repose and consistency of flow in contour, and very slowly began to quit my bars and dots, and draw curves where they were necessary, with a gentler and greyer line." (35:623)

During the time that Ruskin was an undergraduate at Christ Church, Oxford, from 1837 to 1840, his style of drawing represented an amalgam of influences and impressions. For the time being he continued to look at subjects through the eyes of the artists whose works he had studied and in terms of the poetical descriptions of nature of William Wordsworth and others. He continued to exaggerate the forms of nature so as to make scenes especially impressive.

In the early 1840s, however, Ruskin discovered a new sense of purpose in his drawing. All diffidence about the processes of representing landscape or architectural subjects was swept away in favor of a passionate commitment to the principle of truth to nature. James Duffield Harding, with whom Ruskin first enrolled as a pupil in 1841, was himself progressing toward a fresher and more naturalistic manner of landscape painting—an empirical approach that he laid out in various theoretical treatises and which provided the basis of the lessons he gave. Furthermore, Ruskin was by this time in direct contact with Turner, whom he first met at the house of the picture dealer Thomas Griffith on June 22, 1840. He was to recall how he was "introduced to-day to the man who beyond all doubt is the greatest of the age; greatest in every faculty of the imagination, in every branch of scenic knowledge; at once *the* painter and poet of the day." (35:305)

Soon Ruskin was to become aware of an aspect of Turner's art quite different from the carefully composed and essentially old-fashioned vignettes of Rogers's *Italy*. Griffith showed Ruskin sketches by Turner, which he then found to be spontaneous, intuitive, and unpolished but also full of fluency and glowing with color. These Ruskin dubbed Turner's "delight-drawings," (13:237) recognizing how they originated in the artist's rapt attention to particular aspects of the landscape. Ruskin recalled in *Praeterita*: "I saw that these sketches were straight impressions from nature,—not artificial designs, like the Carthages and Romes. And it began to occur to me that perhaps even in the artifice of Turner there might be more truth than I had understood. I was by this time very learned in *his* principles of composition; but it seemed to me that in these later subjects Nature herself was composing with him." (35:310)

Since early childhood the experience of open countryside had been one of Ruskin's greatest pleasures. In 1872 he was to say of himself: "All my own right art work in life . . . depended not on my love of art, but of mountains and sea. . . . No chance occurred for some time to develop what gift of drawing I had; but I would pass entire days in rambling on the Cumberland hillsides, or staring at the lines of surf on a low sand." (22:153)

In 1842 two incidents, which Ruskin was to glorify as moments of transcendant revelation, demonstrated to him the importance of the direct study of nature. In 1883 he described how forty-one years previously, "In the spring of this year, I made, by mere accident, my first drawing of leafage in natural growth—a few ivy leaves round a stump in the hedge of the Norwood road. . . . I never (in my drawings, however much my writings) *imitated* anybody any more after that one sketch was made; but entered at once on the course of study which enabled me afterwards to understand Pre-Raphaelitism." (4:344) "When it was done," he wrote in *Praeterita*, "I saw that I had virtually lost all my time since I was twelve years old, because no one had ever told me to draw what was really there! All my time, I mean, given to drawing as an art; of course I had the records of places, but had never seen the beauty of anything, not even of a stone—how much less of a leaf!" (35:311) Later in the summer of 1842 Ruskin found himself at Fontainebleau, where, morosely displeased by all the usual tourist sights, he wandered into the surrounding countryside, eventually finding himself "lying on the bank of a cart-road in the sand, with no prospect whatever but [a] small aspen tree against the blue sky." He went on:

> *Languidly, but not idly, I began to draw it; and as I drew, the langour passed away: the beautiful lines insisted on being traced,—without weariness. More and more beautiful they became, as each rose out of the rest, and took its place in the air. With wonder increasing every instant, I saw that they "composed" themselves, by finer laws than any known of men. At last, the tree was there, and everything that I had thought before about trees, nowhere. (35:314)*

Whether or not these events actually happened, they indicate Ruskin's adoption of a particular stance based on the principle that artists should look for and abide by the laws of nature rather than seek to apply an artificial scheme of beauty to their compositions. A year later, in 1843, he issued the first volume of *Modern Painters*, itself largely an exposition on the virtue of truth in seeing and representation as opposed to the falseness of pictorial convention, at the end of which he made his famous plea to landscape artists, that they "should go to Nature in all singleness of heart, and walk with her laboriously and trustingly, having no other thoughts but how best to penetrate her meaning, and remembering her instruction; rejecting nothing, selecting nothing, and scorning nothing; believing all things to be right and good, and rejoicing always in the truth." (3:624)

Ruskin had come to believe that the artist should strive for an ever closer union with nature. In his drawings he sought to approach his subjects directly and to eliminate anything that was subsidiary or superfluous. In *Praeterita* Ruskin described how and what he drew in the mid 1840s: "I had learned to draw now with great botanical precision; and could colour delicately, to a point of high finish. I was interested in everything, from clouds to lichens." (35:328) Whenever he had the opportunity, he made accurate studies of plants and foliage, as on one occasion he described himself doing while on holiday in Scotland:

> *I always had a fresh-gathered outer spray of a tree before me, of which the mode of growth, with a single leaf full size, had to be done at that sitting in fine pen outline, filled with the simple colour of the leaf at one wash. On fine days, when the grass was dry, I used to lie down on it and draw the*

a.

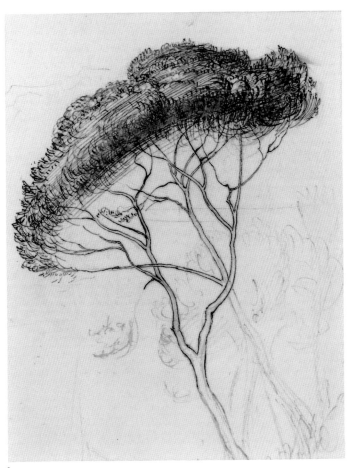

b.

Figures 62 a–j
JOHN RUSKIN (1819–1900)
Ten sketches for *The Elements of Drawing*, published 1857
Pen and ink (see approximate dim. below)
Collection of Mr. and Mrs. Brian Pilkington

a. *Ramification of a Small Stone Pine*, figure 4, 2⅞ × 2½"
b. *Ramification of a Small Stone Pine*, unpublished, 2⅞ × 2½"
c. *Leafage at the Root of a Stone Pine at Sestri, near Genoa*, figure 16, 3½ × 3⅞"
d. *Shoot of a Spanish Chestnut Shedding Its Leaves*, figure 24, 1⅞ × 2½"
e. *A Young Shoot of Oak*, figure 25, 1 × 2½"
f. *Two Swiss Cottages*, figure 30, 1⅝ × 2½"
g. *Branch Ramification Compared to the Ribs of a Boat*, figure 45, ½ × 1⅞"
h. Diagram of the towers of Ehrenbreitstein in Turner's *Coblentz*, figure 35, 2⅞ × 3⅝"
i. Drawing after Turner's sketch *Calais Sands at Sunset*, figure 33, 2⅛ × 3⅛"
j. *Top of an Old Tower*, figure 48, 2¼ × 3⅜"

The Elements of Drawing, Ruskin's handbook for beginning artists, contains visual and manual exercises and moral instruction. The first practices in contour drawing (a., b.) discipline the eye, for "the outline is like a bridle, and forces our indolence into attention and precision." (15:41) The student then studies the vital patterns of growth, always mindful of the unique forms in nature (c., d., e.), and the intel-

87

c.

ligent use of color to suggest shape and texture (f.). Good composition, the last subject, mirrors ideal social harmony: "Everything should be in a determined place, perform an intended part, and act . . . advantageously for everything that is connected with it. Composition . . . is the type, in the arts of mankind, of the Providential government of the world. It is an exhibition, in the order given to notes, or colours, or forms, of the advantage of perfect fellowship, discipline, and contentment." (15:162) The graceful curve is emphasized as the loveliest of lines, lending a sense of unity in apparent variety (g., h.) and a mood of repose in its repetition (i.). Contrast adds interest and emphasis in subtle ways, such as a ring on an old tower opposing the angularity of the battlements and roof (j.). He suggests drawing the tower without it to see what a vast difference this one detail makes in the whole.

d.

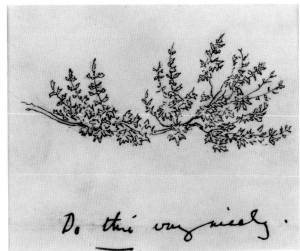

e.

f.

Do me this lower one.

g.

*Make the dots quite
at even distances.*

h.

Dear Miss Byfield.

I have two more and a little one coming
after this. Of course I mean the line to be drawn neatly
round it and no trouble to go over the margin
Truly yours JR

i.

j.

Figure 63
JAMES DUFFIELD HARDING
(1798–1863)
Landscape with Two Chalets, Brunnen.
1856
Pencil, 9¾ × 13⅝″
Birmingham Museum and Art
Gallery, England

Ruskin studied with Harding, and the two sketched together in Italy in 1845. That year, Harding published *The Principles and Practices of Art*, in which he spoke of the importance of accuracy but the impossibility of imitating in art any object seen. Ruskin knew this well, and preached for an art that emulated reality through an understanding of the laws of nature and an appreciation of its variety. Ruskin recognized Harding in the first edition of *Modern Painters* 1 for his handling of trees and running water but later, in *Academy Notes*, the student criticized the master for not observing carefully enough.

blades as they grew, with the ground herbage of buttercup or hawkweed mixed among them, until every square foot of meadow, or mossy bank, became an infinite picture and possession to me, and the grace and adjustment to each other of growing leaves, a subject of more curious interest to me than the composition of any painter's masterpiece. (35:429)

Ruskin's landscape drawings of the second half of the 1840s and the 1850s reveal his absorption in the aspects of nature. Frequently the angle of vision is downward, so that the foreground fills the composition while distant vistas are eliminated entirely or indicated in a perfunctory way. The elements of the landscape are displayed to the viewer at a range and from a viewpoint that suggest that the spectator is exploring the terrain on hands and knees, and the usual sense of atmospheric and perspectival recession gives way to an overall pattern of confused shapes and textures. In drawings such as *Stone Pines at Sestri* (figure 58), done in Italy in 1845, all attempts at conventional naturalism are abandoned as Ruskin's handling of ink, graphite, and monochrome wash alternates between vibrant detail and shadowy breadth to suggest the qualities of intense light, deep shadow, and flickering color. Landscape drawings of this kind are much more than literal representations; rather, they rely on the expressiveness of Ruskin's drawing technique to evoke the sights and sensations of a place.

Nonetheless, Ruskin was concerned to make his drawings accurate and informative descriptions of specific landscapes, and therefore to comply with the truthfulness he demanded in *Modern Painters*. He spent the late summer of 1845 high in the Piedmontese Alps close to the foot of Monte Rosa, where he reflected on how the mountains might be painted or drawn. He made a journey to Saint Gotthard to locate and draw from the viewpoint of Turner's *Pass of Faido* (the watercolor was in his own collection at home in London). He met up with J. D. Harding, who was traveling in Italy, and a direct comparison of his current work with the type of drawing that Harding was doing allowed him to take stock of his progress. It seemed that he and his old master had diverged artistically, according to the different purposes that each ascribed to drawing. Ruskin wrote to his parents:

> *Harding does such pretty things . . . that when I looked at my portfolio afterwards, and saw the poor result of the immense time I have spent— the brown, laboured, melancholy, uncovetable things that I have struggled through, it vexed me mightily; and yet I am sure I am on a road that leads higher than his. . . . His sketches are always pretty because he balances their parts together, and considers them as pictures; mine are always ugly, for I consider my sketch only as a written note of certain facts, and those I put down in the rudest and clearest way as many as possible. Harding's are all for impression; mine all for information. (3:200–201 n.)*

Ruskin's relations with Harding were complicated, bordering on the duplicitous, as he adds: "I am in a curious position with him—being actually writing criticisms on his works for publication, while I dare not say the same things openly to his face." (3:200 n.) On the whole each found the other a pleasant painting companion: "We could always sit down to work within a dozen yards of each other, both pleased. I did not mind his laughing at me for poring into the foreground weeds, which he thought sufficiently expressed by a zigzag, and heartily admired in him the brilliancy of easy skill, which secured, and with emphasis, in an hour or two, the effect of scenes I could never have attempted." (4:353–54) Even at a time when Ruskin was driving home the message of truth to nature of *Modern Painters*, in the private realm of his own draftsmanship he was well aware of the opposing aesthetic demands of fact and expression.

Ruskin was utterly absorbed by geology and the physical sciences. Increasingly he found himself searching in his drawings for the prevailing patterns and rhythms of shape and color that provided evidence of the origins and evolution of the physical world. He found harmony and unison in the mechanism of glaciers and the flow of water over the surfaces of polished stone; he saw each as processes ordained to perfect the beauty of a universal creation, and the drawings that he made in the 1840s of mountains and streams, ice and rock, served to praise God. Gradually, however, his certainties were undermined by his own observation of the physical world.

As Ruskin's faith in God faltered in the 1850s, he came to attach more importance to the aesthetic function of drawing. In the fourth volume of *Modern Painters*, published in 1856, he sought to define certain laws of beauty on the basis of his observation of natural phenomena. All the forms of the landscape were seen as part of an organized whole, subject to stupendous forces and molded together into dense and complex patterns. Ruskin came to see lines as directions of flow, winding and intertwining into

Figure 64
JOHN RUSKIN (1819–1900)
Anaconda. n.d.
Watercolor on blue paper, 6⅞ × 9½″
Ashmolean Museum, Oxford;
Educational Series 172

In March of 1880, Ruskin initiated a series of public talks with a "Lecture on Serpents," intending to compete with a successful set of addresses on snakes by his rival Thomas Huxley. Huxley's observations on snake anatomy and behavior were far different from Ruskin's symbolic and literary discussion of serpents. Ruskin observed that "the characteristics of perfect serpent nature [are] in pattern, motion and poison." (26:314) He believed in the traditionally evil associations of the snake. They threatened him in his dreams during his periods of increasing madness.

intricate arabesques, and as indicators of energy and competing force rather than as mere outlines or conjunctions. Clear divisions hardly occurred, as the very landscape, as he perceived it and as it appeared in his drawings, metamorphosed into rhythmic arrangements of shifting mass and merging form. Ruskin infused an organized quality into his drawings by the use of distinctive strokes and textures suggestive of the flux and fusion of nature. The late 1850s represent the highpoint in Ruskin's belief in the function of art to create and abide by its own laws; for a period at least he was drawn to the idea of art as its own justification without need for practical or spiritual association. In his manual for the use of amateur artists, *The Elements of Drawing*, published in 1857, he explained:

> *The perception of solid Form is entirely a matter of experience. We see nothing but flat colours; and it is only by a series of experiments that we find out that a stain of black or grey indicates the dark side of a solid substance, or that a faint hue indicates that the object in which it appears is far away. The whole technical power of painting depends on our recovery of what may be called the* innocence of the eye; *that is to say, of a sort of childish perception of these flat stains of colour, merely as such, without consciousness of what they signify,—as a blind man would see them if suddenly gifted with sight. (15:27 n.)*

Certain highly worked watercolors of the 1850s, such as *Gneiss Rock, Glenfinlas* (figure 121), signify Ruskin's desire to make pictorially

In December 1838, at age nineteen, Ruskin wrote an article entitled "The Poetry of Architecture" for *Architectural Magazine*. Under the pseudonym Kata Phusin, Ruskin described the unique beauty of Strasbourg's high-rising tower: "No introduction [to a city] can be more delightful than such a tower in the distance as Strasburg, or, indeed, than any architectural combination of verticals." (1:176) Samuel Prout's influence is clear in this early effort by Ruskin, who recommended study of Prout's drawings of Strasbourg to his readers because they excised recent offensive restorations to the building.

complete drawings—and perhaps denote a wish to be taken seriously as a creative artist in his own right. However, his true inclination was moving in the opposite direction; his long meditations on the relationship of nature and art were drawing to a close, and as the delight that landscape had once given him waned, so his propensity to draw subjects for their own sake lessened. Ruskin was moving toward an attitude of mind that placed the interests of humanity higher than a concept of undefiled nature or an abstract ideal of beauty. He did fewer landscapes, while drawings that explored the achievements or the plight of humankind, usually seen through the metaphor of the types of building of a given age, proliferated.

During the 1840s and early 1850s, Ruskin worked on *The Seven Lamps of Architecture* and the volumes of *The Stones of Venice*. He devoted much of his time to drawing architecture, which he considered "an essential part of landscape," the study of which was "one of the necessary functions of the landscape-painter." (5:130) Wherever he went he sought out buildings about which he had read or had seen represented in paintings or engravings. In Venice and Strasbourg, for example, he deliberately matched himself against Prout's style of architectural drawing. Ruskin's view of the Casa Contarini Fasan in Venice (figure 28) was so close in spirit to Prout's work that Prout himself asked to borrow it (figure 27). Ruskin wrote of his early draftsmanship: "I knew absolutely nothing of architecture proper, had never drawn a section nor a leaf moulding; but liked . . . anything that was graceful and rich, whether Gothic or Renaissance; was entirely certain and delicate in pencil-touch; and drew with an acuteness of delight in the thing as it actually stood, which makes the sketch living and like." (35:296) In 1842 the Ruskin family visited Strasbourg, whose buildings were familiar from Prout's *Sketches in Flanders and Germany*, and once again the drawings that Ruskin made, such as *The Tower of Strasbourg Cathedral* (figure 65), were done in conscious emulation of Prout's work.

In 1845 Ruskin traveled abroad to prepare his thoughts for the second volume of *Modern Painters*. The drawings he made in Lucca, Pisa, Florence, and Venice served a somber purpose. Ruskin was aware of the threat that destructive restoration posed to buildings, and he drew to provide records of monuments that he feared would not survive. On September 23, 1845, he wrote to his father from Venice:

> *You cannot imagine what an unhappy day I spent yesterday before the Casa d'Oro, vainly attempting to draw it while the workmen were hammering it down before my face. It would have put me to my hardest possible shifts at any rate, for it is intolerably difficult, and the intricacy and colour of it as a study of colour inconceivable . . . and all the while with the sense that* now one's art is not enough to be of the slightest service, but that in ten years more one might have done some glorious things.[2]

Ruskin's watercolors of the 1840s and 1850s are made delicious to the eye by his discovery of the power of light and color to give depth, volume, and brilliance to architectural subjects. Characteristic of his drawings then is the way in which he arranged the principal elements of the composition four-square to the rectangle of his paper, thus maximizing the area of the sheet given to the main subject and making adjoining buildings or incidental details unimportant. This trait, quite unlike that of the picturesque view painters who tended to place buildings in oblique perspectives or merged them into a wider urban scene, manifests itself again in his *Exterior of the Ducal Palace*, dating from either 1845 or 1852. In 1854 Ruskin corresponded with the Pre-Raphaelite watercolorist George Price Boyce about suitable painting subjects in Venice, recommending that he draw the southwest portico of the basilica of Saint Mark's from the loggia of the Ducal Palace (figure 70): "It answers precisely to your wishes, as expressed in your note, '*near* subject — good architecture — colour — & light & shade.'"[3] Boyce had understood and stated the essential principles of Ruskinian architectural drawing.

The same solemn spirit of objective record-making lay behind the campaign of measuring and drawing buildings and their details that Ruskin

Figure 66
JOHN RUSKIN (1819–1900)
Exterior of the Ducal Palace, Venice.
1845 or 1852
Pencil, pen and ink, and wash,
14¼ × 19⅞"
Ashmolean Museum, Oxford;
Reference Series 67

Ruskin drew this rendering of the Ducal Palace and the Bridge of Sighs, in the shadows to the right, from a hired gondola on the Grand Canal. It depicts the building, which more than any other Ruskin felt was "the principle effort of [Venice's] imagination, employing her best architects in its masonry, and her best painters in its decoration." (10:328) Ruskin preferred the southern European interpretation of the Gothic style to that of his own northern Europe: "The Gothic of the Ducal Palace of Venice is in harmony with all that is grand in all the world: that of the North is in harmony with the grotesque Northern spirit only." (9:188) The immense effort required to record meticulously every intricacy of window tracery and decorative pattern is sustained only in the center of the drawing, contrasting with the suggestive, almost abstract representation of the boats in the foreground, which are reminiscent of Turner.

undertook during the winters of 1849–50 and 1851–52 in preparation for *The Stones of Venice*. He made notional collections of cornices, capitals, moldings, and bases in a series of sketchbooks, to which he gave titles such as *Gothic Book*, *Bit Book*, *Door Book*, and *St M Book*. He regarded every detail as a significant clue to Venice's rise to greatness and her fall, which historical parabola he was charting in his study of her buildings. Ruskin became utterly absorbed in the abstract patterns of color and shape in mosaic and marble decoration; and in his studies of Byzantine carved decoration he found a combination of complete naturalism and "that unity of perfect ease in every separate part, with perfect subjection to an enclosing form or directing impulse." (10:161)

Quite different in spirit are the large pencil and wash views of buildings that Ruskin made to provide illustrations for the volume of plates, *Examples of the Architecture of Venice*. His *Loggia of the Ducal Palace, Venice* (figure 67) demonstrates the technique he devised for this purpose. The densities of the composition are built up in hatched areas of graphite; certain areas, notably the series of Gothic capitals, are worked in more detail; wash is then used to draw the composition together and to lend drama to the effects of light and shade. Ruskin here reverted from the objectivity and detachment of his 1845 drawings to something more romantic and theatrical.

Even in his earliest work on architecture, Ruskin had thought about buildings in terms of the historical evidence they provide. During the 1850s he found himself inspecting the landscape for clues to the way of life of its inhabitants. During a series of visits to Switzerland, he assembled a large group of drawings, watercolors, and sketchbooks, which were to provide him with a store of information as well as to serve as illustrations for a projected but never realized history of the Swiss people based on the architecture of their towns.

Figure 67
JOHN RUSKIN (1819–1900)
Loggia of the Ducal Palace, Venice.
1849–50
Pencil and watercolor, 18½ × 11½″

This large drawing was reproduced as a lithograph in *Examples of the Architecture of Venice*, issued in 1851, a series of plates of "servile veracity" intended as illustrations for *The Stones of Venice*. (11:314) It offers an oblique view of the south side of the basilica of Saint Mark's. Sumptuous, multicolored marbles, such as those on the basilica, often attracted Ruskin's pen and brush. He saw Saint Mark's not as a structure representing the Byzantine style but as an expression of the Venetian Republic's bellicose history. "St. Marks became rather a shrine at which to dedicate the splendor of miscellaneous spoil, than the organized expression of any fixed architectural law or religious emotion." (10:97)

Figure 68
GEORGE PRICE BOYCE (1826–1897)
The Tomb of Mastino II della Scala, Verona. 1854
Watercolor, 15½ × 10⅝″
Private Collection, England

Boyce visited Verona during his 1854 tour in Italy, again following Ruskin's advice. In her biography of her husband's life, Caroline Boyce noted Ruskin's opinion that "the little group of the Scala monuments is altogether unrivalled *in the world* for sweet colour and light and shade, and in these times there is no knowing how long it may stand. Venice will retain some of her canal effects for twenty years yet, but the Scala monuments may be destroyed in a fortnight—as far as their effect goes—by any change in the houses around them." Ruskin also studied the Scala tombs in a series of drawings.

Figure 69
JOHN RUSKIN (1819–1900)
Tomb of Can Mastino II della Scala, Verona. n.d.
Pencil and wash, 18⅛ × 11¾″
Ashmolean Museum, Oxford;
Reference Series 59

Designed by Perino and dated c. 1380, Ruskin claimed that "on the whole [it is] the finest piece of Gothic in Verona." (21.196) He placed the drawing above the entrance doorway at the Ruskin School of Drawing at Oxford, instructed Arthur Burgess to draw details of it, and had photographs and plaster casts done for his students to copy. As with other architectural monuments, Ruskin assigned a moral meaning to the tomb "which stands . . . in the little field of sleep, [it] already shows traces of erring ambition. It is the tomb of Mastino the Second, in whose reign began the decline of his family." (11.89)

Stones of Venice 3 Pl. IV

Figure 70
GEORGE PRICE BOYCE
(1826–1897)
Saint Mark's, Venice, Southwest Angle.
1854
Watercolor, 21½ × 15″
Private Collection, England

Boyce's diaries, kept from 1851 to 1875, record a wealth of information about the art world, including Ruskin's circle. In April 1854, he described a visit by Ruskin and his father. They had come to see Boyce's collection of drawings by Rossetti, and, while there, Ruskin expounded on his theory that art must be objective, not "just simply . . . picturesque scenery or striking atmospheric effects." Following Ruskin's suggestions in Venice later that year, Boyce studied the splendidly colored marbles and porphyry columns of Saint Mark's. He produced this detailed record of the stone structure, with its complexities of light and shade, texture, and varied color.

Left:
Figure 71
JOHN RUSKIN (1819–1900)
Mosaics of Olive Trees and Flowers, Saint Mark's, Venice. 1852–53
Pencil, pen and ink, and wash, assembled on three pieces of paper, 8⅜ × 5″
Education Trust Ltd., Brantwood, Coniston

Ruskin's fascination with the Byzantine basilica of Saint Mark's, Venice, lasted his entire career. The building combined an exotic style and richness of materials that he found disarming: "The whole edifice is to be regarded less as a temple wherein to pray, than as itself a Book of Common Prayer, a vast illuminated missal, bound with alabaster instead of parchment, studded with porphyry pillars instead of jewels, and written within and without in letters of gold." This image was published as plate 4 in the third volume of *The Stones of Venice*. The powerful symbolic meaning that Ruskin assigned to forms derived from nature reaffirmed his belief that the universal Truths binding nature to God could be found in the art of many cultures, most notably that of European Gothic.

Figure 72
JOHN RUSKIN (1819–1900)
Hotel de Ville, Aix-la-Chapelle. 1859
Pencil, brown and black ink, and
watercolor, with touches of opaque
white on faded blue paper, 14⅞ × 12½"
The Fogg Art Museum, Harvard
University Art Museums, Fine Arts
Appropriations Fund

This view of the city hall of the ancient
city of Aix-la-Chapelle was executed
during Ruskin's 1859 continental tour
to Germany. His fully developed gifts
for rendering architecture bring into
focus a series of visual juxtapositions
often found in Ruskin's mature work:
The gothic tower of the Royal Chapel,
the more modern city hall, and the
randomly placed market baskets in the
foreground contrast the nobility of
historic architecture with the less-
than-heroic references to modern life.

Ruskin had the example of Turner in mind as he studied the
architecture of Switzerland. He had made an effort to acquire Swiss watercolor views by Turner, and when, from 1856–1858 he sorted out the mass of
drawings that Turner had left to the nation, Ruskin found himself particularly absorbed by the work done on the artist's late visits to Switzerland.
Ruskin put groups of Turner drawings together to illustrate a typical
journey through the country and to demonstrate what types of building and
scenery meant most to Turner. In his own drawings of Switzerland he
sought to convey the same sense of progression through the landscape and
towns of a beloved region. In *View of Fribourg* (figure 73), and many of the
other drawings Ruskin made of the Swiss towns and landscape in the late
1850s, he exploited and transcended what he had learned from his study of
the drawings that Turner made for the *Liber Studiorum*, in which soft
washes of color are put over hatched textures of graphite and in which the
pen is used to define forms—a style that Ruskin had come to see as
expressive and flexible. Buildings, or parts of them, loom out of expanses of
color that suggest water, mist, or shadow, the abstract quality of which
emphasizes the compositions, specific points of detail. The forms of Ruskin's drawing seem to be in perpetual movement—merging into one another, crystalizing into sharper definition, and fading into hazy

indefiniteness. Visual drama is combined with loving observation, brevity allied with meticulousness of observation, and Turnerian impressionism crossed with Pre-Raphaelite exactitude. Ruskin makes the spectator work to identify a reality that is subtly and temptingly alluded to in the drawing, causing one to look with urgency lest that to which he draws attention should disappear once again into ethereal vagueness.

The year 1860 represented a turning point in Ruskin's life. From this time forward he was much less interested in the contemporary conduct of art, and aesthetic questions faded into relative insignificance. Nonetheless, Ruskin's enthusiasm for drawing remained intense. He continued to regard drawing as vital for the purposes of teaching and record-making. He produced a series of studies to illustrate points in lectures and essays and commissioned works from a succession of professional artists to provide pictorial accounts of places and buildings.

Yet much of Ruskin's work as an artist in the second half of his career was entirely personal, intended as self-investigation or a search for spiritual solace at a time of mental upheaval. Increasingly, Ruskin found himself drawn back to places where he had once been happy, looking again at whatever had inspired and stimulated him previously. In the late 1860s, at the time of his futile love affair with Rose La Touche, he returned both to Switzerland and Normandy, drawing buildings and landscapes to which he was particularly attached; in 1869 he visited Venice for the first time since the early 1850s and also made architectural studies in Verona, where he found himself absorbed again by the Can Grande tombs. Ruskin sought to recall the sense of purpose he had once had in observation and drawing, and on occasions made elaborate studies of architecture and sculpture, such as his sketch of a griffin at Verona (figure 76)—previously drawn to provide an illustration for *Modern Painters*—which compares with the objectivity and monumentality of his Alpine rock studies of the 1850s. Increasingly, however, he was attracted by fine detail and complexity of repeated pattern. He had, he wrote in a passage omitted from the final text of *Praeterita*, "an idiosyncrasy which extremely wise people do not share,—[a] love of all sorts of filigree and embroidery, from hoarfrost to the high clouds," (35:157 n.) which was, according to Kenneth Clark, a "bias of taste which led him to look at detail rather than mass, ornament rather than proportion, Rouen rather than Durham."[4] Drawings such as that of a spiral relief from Rouen Cathedral (figure 78) reveal the delight he took in pure pattern.

Ruskin had long relied on drawing as a distraction from worries; in 1854, for example, he had drawn rock forms at Chamonix to try to forget the humiliation of his failed marriage. In the winter of 1860–61, when he adandoned his interest in the theory of art in favor of economic questions, amid all the stress that this change of direction involved he consoled himself by drawing. As he suffered increasingly from bouts of deep depression, he turned to drawing as an aid to mental stability, as a distraction and succor, and as a pastime in which he could forget himself at least for a while and meditate on a material and unthreatening aspect of the world. In *Fors Clavigera* he asked: "Does it never occur to me . . . that I may be mad myself?" The answer came: "Well, I am so alone now in my thoughts and

Figure 73
JOHN RUSKIN (1819–1900)
View of Fribourg. 1854
Pencil, pen and ink, watercolor,
and body color, 5½ × 7¾″
Courtesy of the Syndics of the
Fitzwilliam Museum, Cambridge,
England

Ruskin composed this watercolor
while staying at the inn he had shared
with his parents on his first trip to the
Continent. He took photographs of
the city's medieval towers and admired
the way the walled city clung to the
steep mountain slopes. He wrote,
"The notablest thing in the town of
Fribourg is, that all its walls have flexible spines, and creep up and down the
precipices more in the manner of cats
than walls." (6:46)

Opposite, above:
Figure 74
THOMAS MATTHEW ROOKE
(1842–1942)
Cottage at Leukerbad. September
1884
Watercolor, 13⅝ × 17¾″
Ashmolean Museum, Oxford;
Reference Series 171

An assistant to Edward Burne-Jones in
the design firm of William Morris,
Rooke was employed by Ruskin as a
copyist in 1879. In the fall of 1884,
Ruskin directed him to come home
from Italy via Switzerland. On his way
Rooke recorded buildings in their settings, in this case a sagging cottage
before the vertical face of a mountain
in the Swiss village of Leukerbad.
Rooke undoubtedly did this highly finished watercolor from sketches after
his return to England.

Opposite, below:
Figure 75
FRANK RANDAL (c. 1858–1901)
*The Rescyone (Regione?) of Lecco, 6:30
P.M.* June–July 1885
Watercolor and body color,
8¾ × 13⅛″
The Ruskin Gallery, Sheffield—The
Collection of the Guild of Saint
George

Randal worked around Lecco, near
Lake Como in Lombardy, during the
spring and summer of 1885. Ruskin
instructed him to record the region's
topography and its unique qualities of
light. In accordance with Ruskin's
wishes, he concentrated on seasonal
changes and atmospheric effects at different times of the day, such as this
effect of light during an early summer
evening.

The Resegone of Lecco. Como.
Sun. July 1855.   6.30 p.m.

Figure 76
JOHN RUSKIN (1819–1900)
Griffin Bearing the North Shaft of the Entrance of the Duomo, Verona. 1869
Pencil, watercolor, and body color, 8⅝ × 14″
Ashmolean Museum, Oxford;
Educational Series 82

Ruskin made use of this drawing in his public lecture, given in London in the winter of 1870, on the architectural wonders of Verona. Later, in his ten lectures on Tuscan art (published in *Val d'Arno*, 1874), Ruskin devoted much space to the inextricable links that bind sculptural ornamentation and architecture into a unified whole. He likened their symbiotic tie to book design: "Perhaps you may most clearly understand the real connection between structure and decoration by considering all architecture as a kind of book, which must be properly bound, indeed, and in which the illumination of the pages has distinct reference in all its forms to the breadth of the margins and length of the sentences." (23:87)

ways, that if I am not mad, I should soon become so, from mere solitude, but for my *work*. But it must be manual work. Whenever I succeed in a drawing, I am happy, in spite of all that surrounds me of sorrow." (28:206) Kenneth Clark, speculating on the personal significance of Ruskin's late drawings, recognized the consistency with which he relied spiritually on the faculty of sight and the processes of observation: "He had stared fixedly at details all his life, and, as he grew older, to look into something intensively was like re-entering a lost Eden."[5] The different styles of drawing that Ruskin used were prompted by fluctuations in his state of mind. The microscopically detailed and intensely colored drawings—often of stones, leaves, flowers, feathers, or other specimens (such as figures 79, 81, 82)—stemmed from moods of calm deliberation and may be seen as an attempt on Ruskin's part to establish data about the physical world, upon which he felt he could rely; the opposite type of drawing, in which frenzied patterns of graphite and dashed areas of wash signify buildings and natural forms whose volumes are reduced to seething masses of light and shade, derived either from phases of euphoric delight in the awesome power of the physical world, or from a dread sense of malevolent forces operating against the benign laws of nature.

The American author and educator Charles Eliot Norton was one of the few who understood the intrinsic value and personal importance of Ruskin's drawings. Norton noted: "I use whatever power I have with him to keep him steadily and busily at work."[6] He wrote to Ruskin: "Your influence will be made deeper, more permanent, and more helpful by patient work of this kind, than by your impassioned and impatient appeal to men who will scoff at your words."[7] Ruskin gave Norton bundles of his old drawings and made new ones to send him. He was delighted to have found someone who appreciated his work as a draftsman, as he wrote:

My dearest Charles,—I took out a feather to begin for you this morning; but shyed it—and took to sorting out sketches. I have found some that I am sure you will think useful; others which I believe you may take some pleasure in, partly in friendship, partly in knowledge of the places. . . . They will be more useful in your hands than any one else's, and perhaps of more in America than in England. (37:275–76)

In 1873, as the warning signs of Ruskin's mental decline showed more clearly, Norton suggested that Ruskin make a series of self-portraits. In

Figure 77
JOHN RUSKIN (1819–1900)
Self-Portrait. 1874
Watercolor, 15 × 9⅞″
Wellesley College Library, Special Collections, Ruskin Collection, Gift of Charles E. Goodspeed

At the request of his American friend and admirer Charles Eliot Norton, Ruskin executed a number of self-portraits. It was an enterprise he did not much enjoy. Ruskin wrote to Norton from Pisa on April 9, 1874: "All that is good in me depends upon terrible subtleties. . . . I let these failures be sent to show I have been trying." (37:92) The self-portraits have penetrating gazes, and Ruskin confessed that "whatever of good or strength there is in me comes visibly, as far as I know myself, only sometimes into the grey of my eyes." (36:219) As with all artistic genres, Ruskin assigned important moral significance to portraiture. He remarked, "The effort at portraiture is good for art if the men to be portrayed are good, not otherwise." (20:281)

Figure 78
JOHN RUSKIN (1819–1900)
Carving Detail of the Spiral Relief from the North Transept, Rouen Cathedral. February 1882
Sepia and white on cream card,
11½ × 8½"
Ruskin Galleries, Bembridge School, Isle of Wight

For Ruskin, Rouen was a superb example of the Northern Gothic style. He took "especial delight in [the] multiplication of small forms, as well as in [the] exaggerated points of shade and energy" in the carving. (9:187–88) He thought so highly of Rouen's sculpted facades that he hired Arthur Burgess in 1880 to supervise the taking of photographs from a scaffolding Ruskin had erected on its north and west fronts. (14:355) Ruskin also ordered casts of some of the carvings for his students and followers to study. The texture and the volume of the carved ridges in this two-dimensional study emphasized the sculptural energy of just one detail on the cathedral's north facade.

Figure 79
JOHN RUSKIN (1819–1900)
*Study of Kingfisher, with Dominant
Reference to Color*. 1870–71
Pencil, watercolor, and body color,
10⅛ × 8⅝″
Ashmolean Museum, Oxford;
Rudimentary Series 201

Ruskin was attracted to this subject as
much as by its inherent beauty as from
scientific curiosity. He found wonder
in the kingfisher's intricate, colorful
plumage, but he had no interest in exploring the bird's bone structure, the
physiological source of its song, or its
nesting habits. (25:94) Though he ab-
horred the hunting of these small
birds, Ruskin admitted that he worked
from a stuffed specimen. (28:606)

Figure 80
J. M. W. TURNER (1775–1851)
Dead Pheasant. c. 1815–18
Watercolor and pencil with
scratching-out, 11⅛ × 14⅞″
The Whitworth Art Gallery,
University of Manchester, England

Turner made a number of studies of
dead birds, particularly when staying
at Farnley, the home of Walter Fawkes,
who recruited Turner for a natural-
history project resulting in an album
titled *Ornithological Collection.* Ruskin,
who owned this drawing, placed it in
his 1869 sale describing it in the catalogue as "finished study, superb." He
admired the scrutiny and accurate depiction of Turner's bird drawings, and
his own studies of birds were clearly
influenced by them.

Figure 81
JOHN RUSKIN (1819–1900)
*Feathers of the Kingfisher's Wing and
Head, Enlarged, and a Group of the
Wing Feathers, Real Size.* n.d.
Pencil and watercolor, 14¾ × 10″
Ashmolean Museum, Oxford;
Rudimentary Series 204

This drawing followed *Study of Kingfisher* in the Rudimentary Series, one of
four separate groups of objects compiled by Ruskin while Slade Professor
of Art at Oxford. The Rudimentary
group was intended for beginning students. Ruskin hoped that the examination and copying of these carefully
rendered drawings would educate the
students' eyes and hands. The Rudimentary Series was divided into cate-
gories such as heraldry, Greek and
medieval design, birds, grasses and
foreground materials, and tree drawing. Other series included the Standard
Series, a pictorial history of art; the
Reference Series, used in connection
with Ruskin's lectures; and the Educational Series, for advanced students.

these (figures 1 and 77) Ruskin sought to capture his own chance expressions, which he knew his friend would recognize and value, but he found the task immensely difficult. The intense images that resulted speak of unhappiness and frustration. As the artist looked at himself, he was confronted by the reality of his own isolation.

In the 1850s Ruskin came to be regarded as an authority to whom all should defer in matters relating to the arts. While teaching at the Working Men's College and preparing his book *The Elements of Drawing*, he devised a theory of art teaching based on the accurate observation of nature. Furthermore, his criticism in *Academy Notes* and his contact with contemporary artists meant that he was in a position to influence directly the way drawing and watercolor painting were practiced. The conviction in his statements owed much to a practical understanding of technical demands and difficulties, gained in the course of his own work as a draftsman. As he said in the preface to the first edition of *Modern Painters* 1: "Yet it is proper for the public to know that the writer is no mere theorist, but has been devoted from his youth to the laborious study of practical art." (3:5) As artistic patriarch, a position Ruskin maintained at least by reputation until the 1880s, he explained the virtues and limitations of the different mediums. On one occasion Ruskin pointed out the unsuitability of watercolor for professional artists: "The extended practice of water-colour painting, as a separate skill, is in every way harmful to the arts: its pleasant slightness and plausible dexterity divert the genius of the painter from its proper aims, and withdraw the attention of the public from excellence of higher claim." (20:120) A letter to the *Times* of 1896 stated, however:

> *There is no china painting, no glass painting, no tempera, no fresco, no oil, wax, varnish, or twenty-chimney-power-extract-of-everything painting which can compare with the quiet and tender virtue of water-colour in its proper use and place. There is nothing that obeys the artist's hand so exquisitely; nothing that records the subtlest pleasures of sight so perfectly. All the splendours of the prism and the jewel are vulgar and few compared to the subdued blending of infinite opalescence in finely inlaid water-colour; and the repose of light obtainable by its transparent tints and absolutely right forms, to be rendered by practised use of its opaque ones, are beyond rivalship, even by the most skilful methods in other media. (13:590)*

Ruskin believed that certain shapes and patterns were particularly beautiful, and in the practical instruction he gave he pointed to the abstract pictorial qualities artists should look for, each quality manifesting a law of nature:

> *It is in the perfect acknowledgement and expression of these* three *laws that all good drawing of landscape consists. There is, first, the organic unity; the law, whether of radiation, or parallelism, or concurrent action, which rules the masses of herbs and trees, of rocks, and clouds, and waves; secondly, the individual liberty of the members subjected to these laws of unity; and lastly, the mystery under which the separate character of each is more or less concealed. (15:115–16)*

Figure 82
JOHN RUSKIN (1819–1900)
Study of a Peacock's Breast Feather.
1873
Watercolor, 8⅝ × 5⅝"
The Ruskin Gallery, Sheffield—The Collection of the Guild of Saint George

Such small intense studies of "fragments from nature" are not uncommon among the drawings of Ruskin. They served two purposes: They evidenced to students and to followers the microscopic beauties in the world, and they were visual notations of Ruskin's own intense observations of natural phenomena.

This amounts to a decree that artists should reproduce the aspects of nature that suggest the consistency, variation, and living quality of the natural world and by these means draw their compositions together into harmonious and living completeness. According to Ruskin, natural beauty depended on the combination of two abstract principles: unity and infinity.

A conventional sense of the scale of landscape was unimportant for Ruskin, who, in his desire to identify those dominant characteristics that give consistently to the forms of nature, equated objects of widely differing sizes. His studies of pebbles are treated with the same patterns of shape and color as mountain ranges, and in them the aesthetic theory that Ruskin had devised in the course of his study of entire landscapes gained its ultimate proof and fulfillment. In *Modern Painters* 4 he made the point: "A stone, when it is examined, will be found a mountain in miniature. The fineness of Nature's work is so great, that into a single block, a foot or two in diameter, she can compress as many changes of form and structure, on a small scale, as she needs for her mountains on a large one." (6:368) In *Modern Painters* 5 he asked: "Do you think that I am irreverently comparing great and small things? The system of the world is entirely one; small things and great are alike part of one mighty whole." (7:452)

Ruskin insisted that color should be gradated in tone and intensity, so that compositions would appear vibrant and alive. Small particles of color were to be blended into complex patterns, as in nature, "not . . . raw or monotonous, but composed—as all beautiful colour must be composed—by mingling of many hues in one." (6:139) Similarly, line represented the infinity of nature in the constant variety and unpredictability of its curvature, which was, according to Ruskin, "the first element of all loveliness in form." (6:348)

The subjects that most appealed to Ruskin were those in which he had the opportunity to explore a theory of beauty that delighted in both consistency and variety—flowers with petals of equal size that formed unbroken rings, and yet in which minute variations of color and form were to be observed; mineral fragments whose shapes and patterns suggested entire mountain ranges and yet in which the trained eye might recognize myriad conflicting physical characteristics; or the patterns of clouds or water, subject to prevailing winds or currents but infinitely various in their forms. Finally, Ruskin believed that all subjects should be treated with refinement and moderation; in terms of color for example: "The finer the eye for colour, the less it will require to gratify it intensely. But that little must be supremely good and pure." (16:424) By these means aspects of nature might be seen to have a greater significance and more intense beauty than by their mere naturalistic replication. As he wrote in *The Elements of Drawing*: "Every line and colour is so arranged as to advantage the rest. None are inessential, however slight; and none are independent, however forcible. It is not enough that they truly represent natural objects; but they must fit into certain places, and gather into certain harmonious groups." (15:162–63)

For Ruskin the idea that a drawing expressed was more important than any conventional concept of technical completeness or finish; as he wrote in *The Stones of Venice*: "Always look for invention first, and after that, for such execution as will help the invention, and as the inventor is capable of without painful effort, and *no more*. Above all, demand no refinement of execution where there is no thought, for that is slaves' work, unredeemed." (10:199)

Ruskin found it easier to start things than to finish them; throughout his life he embarked upon projects that he later struggled to conclude. In *Praeterita* he described his "evermore childish delight in beginning a drawing; and usually acute misery in trying to finish one." (35:368) Because he took little account of the result as a work of art, he felt free to leave his drawings unfinished and incomplete: "From this time forward, my drawing was all done that I might learn the qualities of things, and my sketches were

113

left miserably unfinished, not in idleness,—but because I had to learn something else." (13:508–9) Ruskin knew how to suggest the complete forms of landscapes or buildings, even when represented only in parts. When drawing the arcaded walls of a Gothic palace, he did not attempt to replicate the patterns of columns and window openings across the width of the sheet, nor to represent minutely the carved decoration of each capital. When drawing landscapes he seldom worked up his compositions to a uniform degree of finish but preferred to concentrate on parts that might be regarded as indicative of the whole. A salient or carefully drawn detail may be surrounded by areas that are summarily blocked out in color or drawn across in a perfunctory way.

As an artist Ruskin knew how to reconcile overall impression with precision of detail, and in his drawings he intuitively simulated the very process of seeing. Just as the eye focuses on a point of detail in a view and understands how a pattern of which that detail is part extends over a larger area, he knew how much information he needed to provide to stimulate the visual processes of the viewer. He collected photographs of buildings and architectural decoration, but he maintained that a sketch might give a more truthful account of a subject. In *Modern Painters* 4 Ruskin compared a drawing he had made of Fribourg with his daguerreotype of the same subject: "But the first sketch nevertheless conveys, in some respects, a truer idea of Fribourg." (6:46)

Ruskin accepted the traditional hierarchy that established the relative importance of the different genres of art, which had originated in the writings of the sixteenth-century art historian Giorgio Vasari and which had been restated nearer Ruskin's time in the *Discourses* of Sir Joshua Reynolds. He considered that works of art were necessarily complete and self-contained. Ruskin had no professional ambitions as an artist. He thought of himself as an amateur and valued the work he did accordingly: "The best that you can do in the production of drawing, or of draftsmanship, must always be nothing in itself, unless the whole life be given to it. An amateur's drawing, or a workman's drawing—anybody's drawing but an artist's, is always valueless in itself." (16:182) His own drawings were seldom seen by the public at large in his lifetime. It was only in 1879, on the occasion of an exhibition of Ruskin's drawings in America, that anyone tried to explain why the works were so peculiarly interesting. Charles Eliot Norton wrote of them:

> *These drawings are not the work of an artist by profession; there is not a picture among them. They are the studies of one who, by patience and industry, by single-minded devotion to each special task, and by concentrated attention upon it, has trained an eye of exceptional keenness and penetration, and a hand of equally exceptional delicacy and firmness of touch, to be the responsive instruments of faculties of observation and perception such as have seldom been bestowed on artist or on poet. Few of these drawings were undertaken as an end in themselves, but most of them as means by which to acquire exact knowledge of the facts of nature, or to obtain the data from which to deduce a principle in art, or to preserve a record of the work of periods in which art gave better expression to the higher interests and motives of life than at the present day. (13:583)*

114

A more severe response to Ruskin's style of drawing came from the *Art Journal* in 1884, on the occasion of his showing of architectural studies at the Royal Water-Colour Society winter exhibition: "Professor Ruskin must adjust with himself the motives which permit him to exhibit drawings in the unfinished state he condemns in others."[8] In the preface of *Modern Painters 3* Ruskin stated the requirements that he placed on his art:

> *The first, that they ought at least to show such ordinary skill in draughtsmanship, as to prove that the writer knows* what *the good qualities of drawing* are; *the second, that they are never to be expected to equal, in either execution or conception, the work of accomplished artists—for the simple reason that in order to do* anything thoroughly well, the whole mind, and the whole available time, must be given to that single art. *(5:10)*

At the same time Ruskin made clear that he set no great store on his own ability but simply offered his efforts to friends and followers without fanfare or flourish. "As for the merit or demerit of these or other drawings of my own . . . I leave, as most readers will think I ought, such judgement to them." (5:10) In conversation in 1884 he said: "I wish I could have drawn more myself—not that I should have done anything great; but I could have made such beautiful records of things. It is one of the greatest chagrins of my life." (34:668) In 1886 he wrote to a friend who had admired his drawings: "They are all such mere hints of what I want to do, or syllables of what I saw, that I never think, or at least never thought, they could give the least pleasure to any one but myself." (37:566)

Ruskin's drawings served, as has been seen, a wide variety of purposes, from the starkly practical function of recording factual information about the physical world—"the more facts you give, the greater you are; and there is no fact so unimportant as to be prudently despised, if it be possible to represent it" (5:173)—to the purely aesthetic; as he said, a landscape painter "must be capable of experiencing those exquisite and refined emotions which nature can arouse in a highly intellectual mind." (1:279) It was the experience of looking and responding that was of vital importance—the drawing that resulted might be regarded as ephemeral. All self-consciousness or instinct to admire the product of one's own endeavor was disallowed: "If you desire to draw, that you may represent something that you care for, you will advance swiftly and safely. If you desire to draw, that you may make a beautiful drawing, you will never make one." (15:354) The object of the painter or draftsman was to be honest and true, and to respond in a straightforward way to the subject—with clarity and objectivity, and with affection. Ruskin's own drawings fulfill this requirement, for in them he revealed his passionate interest in and involvement with his physical surroundings: landscape and nature, the movement of water and clouds, the effects of light and atmosphere, and buildings and all manifestations of the human spirit. The process of drawing allowed him to enter a state of heightened receptivity to phenomena and sensations; and as an artist his mind and faculties were engaged in a search for closer unity with those things he loved.

NOTES

1. The letter, dated June 2, 1852, was sent from Verona. Quoted in E. T. Cook, *The Life of John Ruskin*, 2 vols. (London, 1911), vol. 1, 263.
2. *Ruskin in Italy, Letters to His Parents, 1845*, ed. H. I. Shapiro (Oxford, 1972), 209.
3. *The Diaries of George Price Boyce*, ed. Virginia Surtees (Norwich, 1980), appendix, 119–20.
4. Kenneth Clark, *Ruskin Today* (London, 1964), 352.
5. *Ibid.*, 351.
6. *Letters of Charles Eliot Norton*, 2 vols. (Boston, 1913), vol. 1, 430.
7. *Ibid.*, vol. 2, 46.
8. *Art Journal* (1884), 29.

HEARTSIGHT DEEP AS EYESIGHT: RUSKIN'S ASPIRATIONS FOR MODERN ART

Susan Phelps Gordon

The nocturnes by the American expatriate Whistler were extraordinarily original. Like many truly innovative works, they were denounced by many when first displayed in the 1870s. This scene of fireworks in Cremorne Gardens falling into the Thames River became the most famous of the nocturnes as a result of Ruskin's particularly uncharitable remarks upon it and the subsequent Whistler versus Ruskin trial. The painting was the product of immense study, reflection, and effort, but Ruskin could see it only as an impertinent attempt to defraud the public. Although the two men shared many friends and acquaintances, they apparently never met.

In his *Fors Clavigera* letter of June 18, 1877, John Ruskin reviewed the exhibition at Sir Coutts Lindsay's newly opened Grosvenor Gallery. He spoke with words of both commendation and condemnation, as he often had during his career as an art critic, historian, and theoretician. Ruskin applauded Sir Coutts Lindsay's "true desire to help the artists and better the art of his country," and he largely approved of the artists invited to display there. (29:157) They included James Tissot, Albert Moore, James Abbott McNeill Whistler, and two of Ruskin's good friends, George Frederic Watts and Edward Burne-Jones. Ruskin had never spoken publicly about Burne-Jones's work, and he took this opportunity to praise it as "'classic' in its kind,—the best that has been, or could be." (29:159)

In response to those who, he admitted, found Burne-Jones's style "repulsive . . . indeed reprehensible," Ruskin replied that any faults or errors of execution resulted from the force of his imagination. (29:159) No matter how strange these eccentricities appeared to be, he continued, they were sincere expressions of a distinct personality and never intentionally affected or indolent. Ruskin could not say the same of others whose cleverness and eccentricity were gratuitous and insincere. James Abbott McNeill Whistler's 1875 painting, *Nocturne in Black and Gold: The Falling Rocket*, served as a convenient example: "For Mr. Whistler's own sake, no less than for the protection of the purchaser, Sir Coutts Lindsay ought not to have admitted works into the gallery in which the ill-educated conceit of the artist so nearly approached the aspect of wilful imposture. I have seen, and heard, much of Cockney impudence before now; but never expected to hear a coxcomb ask two hundred guineas for flinging a pot of paint in the public's face." (29:160)

Whistler sued Ruskin for that libelous remark, embroiling the two in a highly publicized, personally devastating trial in November 1878, in which *Nocturne in Black and Gold* was displayed as evidence.[1] Lawyers on both sides brought up issues rarely submitted for judicial inquiry, such as artistic quality and purpose and the rights of a critic. The plaintiff contended that Ruskin damaged Whistler's reputation unjustly and maliciously, to the point of affecting the sale of his work; the defense countered that Ruskin's criticism was an impartial and accurate assessment of a painting placed on public display, and so subject to critical judgment. The painting was called incomprehensible, unfinished, a mere sketch dashed off in two days' time. The price of two hundred guineas was unconscionable. The plaintiff argued in turn that it was a legitimate work of art, intended to be an arrangement of light, form, and color, and that Ruskin's "reckless and

Figure 84
Sir Edward Burne-Jones
(1833–1898)
Orpheus Leading Eurydice from Hades.
c. 1875
Pencil, 10⅞ × 10⅞"
Ashmolean Museum, Oxford

The opinions on art, craftsmanship, and social reform elaborated in *Modern Painters* and the chapter "The Nature of the Gothic" in *The Stones of Venice* influenced both Burne-Jones and his friend and collaborator William Morris. Those ideas ultimately inspired Morris's design and the Arts and Crafts Movement. This drawing depicts an episode in the Greek myth of Orpheus, who rescued his wife Eurydice from Pluto's underworld. The Orpheus series ornamented a piano commissioned by William Graham, whose daughter, Frances, modeled for Eurydice.

unfair attacks [were] merely for the love of exercising his power of denunciation." (29:584) As to the fairness of the price, Whistler, by his own account, summed up the painting's worth neatly:

> *Defense: "Oh, two days! The labour of two days, then is that for which you ask two hundred guineas!"*
> *Whistler: "No;—I ask it for the knowledge of a lifetime." (Applause)[2]*

Had Ruskin spoken on his own behalf, the verdict might have been different, but he was recovering from a breakdown and was considered too weak to appear. Others, notably Burne-Jones and W. P. Frith, spoke in Ruskin's defense, but their testimony was uninspired compared to Whistler's brilliant repartee. The jury decided on Whistler's side, but it awarded him only one farthing and required him to pay his court costs, which later led to his bankruptcy. Yet Whistler felt vindicated by his moral victory. He publicized it further the next month in his pamphlet *Whistler versus Ruskin: Art and Art Critics* by declaring that critics "are not a 'necessary evil,' but an evil quite unnecessary, though an evil certainly."[3] Demoralized, Ruskin immediately resigned his position as Slade Professor of Art at Oxford University, explaining, "I cannot hold a Chair from which I have no power of expressing judgement without being taxed for it by British Law." (29:xxv)

The Whistler-Ruskin case is one indication of the sharp divisions in the Victorian art world in the late 1870s and 1880s, some of which were reactions against Ruskin's ideas and attitudes. Most controversial was the

Figure 85
JAMES TISSOT (1836–1902)
The Convalescent. c. 1875–76
Oil on canvas, 30¼ × 39¼"
Sheffield City Art Galleries, The
Mappin Art Gallery

Tissot was known for his scenes of opulent Victorian high society. He was a close friend of Whistler's and participated in the Grosvenor Gallery exhibit reviewed in Ruskin's *Fors Clavigera* letter number 79. Ruskin blasted Whistler's paintings but complimented Tissot's dexterity and brilliance. Still, he qualified his praise and reflected his lifelong dislike of popular and fashionable social affairs by concluding that "most of [Tissot's paintings] are unhappily mere colored photographs of vulgar society." (29:161)

idea of "art for art's sake," divorced from the social, didactic, or representational concerns so crucial to the Victorian ethics of practicality and morality that Ruskin supported. The trial also highlighted Ruskin's seemingly contradictory opinions. His career, after all, had begun with an aggressive defense of J. M. W. Turner, who had confounded the art world more than forty years earlier with his own curious paintings. Ironically, critics had lambasted his vaporous atmospheric effects, bursts of light and color, and lack of detail in words similar to those Ruskin used against Whistler. A striking example is Turner's *Rockets and Blue Lights (Close at Hand) to Warn Steamboats of Shoal Water* of 1840. One reviewer suggested that the picture had been produced by firing a blunderbuss full of pigment at the canvas, and another wondered if "the Artist meant the title and the subject as a sarcasm upon the style?"[4] Another concluded that it was remarkable as an example "of colour and prodigious as eccentric flights of genius. [It] would be equally effective, equally pleasing, and equally comprehensible if turned upside down."[5]

How could Ruskin unflaggingly defend the work of Turner and yet be so insensitive to that of Whistler? Before that, by what logic had Ruskin reasoned Turner to be the "first Pre-Raphaelite," or in any way associated with the sharp-focus realism and narrative themes of the Pre-Raphaelite

J. M. W. TURNER (1775–1851)
Rockets and Blue Lights (Close at Hand) to Warn Steamboats of Shoal Water. Exhibited 1840
Oil on canvas, 36 1/16 × 48 1/8"
Sterling and Francine Clark Art Institute, Williamstown

Opposite, above:
Figure 86
J. M. W. TURNER (1775–1851)
Llanthony Abbey, Monmouthshire.
c. 1834
Watercolor and body color over pencil, 11 7/8 × 16 3/4"
Copyright 1992: Indianapolis Museum of Art, Bequest of Kurt F. Pantzer, Sr.

Llanthony Priory in southern Wales dates from the twelfth century. Turner first visited the ruin in 1792. Ruskin owned and prized this watercolor, using it as an example of Turner's ability to capture the true qualities of changing clouds and torrential water.

Opposite, below:
Figure 87
J. M. W. TURNER (1775–1851)
A First Rate Taking in Stores. 1818
Pencil and watercolor, 11 1/4 × 15 5/8"
The Trustees, The Cecil Higgins Art Gallery, Bedford, England

Ruskin cited this work as proof of Turner's mastery of composition. In November 1818 Turner was staying with his patron Walter Fawkes. One morning Fawkes asked the artist for a drawing that would give him an idea of the size of a man-of-war (warship). Turner allowed Fawkes's fifteen-year-old son to observe him, and later the boy described Turner at work: "He began by pouring wet paint onto the paper until it was saturated, then he tore, he scratched, he scrabbled at it in a kind of frenzy . . . but gradually and as if by magic, the lovely ship . . . came into being and by luncheon time the drawing was taken down in triumph." (12:386)

Brotherhood? And how could he champion the Pre-Raphaelites, so progressive in comparison to the precepts of the Royal Academy, yet remain devoted to older artists such as Samuel Prout and William Henry Hunt, or later to the sentiments of Kate Greenaway and Helen Allingham? Ruskin answered these questions himself in thousands of pages of public proclamation on the state of British art, its place in history, and his hopes for it. Much of this text was produced between 1843 and 1860, from the publication of the first to the last volume of his monumental series *Modern Painters*, when his attention fixed primarily on these topics. Writing with the evangelical zeal and earnestness of his Victorian era, he intended to inspire his audience, artist and nonartist alike, and to teach it how to see the visual art of its own day and, indeed, the world around it. His objective was to ensure the continuation of Turner's legacy and to resuscitate a moribund English school. The task was difficult: "Art, properly so called," he stated unequivocally, "is no recreation; it cannot be learned at spare moments, nor pursued when we have nothing better to do." (4:26)

The five-volume *Modern Painters*, originally subtitled *Their Superiority in the Art of Landscape Painting to All the Ancient Masters*, began as a rebuttal to critics who accused Turner of being untrue to nature. Ultimately it explored the theoretical and formal aspects of great art and its informative, interpretive role in understanding the relationships between God, nature, humanity, and society. Its foundation rested upon Ruskin's conviction that all real and vital knowledge—hence, truth—was revealed visually to the eyes and minds of only a few artists. "The greatest thing a human soul ever does in this world is to *see* something," he explained, "and tell what it *saw* in a plain way. Hundreds of people can talk for one who can think, but thousands can think for one who can see. To see clearly is poetry, prophecy, and religion—all in one." (5:333)

Volume 1 begins with the proclamation that "the art is greatest which conveys to the mind of the spectator, by any means whatsoever, the greatest number of the greatest ideas." (3:92) These ideas, encompassing the concepts of power, imitation, beauty, relation, and, most important, truth, elevated art from the function of mere decoration to the expression of profound thoughts conveyable visually and only through art. Truth as applied to art, Ruskin said, "signifies the faithful statement, either to the mind or senses, of any fact of nature. . . . There is a moral as well as material truth,—a truth of impression as well as of form,—of thought as well as of matter." (3:104) Ruskin's explanation and interpretation of these initial precepts evolved and matured over the years, but he stood by them in principle throughout his life.

Turner, despite every charge to the contrary, was "the only man who has ever given an entire transcript of the whole system of nature, and is, in this point of view, the only perfect landscape painter whom the world has ever seen." (3:616) Turner earned this acclaim by realizing in his work, as much as was humanly possible, the impressions of tone, color, chiaroscuro, and space, and the specifics of sky, earth, water, and vegetation. To prove this achievement, Ruskin repeatedly compared Turner's works with those of popular Dutch, French, and Italian masters. The conclusion was the same in case after case: Turner was undeniably more factual than all others.

In one of these tests for accuracy, the rain clouds in *Llanthony Abbey, Monmouthshire* (figure 86) were compared to a work by the seventeenth-century painter Gaspar Dughet. "Throughout the whole range of ancient landscape art there occurs no instance of the painting of a real rain-cloud," Ruskin asserted. Dughet's clouds were "massive concretions of ink and indigo, wrung and twisted very hard, apparently in a vain effort to get some moisture out of them." (3:396) Entering the scene in *Llanthony Abbey*, verbally repainted for the reader, one found:

> *The shower is here half exhausted, half passed by, the last drops are rattling faintly through the glimmering hazel boughs, the white torrent, swelled by the sudden storm, flings up its hasty jets of springing spray to meet the returning light; and these, as if the heaven regretted what it had given, and were taking it back, pass as they leap, into vapour, and fall not again, but vanish in the shafts of the sunlight; hurrying, fitful, wind-woven sunlight, which glides through the thick leaves, and paces along the pale rocks like rain; half conquering, half quenched by the very mists which it summons itself from the lighted pastures as it passes, and gathers out of the drooping herbage and from the streaming crags; sending them with messages of peace to the far summits of the yet unveiled mountains, whose silence is still broken by the sound of the rushing rain. (3:402)*

Llanthony Abbey also stood as the standard of torrent drawing. Ruskin forcibly described the gushing river as "green and clear, but pale with anger, in broad, unbroken, oceanic curves, bending into each other without break . . ., one united race of mad motion; all the waves dragged . . . into lines and furrows by their swiftness; and every one of those fine forms is drawn with the most studied chiaroscuro of delicate colour, greys and greens." (3:557–58)

Any attempt to imitate nature, literally to transcribe reality, was valuable as an exercise, but it was doomed to failure because it was impossible. Ruskin admitted that trompe l'oeil mimicry was always enormously popular, but it was a low form of art. In attempting to deceive the viewer, "it derives its pleasure, not from the contemplation of a truth, but from the discovery of a falsehood. . . . No picture can be good which deceives by its imitation, for the very reason that nothing can be beautiful which is not true." (3:108) Turner's works were the result of his complete understanding of nature's forms, its slow processes, and its great moments. Through his knowledge and his own deeply felt emotions, Turner roused ideas and insights far beyond the merely material aspects of his subject. The swiftly moving clouds and the swollen torrent in *Llanthony Abbey* were witnessed by the ancient, ruined abbey and the fishermen. The past and the present human activities created a history of the place as well as an evocation of its fluctuating appearance at a specific moment in that history.

Turner's grasp of an accurate image infused with subtle but significant meaning amazed Ruskin; no less incredible was the ease with which Turner conceived his best works. They were sudden and complete, never strained or forced. Ruskin attributed this largely to the retentive, synthesizing power of a memory capable of recalling a scene witnessed long before and instinctively adjusting of scale, form, color, and composition to correspond with that element of beauty or interest most attractive to him. This

Figure 88
J. M. W. TURNER (1775–1851)
*Calais Sands, Low Water, Poissards
Collecting Bait*. Exhibited 1830
Oil on canvas, 28½ × 42″
Bury Art Gallery and Museum,
England

Turner visited Calais numerous times, making many studies. The vastness and serenity of the scene is distinguished by passages of energetic brushwork and glowing color characteristic of his mature work. Anticipating a wave of criticism in the next decade, *The Morning Chronicle* attacked Turner for "taking an unpardonable liberty with the public" but allowed that *Calais Sands* was "excusable in its slightness—it is literally nothing in labour, but extraordinary in art." Ruskin viewed Turner's Calais subjects as "records of successive impressions, as plainly written as ever a traveler's diary. All of them pure veracities. Therefore immortal." (12:381)

spontaneously selective recollection was witnessed as the artist painted *A First Rate Taking in Stores* (figure 87). The hull of a ship, gigantic next to the other boats, occupies nearly half of the picture. Ruskin, fascinated by this remarkable perspective, the minutiae of rigging and cannons, the dancing sea and the correspondingly complex sky, impressed upon his readers the facility with which this was achieved: "It might appear no small exertion of mind to draw the detail of all this shipping down to the smallest ropes, from memory, in the drawing-room of a mansion in the middle of Yorkshire, even if considerable time had been given for the effort. But Mr. Fawkes sat beside the painter from the first stroke to the last. Turner took a piece of blank paper one morning after breakfast, outlined his ships, finished the drawing in three hours, and went out to shoot." (12:386)

Memory, informed by direct observation and enriched by time, also created the melancholy but luminous *Calais Sands, Low Water, Poissards Collecting Bait*, exhibited in 1830. Ruskin described it as a remembrance from Turner's first visit to Calais in 1802.[6] Taking an evening walk at low tide, Turner watched fisherwomen scattered over the beach before a glorious sunset. The resulting painting is aglow with last light. The rhythmic placement of the laboring figures, their distorted shapes echoed in the foreground barrel and distant cloud formations, contrasts with the vastness of beach and sky.

These works fulfilled Ruskin's two goals of landscape painting. The first was "to induce in the spectator's mind the faithful conception of any natural objects whatsoever," and the second was "to guide the spectator's mind to those objects most worthy of its contemplation, and to inform him of the thoughts and feelings with which these were regarded by the artist himself." He explained that "in attaining the first end the painter only places the spectator where he stands himself; he sets him before the landscape and leaves him. The spectator is alone. . . . The artist is his conveyance, not his companion, — his horse, not his friend. But in attaining the second end, the artist not only *places* the spectator, but *talks* to him; makes him a sharer in his own strong feelings and quick thoughts; hurries him away in his own enthusiasm; guides him to all that is beautiful; snatches him from all that is base; and leaves him more than delighted, — ennobled and instructed." (3:133–34) He warned that dedication only to the first goal was dangerous; the artist could lapse into pleasant—but tiresome and repetitious—scenes simply by using formulae for composition and color that seemed successful but that were ultimately facile and unenduring. Rules and patented solutions for the attainment of visual effects were anathemas to Ruskin.[7] Whether learned through academic tradition or individual cleverness, they detached the artist from the particular and the varied yet enduring forms of nature. By contrast, those striving for the

Figure 89
DAVID COX (1783–1859)
The Mill. 1853
Watercolor heightened with white, 12¼ × 14¼″
The Trustees, The Cecil Higgins Art Gallery, Bedford, England

Although he was not a member of the Pre-Raphaelite Brotherhood, Cox was one of the masters of landscape watercolor painting in whom Ruskin saw the promise of English art and the synthesis of accuracy and feeling so crucial to his program. Cox's watercolors are remarkable for their freedom and spontaneity, especially in their depiction of the effects of weather. Like Turner, Cox imbued nature with a sense of energy and atmosphere that anticipated Impressionism. Ruskin admired his loose and blotted handling, qualities that responded "gracefully to the accidental part of nature herself." (3:195)

125

Figure 90
J. M. W. TURNER (1775–1851)
The Ruined Abbey at Haddington.
1793–95
Watercolor over pencil, 7 × 9″
Ashmolean Museum, Oxford

Ruskin prized the work so highly that he gave it to his School of Drawing at Oxford to be copied in examinations as a test of skill. He was unaware that it was a copy itself, based on an engraving by W. Byrne after Thomas Hearne. Ruskin described it as a demonstration of Turner's perfect technique: "This I put . . . to be a witness to you once for all, of the right way to work: do nothing without a clearly formed intention, nothing in a hurry, nothing more wrong than you can help, all as tenderly as you can, all as instantly as you can, all thoughtfully, and nothing mechanically. Take those laws for absolute ones, in art and life." (21:128)

second and higher goal looked always with fresh, innocent eyes at nature and chose subjects for meaning and character first, beauty second. Ruskin wanted both the artist, and his audience, to be thoughtfully but actively engaged with each work of art, so that "we feel, in each of its results, that we are looking, not at a specimen of a tradesman's wares, of which he is ready to make us a dozen to match, but at one coruscation of a perpetually active mind, like which there has not been, and will not be another." (3:135)

The young artist could not hope to reach the second goal without accomplishing the first. Ruskin insisted that young artists train their eyes and hands by studying nature's lessons only, and that they must refuse to succumb to habits, conceits, and customs. This was the foundation upon which the artist's true and noble work would stand. In his famous charge to modern artists, Ruskin challenged the young in a fervent voice to begin humbly but, in a crescendo of words, to persevere in their efforts to reach the loftiest and noblest ends:

From young artists nothing ought to be tolerated but simple bôna fide *imitation of nature. They have no business to ape the execution of masters . . . and, making the early works of Turner their example, as his latest are to be their object of emulation, should go to Nature in all singleness of heart, and walk with her laboriously and trustingly, having no other thoughts but how best to penetrate her meaning, and remember her instruction; rejecting nothing, selecting nothing, and scorning nothing; believing all things to be right and good, and rejoicing always in the truth. Then, when their memories are stored, and their imaginations fed, and their hands firm, let them take up the scarlet and gold, give the reins to their fancy; and show us what their heads are made of . . . throw, if he will, mist round it, darkness, or dazzling and confused light, whatever, in fact, impetuous feeling or vigorous imagination may dictate or desire; . . .*

The artist who thus works will soon find that he cannot repeat himself if he would; and new fields of exertion, new subjects of contemplation, open to him in nature day by day; and that, while others lament the weakness of their invention, he has nothing to lament but the shortness of life. *(3:623–28)*

Ruskin asked that artists follow Turner's program of lifelong study, reflection, assimilation, and achievement. His great concern for students motivated his generous gift of seventy-seven Turner drawings and watercolors to Oxford University in 1861, today held in the Ashmolean Museum. In that collection one can follow Turner's independent course, from his early student years when he carefully copied, penciled, and colored *The Ruined Abbey at Haddington* to the more assured and inventive handling of medium in *Sunshine on the Tamar*, done about twenty years later. Ruskin felt that Turner's style crystallized in the 1820s when, completely adept at revealing all he saw, he expressed the mood and essence of his subjects. *Scene on the Loire*, composed in the subtlest blues and golds, evokes the quiet

Figure 91
J. M. W. TURNER (1775–1851)
Sunshine on the Tamar. c. 1813
Watercolor with scratching-out,
8½ × 14½"
Ashmolean Museum, Oxford

In a letter of 1886, Ruskin referred to this scene as "Pigs by Sunlight," a rather humble title, yet he paid a great deal of money for it. It was included in the Fine Arts Society exhibition of 1878. Ruskin's accompanying catalogue wryly comments, "It shows already one of Turner's specially English (in the humiliating sense) points of character that . . . he could draw *pigs* better than any other animal. . . . Sunshine and rivers, and sweet hills, yes, and who is there to see or care for them?—Only the pigs." (13:435)

127

Figure 92
J. M. W. Turner (1775–1851)
Scene on the Loire. 1826–30
Watercolor and body color on blue-gray paper, 5½ × 7½"
Ashmolean Museum, Oxford

Conceived for Turner's engraved series *The Rivers of France*, this drawing was never published. Of all those from the series Ruskin donated to Oxford, it remains the freshest in color. Ruskin considered it a gem and described it as a "very precious, and I believe unsurpassable example of watercolour painting." Often accused of having interest only in imitative and narrative art, Ruskin's comments reveal his sensitivity to the emotional power of color. Here the washed tones evoke "the warmth of a summer twilight with a tinge of colour on the grey paper so slight that it may be a question with some of you whether any [color] is there. . . . The value of it depends never on violence, but always on subtlety." (22:56)

contentment and warmth of a summer sunset. *Mount Lebanon and the Convent of Saint Antonio*, from the same period, was done from another artist's topographical sketch, but Turner added drama and majesty to the scene by manipulating the scale of the mountainous setting. His continental tours in the early 1840s resulted in many of his freest, most unconventional images, vivid color impressions with virtually no descriptive detail. *Venice: The Accademia* (figure 57) is among the late works that Ruskin described as bearing "the same relation to those of the rest of his life that the colours of sunset do to those of the day." (12:391)

Observation, training, thought, and stored memories were all essential components of Turner's mastery, but his greatest powers could not be learned. They were innate. Ruskin maintained that every great artist was distinguished by a personal character that compelled him to choose right and worthy subjects of human significance; to seek and evoke the true beauty in those subjects; and to relay his messages lucidly and sincerely. This noble character was crowned by "that penetrating, possession-taking power of the imagination . . . the very life of the man, considered as a *seeing* creature." (5:177) Imagination was not distinct from either the act of sight or recollection; rather, in a great mind and the great works it produced, imagination permeated and effected perception: "Observe," Ruskin appealed, "these are nothing more than a greater apprehension of the *facts* of

Figure 93
J. M. W. TURNER (1775–1851)
Mount Lebanon and the Convent of Saint Antonio. c. 1835
Watercolor over pencil with pen and ink, 5¾ × 7⅞"
Ashmolean Museum, Oxford

This work was one of twenty-six designed by Turner for *The Biblical Keepsake or Landscape Illustrations of the Most-Remarkable Places Mentioned in the Holy Scriptures*, first published in 1836 by W. and E. Finden and John Murray. Because Turner never visited the Middle East or Greece, this series was based on topographical views by other artists and infused with his own religious feeling and experience. Ruskin explained that Turner chose

Mount Lebanon to represent the beneficent influence of the Gospel in which "every ravine is filled, every promontory crowned, by tenderest foliage, golden in slanting sunshine." (7:192) It was equally remarkable as an example of Turner's knowledge of geological structure: "There is not one shade nor touch on the rock which is not indicative of the lines of stratification, and every feature is marked with a straightforward simplicity which makes you feel that the artist has nothing in his heart but a keen love of the pure unmodified truth. . . . The rocks are laid one above another with unhesitating decision, every shade is understood in a moment." (3:454)

129

the thing. We call [that] power 'Imagination,' because it imagines or conceives; but it is only noble imagination if it imagines or conceives *the truth*." (5:178) The complete expression of this individual mind was inimitable and magnificent: "Hence we see why the word 'Great' is used of this art. It is literally great. It compasses and calls forth the entire human spirit, whereas any other kind of art, being more or less small or narrow, compasses and calls forth only *part* of the human spirit." (5:66)

Turner, that artist gifted with "heartsight deep as eyesight," died in 1851. (7:377) The light that Ruskin felt could lead his nation to glory was extinguished. Looking about at contemporary art and society in 1856, Ruskin lamented that the term "Dark Ages" applied more to his own than to the medieval period. "They were, on the contrary, the bright ages; ours are the dark ones. . . . These are much *sadder* ages than the early ones; not sadder in a noble and deep way, but in a dim wearied way,—the way of ennui, and jaded intellect, and uncomfortableness of soul and body." (5:321) Yet Ruskin had already begun his search for the next great luminary. He was encouraged when he encountered the members and associates of the Pre-Raphaelite Brotherhood, who shared his ideas on truth to nature and his anti-academic attitudes.

Although the Pre-Raphaelite Brotherhood had formed in 1848, Ruskin had never met any of those involved when, as he had for Turner, he defended them against violent critical attack. The press vilified paintings by members of the Brotherhood, including John Everett Millais, William Holman Hunt, Dante Gabriel Rossetti, and James Collinson. In 1850 Charles Dickens wrote in his journal *Household Words* that the two central figures in Millais's *Christ in the House of His Parents* looked like "a hideous, wry-necked, blubbering, red-haired boy in a nightgown, who appears to have received a poke playing in an adjacent gutter, and to be holding it up for the contemplation of a kneeling woman, so horrible in her ugliness that (supposing it were possible for any human creature to exist for a moment with that dislocated throat) she would stand out from the rest of the company as a monster in the vilest cabaret in France or in the lowest gin-shop in England."[8] A *Times* reviewer the next year soundly condemned Millais's *The Woodman's Daughter* and other Pre-Raphaelite paintings, saying, "We cannot censure at present as amply or as strongly as we desire to do, that strange disorder of the mind or the eyes, which continues to rage with unabated absurdity among a class of juvenile artists who style themselves P. R. B., which, being interpreted, means Pre-Raphaelite Brotherhood."[9] Ruskin responded first with two letters to the paper, later with more elaborate replies to this disheartening criticism. He felt that these artists ought to be encouraged for two reasons: their degree of realism put them "above the level of mere contempt," and, being young, they needed nurturing at this crucial, developmental point in their careers. (12:319)

Ruskin agreed that the Renaissance master Raphael was pivotal in the history of art. Art before Raphael was honest, sincere, and dedicated both to praise and instruction; after him, Ruskin contended, artists pursued an artificial beauty rather than truth, with a desire to make "fair pictures, rather than represent stern facts." (12:322) Art declined as a result. Ruskin acknowledged certain faults among the Pre-Raphaelites: Millais's unfortu-

Figure 94
SIR JOHN EVERETT MILLAIS
(1829–1896)
The Woodman's Daughter. 1850–51
Oil on canvas, 35 × 25½"
Guildhall Art Gallery, Corporation of London

Millais entered the Royal Academy as a child prodigy and displayed his first work there at age sixteen. It was he who, with his friends Holman Hunt and Rossetti, formed the Pre-Raphaelite Brotherhood in 1848. Millais, devastated by the critical cry against this and his other Pre-Raphaelite paintings, urged Coventry Patmore to recruit Ruskin's support for the movement. Patmore's poem "The Woodman's Daughter" was the inspiration for this painting. It tells of the first meeting of Maud, a woodman's daughter, and a squire's son. Tossing aside Victorian mores and class distinctions, they had a love affair. Maud gave birth to an illegitimate child, drowned it, and slipped into madness. Millais labored for accuracy in his portrayal of this fateful moment in Patmore's poem. Striving for visual truth, every detail is meticulously described, from the strawberries purchased in Covent Gardens to the setting based on studies at Botley Park, near Oxford.

Figure 95
Sir Charles Eastlake
(1793–1865)
The Salutation to the Aged Friar.
Exhibited 1840
Oil on canvas, 37¼ × 44½"
The FORBES Magazine Collection,
New York

Eastlake was elected president of the
Royal Academy in 1850 and director of
the National Gallery in 1855. He was
renowned for the beauty and physical
grace of his figures and the touching
religious sentiment of his biblical and
genre subjects, all exemplified by *The
Salutation to the Aged Friar*. The Pre-
Raphaelite artists' refusal to refine and
idealize the appearance of their models
contrasted dramatically with this academic style.

nate choice of very plain models for holy persons; Holman Hunt's exaggeration of reflected lights; and the unrelieved intensity of brilliant light
characteristic of most of their paintings. Nonetheless, he found their attention to minute detail and their humble exploration of nature's variety
captivating, and their portrayal of historical events in real and believable,
rather than ideal and remote, terms very refreshing. Obviously excited by
their ability to fulfill the first artistic goal, material truth, and their potential
to reach the second, moral truth, he saw the Pre-Raphaelites as the heirs of
Turner. Ruskin hoped that, given guidance and support, they might provide
the foundation of the most noble school of art the world had seen in three
hundred years, since before Raphael.

Ruskin's personal and professional relationships with the Pre-
Raphaelites surely helped him to clarify his views concerning contemporary British art and artists. In both his 1851 pamphlet *Pre-Raphaelitism* and
his 1853 lecture on the same topic, he concentrated on placing these artists
and their predecessor, Turner, into social, stylistic, and historical contexts,
and he developed his definition of the noble artistic character.[10] Ruskin
introduced the 1851 pamphlet by stating that God intends every man to be
happy in his work. For that, he must be fit for it; he must not do too much of

Figure 96
WILLIAM HENRY HUNT
(1790–1864)
The Shy Sitter. c. 1832
Watercolor heightened with white,
surface scratching,
9 × 7¼"
Harris Museum and Art Gallery,
Preston, England

Among the best of Hunt's works, according to Ruskin, were "drawings illustrative of rural life in its vivacity and purity, without the slightest endeavour at idealization and still less with any wish either to caricature or deplore its imperfections." (14:422) *The Shy Sitter* was listed as one of the best in this class in Ruskin's 1879–80 *Notes by Mr. Ruskin on Samuel Prout and William Hunt.* The direct but innocent gaze of the child, seated politely yet stiffly in her chair, meets the viewer's eye. Ruskin described this work as among a group of "things that the old painter was himself unspeakably blessed in having the power to do. The strength of all lovely human life is in them; and England herself lives only, at this hour, in so much as, from all that is sunk in the luxury, sick in the penury, and polluted in the sin of her great cities, Heaven has yet hidden for her old men and children such as these." (15:448)

it; and he must enjoy a sense of personal success in it aside from what others may say to encourage or dissuade him. As Ruskin developed his argument, he clarified his line of thought: A true artist discovers his fitness for this pursuit. He is born with genius but he must be humble and steady in "accumulating and disciplining its powers, as well as by its gigantic, incommunicable facility in exercising them." (12:345) His work is not labored and difficult because, once again, *"No great intellectual thing was ever done by great effort."* (12:344) The artist cannot be trained for his profession by the Royal Academy's insistence upon conformity and rule, nor can he be discouraged by it. Thus, Turner was "the first and greatest of the Pre-Raphaelites." (12:159) Others might join him including the very promising John Everett Millais, Ruskin's first protégé. Both Turner and Millais "defied all false teaching, and have therefore, in great measure, done justice to the gifts with which they were intrusted." (12:360–61) Turner's sight was free but accurate, unified by memory, and instilled with a sense of mystery and sacredness; Millais's was sharp, attentive to the minutia and color of life, but not yet completely imaginative.

After Turner and Millais, Ruskin arranged the work of several other living artists, from noble to pedestrian, who each nurtured his own vision according to his own talent. William Henry Hunt was the first named. Hunt devoted himself to the loving, unpretentious depiction of rural life such as *The Shy Sitter* (figure 96) and *Barn Interior*. He was, in Ruskin's opinion, the best painter of still life that had ever existed. His rich color and delicate touch gave the products of nature, seen in *Two Apples and a Snail Shell*, a sense of magic and mystery that put them above the level of imitation. Next to Hunt was Samuel Prout, a bouyant man who industriously recorded the ancient monuments of England and Europe. These once grand but now moldering ruined memories of the past faced destruction or the even greater devastation of ill-conceived modern restoration. Prout drew both factual documents like *Saint Omer, the Abbey Church of Saint Bertin: View of Nave and North Transept from the Crossing* (figure 99), and, in works such as *Rome, the Arch of Constantine from the Southeast* (figure 100), more picturesque depictions of locale. John Frederick Lewis held the middle position. The independent Lewis lavished his factual glimpses

Figure 97
WILLIAM HENRY HUNT
(1790–1864)
Barn Interior. 1836
Watercolor and body color with scratching-out, 13¾ × 9⅝″
Yale Center for British Art, Paul Mellon Collection

In the 1879–80 exhibition catalogue *Notes by Mr. Ruskin on Samuel Prout and William Hunt*, Ruskin divided Hunt's work into six classes, with views of rural life comprising three. Those distinguished by a sense of liveliness and honesty, such as this simple but fresh interior of a barn, stood above others that were marred by obvious sentimentality or, even worse, those focused on peasant "gluttony, cowardice, or rudeness." (14:442) The other classes included flower pieces, fruit pieces, and dead animals.

of Egyptian life with an exquisite drawing style, an inimitable suggestion of light, and an enormous talent for color and composition (figure 102). Below Lewis was William Mulready, an artist whose consummate skill frustrated Ruskin because, he said, it was wasted on subjects that were either uninteresting, beyond his capabilities, or simply improper. *The Butt—Shooting the Cherry* (figure 101) exemplifies Mulready's beautiful technique dedicated to a subject that in Ruskin's opinion was one step above worthless depictions of brutality and vice. (5:49) Sir Edwin Landseer was the last named. Ruskin commented, "It was not by the study of Raphael that he attained his eminent success, but by a healthy love of Scotch terriers." (12:365) Among the seven artists named in the pamphlet, only Turner had reached the complete integration of hand, sight, insight, and noble theme.

One of the first Pre-Raphaelite masterpieces to win his complete praise was Holman Hunt's *The Light of the World* (figure 103), the subject of an 1854 letter to the *Times* and an often-cited example of noble art: perfect in theme, feeling, and execution. It was of the highest order in the hierarchy of subjects, those appealing to the most noble thoughts, and Ruskin discovered a wealth of quiet messages within it as he explored its every aspect for hidden meaning. For example, he saw Christ's crown of thorns, sprouting

Figure 98
WILLIAM HENRY HUNT
(1790–1864)
Two Apples and a Snail Shell. c.1860
Watercolor, 5¼ × 7⅜"
Harris Museum and Art Gallery, Preston

Hunt's reputed naïveté was not an artistic one. Simple subjects such as *Two Apples and a Snail Shell* are made magical and quite out of the ordinary by his sensitive placement of shapes and sizes, by the delicate touches of color and light that mold and enrich tiny surfaces, and by the heightened sense of tangibility of the objects.

Figure 99
SAMUEL PROUT (1783–1852)
Saint Omer, the Abbey Church of Saint Bertin: View of Nave and North Transept from the Crossing. n.d.
Hard and soft pencil on cream wove paper, stump with rubbing,
16¼ × 10¾"
By Courtesy of the Board of Trustees of the Victoria and Albert Museum, London

This drawing, probably executed in 1822, contains a detail that seems to confirm one of Ruskin's greatest fears: The glories of the past were fast disappearing, often through the indifference and the destruction of the society that inherited them. Within the noble but ruined interior of Saint Omer, workmen cart off the stones for other uses.

Figure 100
SAMUEL PROUT (1783–1852)
Rome, The Arch of Constantine from the Southeast. c. 1826
Pen and ink, watercolor, and body color on cream wove paper, lights reserved, 14¼ × 10¼"
By Courtesy of the Board of Trustees of the Victoria and Albert Museum, London

Prout first visited the Continent in 1819 and found subjects there to occupy him for the rest of his life. He recorded monumental and humble sites in his distinctive calligraphic

style. Ruskin, devoted to Prout personally, was ambivalent toward his often mannered style. Nonetheless, Ruskin said: "We owe to Prout, I believe, the first perception and certainly the only existing expression of precisely the characters which were wanting to old art, of that feeling which results from the influence, among the noble lines of architecture, of the rent and the rust, the fissure, the lichen and the weed. . . . There is *no* stone drawing, *no* vitality of architecture like Prout's." (3:216–17)

Figure 101
WILLIAM MULREADY
(1786–1863)
The Butt—Shooting the Cherry.
Exhibited 1858
Oil on canvas, 15¼ × 18″
By Courtesy of the Board of
Trustees of the Victoria and Albert
Museum, London

Mulready was an enormously successful Irish painter of genre scenes. He
began this painting in 1822 and finished it in 1857, after the dusty, damaged canvas was discovered in his
studio by a friend. Such humorous depictions of boys' games did not appeal
to Ruskin, who felt that Mulready only
wasted his talent on these trivial subjects. He considered Mulready a superb technician and colorist, indeed,
his use of a white ground and luminous
colors preceeded that of the Pre-
Raphaelites. Ruskin considered the use
of color in *The Butt* to be exceptional,
despite its low subject.

Figure 102
JOHN FREDERICK LEWIS
(1805–1876)
Interior of a School, Cairo. n.d.
Watercolor, 13 × 17⅜″
By Courtesy of the Board of
Trustees of the Victoria and Albert
Museum, London

Lewis, a member of both the Royal
Society of Painters in Water-Colours
and the Royal Academy, was a meticulous painter of exotic subjects. Famed
for his Egyptian scenes, he portrayed
interiors such as this in jewel-like colors, with complicated patterns of light
and shade and detailed costumes and
settings. His style anticipated Pre-
Raphaelitism, and Ruskin named him
a leading Pre-Raphaelite although
Lewis was never actually associated
with the movement.

new verdant leaves, as signifying the healing of nations. Equally important
to this inspiring theme of Christian hope was the painting's superb finish,
its accurate rendering of each object throughout the composition, and the
mystery of its colors. Ruskin later emphasized the importance of Holman
Hunt's skill, insisting "a painter's business is first to *paint*. No one could
sympathize more than I with the general feeling displayed in the 'Light of
the World'; but unless it had been accompanied with perfectly good nettle
painting, and ivy painting, and jewel painting, I should never have praised
it." (14:65)

By 1855 Ruskin was the preeminent living authority on art in Britain and
his views on contemporary art were sought eagerly. To meet these requests,
he assumed the true position of a critic and began to write *Academy Notes*,
brochures offering his opinions on the annual Royal Academy and other
exhibitions. The *Notes*, published from 1855 to 1859 and again in 1875,
included only the pictures Ruskin felt to be the most worthy of mention.
From those chosen, he hoped to determine each artist's goal and his degree
of success in meeting it. Ruskin claimed total impartiality, insisting that he

Figure 103
WILLIAM HOLMAN HUNT
(1827–1910)
The Light of the World. c. 1852
Oil on canvas, 19¾ × 10⅜″
Manchester City Art Galleries,
England

This famous image illustrates Revelation 3:20, "Behold, I stand at the door, and knock: if any man hear my voice, and open the door, I will come in to him, and will sup with him, and he with me." Holman Hunt painted three versions of *The Light of the World*: the original, in Keble College, Oxford, done 1851–53, the second, illustrated here, and the third and largest, in Saint Paul's Cathedral, London, done 1900–1904. Upset about the cursory glances given to the first when it was exhibited at the Royal Academy in 1854, Ruskin wrote a sermonizing interpretation of the painting to the *Times*: "For my own part, I think it one of the very noblest works of sacred art ever produced in this or any other age." This second and smallest version was painted with the assistance of another Pre-Raphaelite artist, F. G. Stephens (1828–1907). Holman Hunt was inspired in his realistic but highly symbolic compositions by his reading of *Modern Painters* 2.

139

Figure 104
WILLIAM POWELL FRITH
(1819–1909)
For Better, For Worse. 1881
Oil on canvas, 61 × 49″
The FORBES Magazine Collection,
New York

Frith spoke of this painting in his
Memoirs, describing the incident that
inspired it with a typically Victorian
moral tone: He contrasted the affluent
newlyweds about to enter their
brougham in Cleveland Square, London, with a family of beggars in the left
foreground. Frith's technical dexterity
and his ability to compose large figural
groups made him the foremost contemporary genre painter of his day.
Ruskin admired his depictions of contemporary life as records for posterity.

sought only to make observations for the reader to accept or reject.
Nonetheless, he obviously saw the *Notes* as a means of promoting the Pre-
Raphaelite style and advancing his own program for the future of British
art. Speaking confidently, he took the opportunity both to praise and to
correct any work, whether by a notable academician or a young artist, and
to urge upon each Pre-Raphaelite accuracy and sincerity.

Ruskin spoke of the variety present in the 1855 exhibition, noting
those pieces that appeared exceptional to him. Millais and his Pre-
Raphaelite brother James Collinson were singled out as successes. He eyed
carefully the work of twenty-five-year-old Frederic Leighton, admiring his
elegant finish and his delicate yet underivative "Venetian simplicity." Ruskin predicted greatness for Leighton if he could avoid the temptation of
affectation. An example of what to avoid might have been the painting by
Sir Charles Eastlake, who, Ruskin felt, merely copied Venetian art, per-
petuating errors rather than virtues. In the 1855 *Notes*, Ruskin recommended that Sir Charles, then president of the Royal Academy and director
of the National Gallery, study nature anew. In a direct attack on the enemies
of Pre-Raphaelitism, the work of the highly respected Daniel Maclise was
dismissed as "energetically or actively bad." (14:9) These comments

brought immediate reactions from academicians, their friends, and patrons. Ruskin responded to their outrage with enormous self-assurance. Insisting that he spoke only of the major defects in each work, he wrote in a supplement to the same *Notes*: "I never say half of what I could say in its disfavor; and it will hereafter be found that when once I have felt it my duty to attack a picture, the worst policy which the friends of the artist can possibly adopt will be to defend it." (14:35)

Ruskin was jubilant in 1856. A vast change had come about, and the Pre-Raphaelite style was predominate. He saw all artists "struggling forward out of their conventionalism to the Pre-Raphaelite standard." Proclaiming victory prematurely, as it turned out, Ruskin declared, "The meaning of this is simply that the battle is completely and confessedly won . . . that animosity has changed into emulation, astonishment into sympathy, and that a true and consistent school of art is at last established in the Royal Academy of England." (14:47) Among those complimented for their turn to Pre-Raphaelitism, as he saw it, were the very popular and successful Richard Redgrave and W. P. Frith. Welcome praise was given to the young Alfred William Hunt who, with this encouragement from the eminent Ruskin, continued to pursue a career in art.

If anyone dared to question Ruskin's impartiality, he needed only to consider Ruskin's appraisal of figure painting in 1856. For the second time since his wife left him in 1854 to marry Millais in 1855, Ruskin publicly and lavishly praised Millais's works in *Academy Notes*. The two

Figure 105
ALFRED WILLIAM HUNT
(1830–1896)
A Welsh Scene: A Runlet Babbling down the Glen. 1858
Watercolor, 9⅞ × 14¼"
Ashmolean Museum, Oxford

Encouraged by Ruskin's praise of his work in the 1856 *Academy Notes*, Hunt abandoned an academic career for art. Ruskin noted that, like Turner, Hunt managed to unite "subtle finish and watchfulness of Nature, with real and rare power of composition." (14:50–51) The intricate path of the brook and minutiae of vegetal and rocky texture in this massive landscape are realized with Pre-Raphaelite precision.

Figure 106
Frederic, Lord Leighton
(1830–1896)
Portrait of Nanna Risi, a Roman Lady.
Exhibited 1859
Oil on canvas, 31½ × 20½″
Philadelphia Museum of Art: The
Henry Clifford Memorial Fund
Supplemented by the John D.
McIlhenny Fund

Leighton met Nanna Risi, the beautiful wife of a Roman cobbler, three years after his spectacular debut in the Royal Academy in 1855. She was a professional model whose striking appearance inspired others as well. Leighton's Venetian sensuousness and color, apparent in this portrait, were praised by Ruskin, who was one of the artist's early and vocal supporters. Ironically, Leighton was the newly elected president of the Royal Academy at the time of the Whistler-Ruskin trial. Even so, Ruskin named him leader of the "Classic Schools of Painting" in his 1883 Oxford lecture.

Opposite:
Figure 107
Sir John Everett Millais
(1829–1896)
Peace Concluded. 1856
Oil on canvas, 46¼ × 36″
The Minneapolis Institute of Arts;
The P. D. McMillan Fund

Millais played a central role in Ruskin's program and hopes for British art; he was Ruskin's first protégé. Ruskin extolled this painting, popularly known as *The Return from the Crimea,* as one of Millais's finest. In his *Academy Notes* of 1856 Ruskin predicted, it "will rank in future among the world's best masterpieces." (14:56) Lady Millais modeled for the wife in the picture.

entries, *Autumn Leaves* and *Peace Concluded,* eclipsed all others. Ruskin compared Millais's art to that of Titian, saying the pieces were "as brilliant in invention as consummate in executive power. . . . I see no limit to what the painter may achieve." (14:56) His admiration was qualified only by his speculation about Millais's future: would he actually surpass all others in figure painting as Turner had in landscape?

Second in the 1856 exhibition at the Royal Academy was William Windus's *Burd Helen* (figure 108), a work initially passed over by Ruskin because, as he said, he disliked slate gray and girls dressed as pages. Upon reexamination, however, he accepted both the grayness and the clothing as appropriate to the theme, young Burd Helen doggedly running alongside the lover who has spurned her. Windus managed to combine good painting

with suitable but sensitive expressiveness, a balance that Ruskin thought nearly impossible in such a heart-wrenching scene. He detailed the manner in which Windus accomplished this:

> *The pressure of the girl's hand on her side; her wild, firm, desolate look at the stream—she not raising her eyes as she makes her appeal, for fear of the greater mercilessness in the human look than in the glaze of the gliding water—the just choice of the type of the rider's cruel face, and of the scene itself—so terrible in haggardness of rattling stones and ragged heath,—are all marks of the action of the very grandest imaginative power, shortened only of hold upon our feelings because dealing with a subject too fearful to be for a moment believed true. (14:86)*

Ruskin described the fall from expressiveness to emotional overindulgence in *Modern Painters* 3 as the "pathetic fallacy," an imbalance in which an overly empassioned mind creates a distorted, hence false, view of reality. (5:208 ff) This undue exaggeration had been avoided by Turner even during the worst moments of crisis in his life. Ruskin cautiously looked

Figure 108
WILLIAM LINDSAY WINDUS
(1822–1907)
Burd Helen. Exhibited 1856
Oil on canvas, 33¼ × 26¼"
Walker Art Gallery, Liverpool

Windus was one of the most interesting artists of those to submit to the influence of both the Pre-Raphaelites and Ruskin. *Burd Helen* was inspired by a Scottish ballad of that title. Windus chose to depict a moment of despair in which the maiden Burd Helen, vowing to stay by his side, is desperately following her cruel, faithless lover. Typical of many Pre-Raphaelite painters, Windus included lines from the ballad on the frame:

> *Lord John he rode, Burd Helen ran,*
> *A live-lang simmer's day,*
> *Until they cam' to Clyde water,*
> *Was filled frae bank to brae.*

Rossetti, enthusiastic about the work, encouraged Ruskin to look at it. Ruskin decided it was "the second picture of the year, its aim being higher, and its reserved strength greater, than those of any other work except [Millais's] *Autumn Leaves*." (14:86)

Figure 109
SIR JOHN EVERETT MILLAIS
(1829–1896)
The Escape of the Heretic, 1559.
Exhibited 1857
Oil on canvas, 42 × 30″
Museo de Arte de Ponce, Luis A.
Ferré Foundation, Inc., Ponce,
Puerto Rico

Ruskin's comments about this work, in
the 1857 *Academy Notes*, marked a
turning point in his judgment of
Millais's art. He began to accuse
Millais of wasting his superb talent by
painting in a coarse style and choosing
grotesque subjects. Millais's success
continued unabated despite Ruskin's
assessment and, in 1896, he was elected
president of the Royal Academy. *The
Escape of the Heretic* may reflect a general Victorian animosity toward anything "Papist." The female heretic is
dressed in a penitential or sambenito
garment with black demons and lurid
yellow flames. Her hero is a young no-
bleman disguised in a monk's habit.
Symbolically, the jailer has been
gagged and bound by his own rosary.

for any signs of it among those less practiced than Turner. They would
surely begin to instill their work with feeling, now that they were mastering
accurate visual description. Not all would be as successful in avoiding the
pathetic fallacy as Windus.

William Dyce's *Titian Preparing to Make His First Essay in Coloring*
(figure 110) was the picture of the year in 1857, and the only work Ruskin
found up to the highest of Pre-Raphaelite standards. He wondered in
passing about Dyce's selection of landscape setting and the colorless stone
figure of the Virgin as the object of Titian's lessons, but this was incidental
to Ruskin's appraisal of the painting. Rendered with "boundless love and
patience," it overcame difficulties that plagued those who worked too hard
for brilliant color and effects of light at the expense of volume and
space. (14:98) Dyce was not a natural colorist, Ruskin observed, but as a
result he had produced the first Pre-Raphaelite work to be infused with a
sculptural sense of form. The intense observation of texture and shape, the

Figure 110
WILLIAM DYCE (1806–1864)
Titian Preparing to Make His First Essay in Coloring. 1856–57
Oil on canvas, 39½ × 31⅛″
City of Aberdeen Art Gallery and Museum Collections, Scotland

Ruskin was first introduced to Pre-Raphaelitism by the eminent Scottish painter Dyce, "who dragged me, literally, up to the Millais picture of the *Carpenter's Shop*, which I had passed disdainfully, and forced me to look for its merits." (37:427–28) One of the few members of the Royal Academy to sympathize with the Pre-Raphaelites, Dyce's own work was influenced by them in turn. This depiction of the young Titian was one of his masterpieces: "Well done! Mr. Dyce, and many times well done!" Ruskin sang, "though it is of little use for any of us to say so to you, for when a man has gone through such a piece of work as this he knows he is right, and knows it so calmly that it does not matter much to him whether people see it or not." (14:98)

Opposite:
Figure 111
SIR JOSEPH NOEL PATON
(1821–1901)
The Bluidie Tryste. 1855
Oil on canvas, 31½ × 27⅞″
Glasgow Art Gallery and Museum

Ruskin's response to *The Bluidie Tryste,* in the *Academy Notes* of 1858, reflects the duality of his criticism. His sharp reproach, "There was no need, as far as I can see, or feel, for the defilement of this sweet dell with guilt," is countered by his pointing to small areas in the same work that prove Paton "to be capable of all perfection." (14:156–57) Portraying a scene from a Scottish poem, *The Harte and the Hynde*, which tells the story of a lover murdered by the brothers of a seduced maiden:

> They shot him dead at Nine-Stone
>   Rig,
> Beside the Headless Cross,
> And they left him lying in his blood,
> Upon the moor and moss.

146

finished grace and the lovely line in the oak foliage deserved to be studied carefully; "It will take about an hour to see this picture properly," Ruskin said. (14:100)

In the 1857, 1858, and 1859 *Notes*, he prefaced his remarks by acknowledging that disciples of Pre-Raphaelitism abounded and that the exhibitions displayed ever higher numbers of good works. Artists calmed the "restless and over-excited crowd of London spectators" with useful, worthy glimpses of nature that appealed to every segment of society rather than to connoisseurs exclusively. (14:91, 151–52) Yet, even so, a sense of growing impatience emerges in Ruskin's comments. The all-important ingredient of imagination, required to elevate art beyond the quotidian, was missing in many and misdirected in a few. Furthermore, he was annoyed that some of the finest artists did not submit work, and those who did disappointed him in one way or another.

Overall, Ruskin found the 1857 exhibition of the Society of Painters in Water-Colours pleasantly boring. Niceties of life were supplied

abundantly in pictures "of roses and quinces, of showers and sunbeams." (14:122) Too many artists passively recorded prettiness rather than energetically seeking true beauty. It was not in jest that he warned, "A Society which takes upon itself, as its sole function, the supply of these mild demands of the British public, must be prepared ultimately to occupy a position much more corresponding to that of the firm of Fortnum and Mason, than to any hitherto held by a body of artists; and to find their art becoming essentially a kind of Potted Art, of an agreeable flavour, suppliable and taxable as a patented commodity, but in no wise to be thought of or criticised as *Living* Art." (14:122) The exceptional work in that exhibition was again by his dear friend, William Henry Hunt. He also admired the landscapes of David Cox, which, though not the type that Ruskin ordinarily recommended, were broad, bold, and distinctive "expressions of the feeling of a painter's mind at rest . . . deeply pathetic." (14:122–23)

He found Millais's entries in the 1857 Royal Academy show, *Dream of the Past* and *The Escape of the Heretic* (figure 109) pathetic also, but in quite a different sense. Standing by his earlier praise and still hoping that Millais could join that "great Imaginative group of Masters," Ruskin warned that "as it is possible to stoop to victory, it is also possible to climb to defeat." (14:107) *The Escape of the Heretic* displayed a "warping of feeling . . . the darkest error in judgement—the fatalest failure in the instinct of the painter's mind. At once coarse and ghastly in fancy, exaggerated and obscure in action, the work seems to have been wrought with the resolute purpose of confirming all that the bitterest adversaries of the school have delighted to allege against it." (14:110–11) Millais was accused of painting deliberately ugly figures rather than beautiful ones, especially in the contorted hushing face of the man. This, Ruskin feared, only confirmed the critics' allegations that *Christ in the House of His Parents* was intentionally grotesque; that work had restrained the advance of Pre-Raphaelitism in 1851, but *The Escape of the Heretic* might arrest its growth altogether. Later, Ruskin coupled what he considered to be Millais's willful distortion with a certain "wildness of execution." While acknowledging these could express emotional and physical conflict, Ruskin sensed more and more that Millais simply was not doing his best. He felt it immoral "that any workman capable of so much should rest content with so little. . . . Here, we have a careless and insolent indication of things that might be; not the splendid promise of a grand impatience, but the scrabbled remnant of a scornfully abandoned aim." (14:215)

Other indications of trouble arose again in the 1858 exhibition. "Now . . . the rage is for sentiment . . . exaggeration of sensibility as offensive as the pedantry of science," he complained. (14:152–53) Ruskin noted both extremes in Sir Joseph Noel Paton's scene of tragic love and death, *The Bluidie Tryste* (figure 111). It had a sense of "prevailing gloom" that disturbed him. (14:155) Ruskin wished that, if the artist insisted on painting tragedy rather than the happy and serene themes chosen by the greatest of artists, he would do it consistently throughout his picture. The dead man failed to capture both Ruskin's sympathy and apparently that of nature. "Nature ought to have had more observance of him—the sun ought to have fallen here and there upon his face—yes, and upon his blood; and the hue of the leafage round him should have had, it seems to me, . . . deep sympathy through all its innocent life." (14:156) The dell was remarkable as natural history, complete with oxalis, red fern, and a viper, but it was not a human landscape like those of Turner.

Whether out of exhaustion, exasperation, or simply haste, Ruskin had little new to say in 1859. Many of the major artists were absent again from the Royal Academy. The others were studious in their efforts, yet in one way or another they missed the mark of excellence toward which he had

Figure 112
ARTHUR HUGHES (1832–1915)
The Nativity. Exhibited 1858
Oil on canvas, 24 × 14¼″
Birmingham Museum and Art
Gallery, England

First attracted to Pre-Raphaelitism through his reading of its literary and artistic journal, *The Germ*, Hughes joined the Brotherhood around 1850, early in its history, and became one of its most important adherents. Hughes participated in the Oxford Union mural project, a turning point in Pre-Raphaelitism that signaled the move toward a romantic, medievalizing phase. Ruskin saw in *The Nativity* those qualities for which Hughes is best remembered: brilliant, magical color, poetic imagination, and touching sentiment in the humble attending angel.

been directing them. Where skill was evident, Ruskin saw it wasted on unprofitable themes that neither informed nor inspired the viewer. He could not appreciate the Venetian scenes by David Roberts, one of his early mentors, and J. F. Lewis offered only his perennial Egyptian subject. Mulready continued "in using more skill in painting Nothing than any painter ever spent before on that subject." (14:221–22). Even John Brett's tour de force, *The Val d'Aosta*, painted at Ruskin's recommendation and under his demanding direction, was found somehow lacking. He tempered his praise of it by concluding: "It has a strange fault. . . . It seems to me

Figure 113
DANTE GABRIEL ROSSETTI
(1828–1882)
The Salutation of Beatrice. 1880–82
Oil on canvas, 60¾ × 36"
The Toledo Museum of Art;
Purchased with Funds from the
Libbey Endowment, Gift of Edward
Drummond Libbey

Ruskin admired Rossetti's early Dante and Beatrice subjects and commissioned several of them for his own collection. Even before Siddal's death, Rossetti became infatuated with Jane Morris, the wife of William Morris. Rossetti saw his adoration for Jane paralleled in Dante's love of Beatrice. Jane's face dominates this image of Beatrice and many of the late, sensual oil paintings and "symbolic" portraits that so disturbed Ruskin.

Opposite:
Figure 114
DANTE GABRIEL ROSSETTI
(1828–1882)
La Pia de' Tolomei. 1868–81
Oil on canvas, 41½ × 47½"
Spencer Museum of Art, The
University of Kansas, Lawrence

Despite the differences between them, Ruskin acclaimed Rossetti as the major intellectual force in modern art. Eventually, however, they parted company: Ruskin was moral and didactic, Rossetti impatient and impetuous. By 1865 the critic could no longer accept what he viewed as Rossetti's technical faults or his increasingly voluptuous style resulting from his obsession with a feminine ideal embodied by Jane Morris. She posed for this rendering of Pia de' Tolomei, who, in canto 5 of Dante's *Purgatory*, was imprisoned in a fortress by her husband, where she died of despair.

wholly emotionless. I cannot find from it that the painter loved, or feared, anything in all that wonderful piece of the world. . . . I never saw the mirror so held up to Nature; but it is Mirror's work, not Man's." (14:236–37) The opposite problem plagued Windus's *Too Late*, a picture of a young dying woman and the return of her absent lover, which begged for comparison with his *Burd Helen* of 1856. Ruskin worried that Windus's mind had taken a dreadful, sick turn, and offered advice to those who, like Windus, were either working too hard for expressive impact or not working hard enough. Since noble art could be produced only by noble persons, he prescribed a life-style corresponding to his view of the virtuous artisan who, like William Henry Hunt and Samuel Prout, happily and selflessly labored at his craft: "Young painters must remember this great fact. . . . A stout arm, a

Figure 115
ELIZABETH SIDDAL (1829–1862)
Two Lovers. 1854
Pen and ink with watercolor,
9½ × 11⅞″
Ashmolean Museum, Oxford

After her "discovery" by artist Walter
Deverell, Siddal modeled for several
members of the Pre-Raphaelite Brotherhood and eventually was drawn ro-
mantically to the magnetic Rossetti.
Basically self-taught, her career lasted
about ten years. She worked in a variety
of mediums, from oil to pen and ink.

Though vexed by their bohemian
life-style, Rossetti's waywardness, and
Siddal's melancholia, Ruskin helped
the two, paying them a stipend in exchange for the first right of refusal of
their work. This is one of a number of
poignant double portraits of Siddal
and Rossetti.

calm mind, a merry heart, and a bright eye are essential to a great painter.
Without all these he can, in a great and immortal way, do nothing.... Frequent the company of right-minded and nobly-souled persons;
learn all athletic exercises, and all delicate arts... be kind and just to
everybody; rise in the morning with the lark, and whistle in the evening
with the blackbird; and in time you may be a painter. Not
otherwise." (14:233–34)

Ruskin felt that, despite their progress in accuracy, some of the
most promising artists were insincere, deviant, or even unhealthy in their
outlook. This opinion had grown since he first voiced it several years earlier
in *The Stones of Venice*, and it resounded in the last three volumes of *Modern
Painters*. In reviewing the watercolor societies of 1859, but speaking to
every "modern English exhibition of paintings," he stated outright that
English art was vulgar. (14:242) This vulgarity, he contended, arose from
the absence of "right, and therefore, all softening, or animating motive for
their work... chiefly by the loss of belief in the spiritual world... belief in
some invisible power—god or goddess, fury or fate, saint or de-
mon." (14:243) He pleaded for artists to be, if not actually religious, "so
much of a human creature as to care about the heart and history of fellow-

Figure 116
ELIZABETH SIDDAL (1829–1862)
Pippa Passes. 1854
Pen and ink, 9⅛ × 11¾"
Ashmolean Museum, Oxford

This "problem picture" is one of many Pre-Raphaelite works dealing with the theme of the fallen woman. Four years earlier, Siddal had modeled for Rossetti's work inspired by Robert Browning's poem "Pippa Passes." In her interpretation, Siddal emphasized the innocence and sweetness of the young Pippa, clothed in a simple, habit-like garment and walking demurely, contrasting her demeanor with that of the three wayward girls on the steps. Ruskin was intrigued with Siddal's delicate and highly distinctive drawings. He valued them as products of a rare, untutored talent.

Figure 117
DANTE GABRIEL ROSSETTI
(1828–1882)
Dante's Vision of Rachel and Leah.
1855
Watercolor, 13⅞ × 12⅜"
Tate Gallery, London; Bequeathed by Beresford Rimington Heaton

Ruskin first sought Rossetti's friendship in 1854, and, despite their differences in temperament, they had an odd but close relationship for nearly a decade. Ruskin badgered Rossetti about the quality of his work and his difficulty in completing it yet gave him the financial support that allowed his marriage to Elizabeth Siddal in 1861. *Rachel and Leah*, illustrating canto 27 of Dante's *Purgatory*, was commissioned by Ruskin in April 1855. Siddal modeled for the figure of Rachel on the left, who symbolizes contemplative life; Leah represents active life. Ruskin paid thirty guineas for the work and later gave it to his friend Ellen Heaton of Leeds.

153

Figure 118
ALBERT JOSEPH MOORE
(1841–1893)
A Flower Walk. Exhibited 1875
Oil on canvas, 9⅝ × 4″
The Art Museum, Princeton
University; Gift of the FORBES
Magazine Collection: Malcolm S.
Forbes, Malcolm S. Forbes, Jr., and
Christopher Forbes

Moore, a close friend of Whistler's, concentrated on single figures or grouped figures placed in antique settings. His paintings relate to the Neoclassicism of Alma-Tadema, Leighton, and others, but Moore's true interest was not history, archaeology, or any subject other than the exploration of subtleties of color. Ruskin appreciated Moore's aesthetic sensitivity yet condemned Whistler for a similar "art for art's sake" attitude. Ruskin recommended *A Flower Walk* in his 1875 *Academy Notes* for its "consummately artistic and scientific work. . . . Try the effect of concealing the yellow flower in the hair, in the *Flower Walk* . . . and you ought afterward, if you have an eye for colour, nevermore to mistake a tinted drawing for a painting." (14:272–73)

154

creatures, and to take so much concern with the facts of human life going on around you as shall make your art in some sort compassionate, exhortant, or communicative, and useful to any one coming after you, either as a record of what was done among men in your day, or as a testimony of what you felt or knew concerning them and their misdoings or undoings." (14:244) Without this animating force, the power behind Turner's compassionate and elevating truth, true sentiment and feeling were impossible, and any attempts to display emotion were empty theatrics.

The final volume of *Modern Painters*, published in 1860, gave voice to a strident call to the audience to heed his words, and it revealed his fear that those words were not being heard at all. He wrote despondently:

> *Whatsoever is there of fairest, you will find recorded by Turner, and by him alone.*
>
> *I say you will find, not knowing to how few I speak; for in order to find what is fairest, you must delight in what is fair; and I know not how few or how many there may be who take such delight. Once I could speak joyfully about beautiful things, thinking to be understood;—now I cannot any more; for it seems to me that no one regards them. Wherever I look or travel in England or abroad, I see that men, wherever they can reach, destroy all beauty.* (7:422–23)

Ruskin ultimately concluded that art could not be appreciated if its first inspiration—nature—was not nurtured, and he doubted even that meaningful art could be made where nature was not cherished and protected, where the sanctity of both nature and art went unrecognized. Turner and the Pre-Raphaelites had suffered from such insensitivity; now Turner was dead and Pre-Raphaelitism had succumbed to aesthetic goals different from his own, leaving unfulfilled the promise he had seen in it. Ruskin felt that the problem must penetrate deeply to the heart of profane society. He turned increasingly to issues of broad social concern in an attempt to arrest what he saw as the ignorance and inertia that diverted humanity from its correct path. Laboring over the next twenty-five years to further his mission, quite literally, of opening the eyes and of elevating the sight of his own society, he founded his museum for the Guild of Saint George and he continued to write and lecture on art. His tone, however, was inalterably different. When he last wrote *Academy Notes* in 1875, he still insisted that "all good art is more or less didactic." (14:265) Yet, aside from the mysterious theology of George Frederic Watts, the delicate color sense of Albert Moore's *A Flower Walk*, and the sympathetic landscape of Alfred William Hunt, there was little new for him to admire. His strongest words were again in condemnation of Millais, whom he felt worked now only for money.

In 1883, five years after the Whistler trial, Ruskin resumed the Slade Professorship at Oxford. His lectures of that year, published together as *The Art of England*, comprised reflective histories of the art of his era and summations of various schools he had witnessed.[11] The fourth lecture, entitled "Fairy Land," turned to a genre of art of real interest to him, but one that was new to his reading public: the art of fancy and fantasy about and for children in which two women artists, Kate Greenaway and Helen

Figure 119
HELEN ALLINGHAM (1848–1926)
The Young Customers. c. 1875
Watercolor, 8⅛ × 6⅛"
Private Collection

Ruskin's interest in Allingham's work began with a mention in his 1875 *Academy Notes*; he found this scene consoling in its innocence and technically superb. In 1890 Allingham became the first woman to gain full membership in the Old Water-colour Society.

Allingham, excelled. He acclaimed Allingham's *Young Customers* as "a classic picture, which will have its place among the memorable things in the art of our time, when many of its loudly trumpeted magnificences are remembered no more." (33:341) Greenaway, one of his students, was well known for her endearing scenes of children such as *Child in a White Dress*. Ruskin, quoting French critic Ernest Chesneau, applauded the way in which she, "with a profound sentiment of love for children, puts the child alone on the scene, companions him in his own solitudes, and shows the infantine nature in all its naïveté, its gaucherie, its touching grace, its shy alarm." (33:343) Ruskin reiterated many of his earlier ideas in this lecture: sincere and original sentiment, delicacy in touch and color, and dedication to landscape. Certainly, his interest in Allingham and Greenaway included what he saw as their charm and innocence.

Long before "Fairy Land," Ruskin had dedicated his life and career to the advancement of these beliefs and the others so important to him: requisite training before nature, discovery of truth, humility and communication, portrayal of beauty not as an end in itself but for its moral value, and the obligations of an artist to society and society to its artists. These essential ideas were a part of the fabric of Ruskin and of his Victorian era, and in promoting them he maintained the integrity of both. Clearly, by the time of the infamous trial, both Ruskin's career and his age were drawing to an end. Whistler's *Nocturne in Black and Gold: The Falling Rocket* was not so materially or physically different from many by Turner, but, in terms of purpose and meaning, it belonged to another time. Whistler did not fit Ruskin's portrait of the great and noble artist, and, right or wrong, Ruskin saw indolence in his painting rather than poetry, prophecy, or religion.

NOTES

1. The trial is the subject of Linda Merrill's recently published study, *A Pot of Paint: Aesthetics on Trial in Whistler v. Ruskin* (Washington, 1992).
2. James Abbott McNeill Whistler, *The Gentle Art of Making Enemies* (New York, 1867), 5.
3. *Ibid.*, 30.
4. Martin Butlin and Evelyn Joll, *The Paintings of J. M. W. Turner* 1 (New Haven and London, 1984), 239.
5. *Ibid.*, 239.
6. Butlin and Joll dispute this, *ibid.*, 188.
7. Ruskin knew such rules well; his own early training was in the tradition of the picturesque landscape as described in the essays by Robert Hewison and Christopher Newall in this volume.
8. Cited in Derrick Leon, *Ruskin, The Great Victorian*, (London, 1949), 138.
9. Cited *ibid.*, 137.
10. Ruskin's opinions on artistic character found in the pamphlet and lecture developed as he researched and wrote *The Stones of Venice*. They reappeared in *Academy Notes* and in the third and fourth volumes of *Modern Painters*, both published in 1856, thus signaling his shift in interest from a rather limited interest in art per se to art in its broad social context, and finally to social reform.
11. Rossetti and Holman Hunt represented the Realist School, Burne-Jones and Watts the Mythic School, and Leighton and Alma-Tadema the Classic School.

Figure 120
KATE GREENAWAY (1846–1901)
Child in a White Dress. n.d.
Watercolor and body color,
8¼ × 6⅛"
Harris Museum and Art Gallery, Preston, England; Haslam Bequest

Best known for her illustrations in children's books, Kate Greenaway's art was praised by Ruskin as being "much too good to be used merely for illumination." (33:344) Delighted with her drawings of young girls, Ruskin corresponded frequently with Greenaway from 1882 on. Her drawings exemplify the attitudes of Victorian society toward the proper deportment of children.

157

Sermons in Stone: Ruskin and Geology[1]

Anthony Lacy Gully

The two great quests of John Ruskin's life were to discover the Truth of Art and the Truth of Nature. Geology, as a study of the Earth's structure, was Ruskin's lifelong passion. Writing to a family friend in February of 1858 his father confided: "From Boyhood he has been an artist, but he has been a geologist from Infancy, and his geology is perhaps now the best part of his Art, for it enables him to place before us Rocks and Mountains as they are in Nature, in place of the very bad likenesses of these objects presented to us in most of the old paintings or modern Drawings."[2]

Late in his career Ruskin confessed that he had hoped to attain prominence in the British scientific community: " It was always the summit of my earthly ambition to attain, that of President of the Geological Society." (26:97) He wrote extensively on geological matters. His first published prose essay, on the color of the Rhine River and the twisted strata of Mont Blanc, appeared in the September 1834 issue of the *Magazine of Natural History*. At fifteen he requested as a birthday gift a copy of Horace-Bénédict de Saussure's *Voyages des Alpes*, a volume he kept throughout his life, quoting from it often.

Ruskin's position among the geological community was made difficult by a number of things. His writing style is unabashedly assertive, and many were offended by the authoritative tone of his articles. For instance, in his published essay on agates he boasts that "even to the present day, [it is] the only one which has the slightest claim to accuracy or distinction, or completeness of arrangement." (26:98) Ruskin's systems of classification and his invented nomenclature, which said more of his regard for classical myth than for scientific accuracy, troubled his contemporaries. Perhaps the greatest barrier to the scientific community's acceptance of Ruskin's ideas was his insistence from his earliest writings on the inextricable linkage between science and art. William Whitaker, president of the Royal Geological Society, speaking to the membership, acknowledged Ruskin's unique relation to the scientific community in his eulogy: "We must not forget his services to our science in directing the attention of artists and others to the effect of geological structure, and of the character of rocks, on scenery."[3] Whitaker went on to say that geologists could "read with advantage" the observations on mountain structure in *Modern Painters*. Ruskin's gifts of observation impressed many, among them Charles Darwin, who remarked to Ruskin's American friend Charles Eliot Norton that Ruskin possessed a keen sense of observation and his works displayed scientific proficiency.

Figure 121
John Ruskin (1819–1900)
Gneiss Rock, Glenfinlas. 1853
Pen and ink, wash, china white, and scratching-out, $18\frac{7}{8} \times 12\frac{7}{8}''$
Ashmolean Museum, Oxford;
Reference Series 89

This drawing may have been intended as a guide to Millais for the background of his famous portrait of Ruskin. Ruskin was fascinated with exposed and fractured faces of metamorphic gneiss. He wrote in 1875 that "the undulations of gneiss rock . . . where they are seen, seem to form the world." (6:150 n.) Ruskin often assigned biomorphic meanings to gneiss formations; those of the Black Forest he thought were "coiled like knots of passionate snakes," and formations in the Swiss Alps "wrinkle themselves as if Falstaff's wit had vexed them, or pleased them and made their faces like a wet cloak ill laid up.'" (26:30)

Ruskin scholars have often observed that Ruskin anticipated the writings of Ernst Gombrich on perception and its relationship to art. Indeed, Ruskin was deeply concerned that he educate his audiences so that they might "see" as he saw and understand that art and nature are inseparably bound together. John Ruskin's thoughts were offered to the public in the belief that seeing and reading were a single activity and that "verbal art teaches perceptual skills."[4] His insistence on imposing universal, often symbolic, significance to forms encountered in art is central in appreciating his commentaries on geological phenomena. Ruskin's love of landscape art motivated his intense visual examination of nature. Herbert Read's summary of the way we "see" has bearing on Ruskin's arguments:

> *The whole history of art is a history of modes of visual perception: of the various ways in which man has* seen *the world. The naive person might object that there is only one way of seeing the world—the way it is presented to his own immediate vision. But this is not true—we see what we learn to see, and vision becomes a habit, a convention, a partial selection of all there is to see, and a distorted summary of the rest. We see what we want to see, and what we want to see is determined, not by the inevitable laws of optics, or even (as may be the case in wild animals) by an*

instinct for survival, but by the desire to discover or construct a credible world. What we see must be made real. Art in that way becomes the construction of reality.[5]

It was the *real* world Ruskin wished to reveal. Ruskin's fascination with geological phenomena was inseparable from his concerns about art. In his "Lecture on Landscape" given in London in December of 1884, Ruskin happily observed: "I am proud to think that these drawings of mine, done thirty years ago at the foot of the Matterhorn, are entirely right as examples of mountain drawing, with absolutely correct outline of all that is useful for geological science or landscape art." (33:532)

Ruskin's superb *Gneiss Rock, Glenfinlas* (figure 121) was exhibited with great success, and he allowed photographic prints of it to be sold.[6] It has been argued that the intensely sharp focus of the drawing may reflect Ruskin's fascination with the daguerreotype; Ruskin certainly was interested in photography and one of his great claims was that he was responsible for the first photographic impressions of the Matterhorn and the Swiss Alps.[7] The delicate line in pen and sensitive use of watercolor washes with touches of Chinese white gouache to build up a sense of volume, combined with the striking light effects, show Ruskin at his best.

The drawing will forever be associated with one of the two scandals that rocked Ruskin's personal life. It was made the summer that Ruskin invited his young protégé John Everett Millais to join him and his wife,

Figure 122
Sir John Everett Millais
(1829–1896)
The Waterfall. 1853
Oil on panel, 10½ × 12½"
Delaware Art Museum; Samuel and Mary R. Bancroft Collection

Millais painted *The Waterfall* at Glenfinlas while awaiting the delivery of a canvas for his famous portrait of Ruskin (opposite) set at the same location. This small painting, showing Mrs. Ruskin sitting on the edge of the rocky Glenfinlas torrent, was previously entitled *Original Study for the Background of the Portrait of John Ruskin, Outdoor Study.*

Effie, at Glenfinlas in Scotland for a holiday which resulted in the annulment of the Ruskin marriage a year later.[8] It is closely related to Millais's
famous portrait of Ruskin standing at the same stream's edge, and to a
smaller work by Millais, *The Waterfall* (figure 122), a portrait of the young
Mrs. Ruskin seated among the smooth twisted stones. Ruskin was privileged to watch Millais at work, something Turner never allowed. Millais's
meticulous rendering of the rocky setting accords with Ruskin's advice to
Millais and his Pre-Raphaelite colleagues to be exacting and faithful in their
transcriptions of nature. Ruskin's *Gneiss Rock*, probably made on July 18
when he noted in his diary that he went to paint alone (Millais was
indisposed), concentrates on the writhing rocky strata, encrusted by invading plants and attacked by the turbulent surging stream at the base. Space is
very compressed; the eye is allowed no rest; the sharp clarity accentuates
the abrupt collision of rock and water, plant and stone. The implications of a
vitalism within the stones and the ongoing destruction of matter in nature
are constant themes in Ruskin's art. In Millais's *The Waterfall* the denudation is less emphatically suggested. The openness of the composition does
not produce the claustrophobic sensation of Ruskin's drawing.

Ruskin made many drawings similar to *Gneiss Rock, Glenfinlas*, with
its focus on a small segment of landscape. The smallest, seemingly most
insignificant portion of a scene could reveal many truths to him: "For a
stone, when it is examined, will be found [to be] a mountain in miniature . . . and taking moss for forests, and grains of crystal for crags, the
surface of a stone, in by far the plurality of instances, is more interesting
than the surface of an ordinary hill; more fantastic in form, and incomparably richer in colour."[9] Elsewhere, "A piece of stone 3 in. in diameter,
irregularly fractured, and a little worn by the weather, has precisely the
same character of outline which we should find and admire in a mountain of
the same material 6,000 ft. high." (1:48)

Ruskin's active participation in the debates on the geological origin and
character of Europe spanned his entire career. From his fledgling efforts in
the early 1830s through the mid-1880s, he published an avalanche of essays
on his observations. Ruskin's favorite tutor at Oxford was the Reverend
Doctor William Buckland, canon at Christ Church College. In 1879
Ruskin recalled, "Dr. Buckland kept me not ill-informed on my favourite
subject, the geological, or cystallogical question." (27:637) Ruskin proudly
recalled twice in his uncompleted autobiography *Praeterita* that he produced diagrams and sketches, still in the possession of Oxford University,
that Dr. Buckland used to illustrate his lectures on geology. Later, as Slade
Professor at Oxford and in his many public lectures, Ruskin duplicated this
practice, either producing or often commissioning drawings, by Alexander
Macdonald and others, to accompany his text. Ruskin remembered his
drawing of the "granite veins of Trewavas Head, with a cutter weathering
the point in a squall, in the style of Copley Fielding," his former drawing
master. The effect probably was not dissimilar from Fielding's *Boats in a
Storm, Bridlington Harbor*, the sublime encounter of sea and land exaggerated through dramatic lighting effects and powerful diagonals.

It was in Buckland's home that Ruskin met Charles Darwin for the
first time. He wrote to his father on April 22, 1837, "He and I got together

... and talked all the evening." (26:xx) Ruskin's meetings with Darwin seemed to have been congenial, though Ruskin could never accept Darwin's theories of evolution. He comically warned his good friend Charles Eliot Norton in 1868, when presenting to him a small piece of chalk embedded with fossil remains:

> *But they will show you what kind of things are now under your feet, and in the roadside heaps of stones; and the first time Darwin takes them in his hand they will become* Prim-*Stones to you. . . . The little group of shattered vertebrae in the square piece of chalk may have belonged to some beast of character and promise. When is he [Darwin] going to write—ask him—the "Retrogression" of Species—or the Origin of Nothing? I am far down on my way into [becoming] a flint-sponge." (36:552–53)*

Ruskin joined the Royal Geological Society, serving as a secretary at some of their meetings, and became a member of the Mineralogical Society in 1840. He published in the latter's official *Transactions* (1:206) and wrote ten articles for the *Geological Magazine*. Ruskin was always proud of his published work on geology; he felt that the geological passages of his *Modern Painters* 4 were "the most valuable and least faultful part of the book." (26:568)

Stimulated by the enormous success of his public lectures throughout England, Ruskin brought together the texts of many of his geology

Figure 123
Anthony Vandyke Copley Fielding (1787–1855)
Boats in a Storm, Bridlington Harbor.
c. 1830
Watercolor with surface scratching,
18⅛ × 24½"
The Whitworth Art Gallery,
University of Manchester, England

In *Praeterita* Ruskin described his family's delight in their first purchase of a Copley Fielding. Ruskin studied under Fielding, a leading drawing master in London, when he was fifteen years old. Ruskin commended Copley Fielding's skill as a sea painter in *Modern Painters* 1: "No man has ever given, with the same flashing freedom, the race of a running tide under a stiff breeze, nor caught, with the same grace and precision, the curvature of the breaking wave, arrested or accelerated by the wind." (3:532) Later, Ruskin saw Copley Fielding's picturesque views as facile and repetitive and warned all artists against that danger.

163

lectures at Oxford in the *Deucalion*, published intermittently between 1875 and 1883. Ruskin's writings on geology cannot be approached as straightforward scientific studies. As Ruskin himself explained at one point, his interest was not theoretical but he wished "to see the Alps in a simple, thoughtless, and untheorising manner; but to *see* them, if it might be, thoroughly." (6:475) The title Ruskin gave to his study on geology provided the reader with clues to the multilevel meanings Ruskin assigned to his observations on geological structure. Deucalion is the Greek mythic equivalent of the Old Testament Noah. Surviving the Great Flood, he was instructed by Zeus to cast the bones of his mother down the flank of a mountain; these "lifeless seeds of life" regenerate the human race. The tale of Deucalion, Ruskin warned, was one of "betrayal and redemption." The stones and rocks Ruskin discusses in his essays are tokens of man's fall and redemption. The study of geology becomes a moral parable.

Ruskin, distressed at the inability of his Oxford students to grasp his ideas, lamented in 1874: "Believe me, gentlemen, your power of seeing mountains cannot be developed either by your vanity, your curiosity, or your love of muscular exercise. It depends on the cultivation of the instrument of sight itself, and the soul that uses it." (26:103) Critical visual observation is necessary but it must be tempered by a mind susceptible to reading the deeper meanings of form in nature. Striking a familiar chord, Ruskin announced in the early pages of *Deucalion* that the essays contained his "endeavors to define the laws of mountain-form for purposes of art." (26:101ff)

Ruskin's second volume devoted to earth studies is *The Ethics of the Dust: Ten Lectures to Little Housewives on the Elements of Crystallisation* (1865).[10] The volume, unique in Ruskin's writing, takes the form of an extended dialogue between the "Old Lecturer" (Ruskin) and ten young residents of a girl's boarding school. In fact, the text is based in part on a series of lessons Ruskin gave at Winnington Hall, Cheshire. The headmistress, Margaret Alexis Bell, had first heard Ruskin speak in 1859; deeply moved, she invited him to teach her charges. He enjoyed these forays into the girls' schoolroom and became a patron of the school and a not infrequent visitor. Ruskin was impressed with Bell's curriculum, for it mirrored his own ideas on educating young minds. In his preface Ruskin explains his theory that, through much questioning, the young person's mind is stimulated to learn more about science. *The Ethics of the Dust* was not well reviewed by the critics, who objected to its dialogue format. However, Ruskin's friend Thomas Carlyle wrote to the author on December 20, 1865: "*The Ethics of the Dust*, which I have devoured without pause, and intend to look at again, is a most shining Performance!" (18:1xxiii–xxiv)

Ruskin's presentation of his scientific observations on mineralogy in a Socratic dialogue is the clue to understanding his attitude toward scientific enquiry and explains why he was often dismissed or misunderstood by the scientific community. In Ruskin's many writings on geological matters it is striking how often he presented his observations (from an eye that had been trained to see the physical world intensely) and then asked his listeners or readers to explain the phenomena. Ruskin was not the least interested in using the miscroscope or engaging in any laboratory experiments to test any hypothesis. He readily confessed that he was not interested in studying deeply the disciplines affected by his pronouncements. He asked the questions and waited for an explanation. Ruskin himself acknowledged that his personal method of scientific observation brought his ideas into dispute: "I believe that one of the causes which has prevented my writings on subjects of science from obtaining the influence with the public which they have accorded to those on art, though precisely the same faculties of eye and mind are concerned in the analysis of natural and of pictorial forms, may have been my constant practice of teaching by question rather than assertion."[11]

Ruskin was troubled by the empirical scientist, who isolated himself from the beauties of the world. No doubt offending and confounding many, Ruskin charged that the majority of modern scientists "cannot appreciate the beauties of nature, and they regard the imaginative man—one who can feel the poetry of life—as a donkey regards his rider: as an objectionable person whom he must throw off if he possibly can. . . . The *real* scientific man is one who can embrace not only the laws that be, but who can feel to the full the beauty and truth of all that nature has to show, as the Creator made them." (26:xxxix n.) He then identified the great *real* scientists of the past as the English physicist Sir Isaac Newton, the Swedish botanist Carolus Linnaeus, and the German naturalist Alexander von Humboldt.

Ruskin's prominence as a writer and arbiter of taste attracted attention to all that he wrote. In the late 1860s he found himself embroiled in one of the great geological controversies of the age—the nature of glaciation. Though Ruskin entered the fray, he did not relish public debate. Indeed, he wrote in the *Geological Magazine* in 1865, "It is often said that controversies advance science. I believe, on the contrary, that they retard it—that they are wholly mischievous, and that all good scientific work is done in silence, till done completely." (26:21)

Ruskin's participation in the heated discussions about the historical importance of fossil records, denudation, and glaciation was complicated by his personal religious doubts. Raised an Evangelical Anglican by his devout mother, he gradually came to realize that the explanations of the Earth's history found in Scripture did not accord with his own observations and with those writers on geology to whom he turned: "If only the Geologists would let me alone, I could do very well, but those dreadful Hammers! I hear the clink of them at the end of every cadence of the Bible verses." (36:115) It is too extreme to argue, as some have, that Ruskin lost his faith. Certainly it was shaken, but it was recast into a personal religion. Stripped of his sectarian vision, he developed a tolerance for the spiritual inquiries of all cultures, especially those of ancient Greece. In his lecture "Crystal Best," in *The Ethics of the Dust*, he urged the girls to nurture "the idea of a personal spirit" and posed the question, "Does this spirit exercise its functions towards one race of men only, or towards all men?" (18:350) Ruskin gently argued that all people and cultures are governed by the same Divine principles.

In the mid-nineteenth century the meaning of the fossil record found in the strata of high mountains and the physical nature and dynamics of glaciers and denudation were hotly debated. Questions surrounding mountain elevation were the major issues of concern to British geologists of

Figure 124
JOHN RUSKIN (1819–1900)
Study of Alpine Peaks. c. 1844
Watercolor over pencil, 6⅝ × 10⅛″
Birmingham Museum and Art
Gallery, England

In the Rudimentary Series and in *Modern Painters* Ruskin repeatedly described the beauty of this group of Alpine peaks. Always urging artists to study them, he warned that it was often difficult to complete a sketch because of the constantly shifting clouds that obscured the peaks. (21:277) This composite sketch captures the spine of the Swiss Alps, and it suggests his interest in geological stratification and effects of denudation in a schematic fashion.

the period, who were certainly the most vocal and respected. The British tended to argue for slow, uniform changes whereas their Continental counterparts argued for a more violent history of the Earth. Before the 1960s and the acceptance of plate tectonics, geological theory revolved around debates about stratification. Fossils offered the most perplexing evidence of geological history. At Oxford in the 1830s, the young Ruskin read two major studies that dealt with the fossil record, Gideon Matnell's *The Wonders of Geology: Or a Familiar Exposition of Geological Phenomena: Being the Substance of Lectures Delivered at Brighton* (1836) and Charles Lyell's *Principles of Geology, Being an Attempt to Explain the Former Changes of the Earth's Surface, by Reference to Causes Now in Operation* (1830–33), a three-volume study whose theories were supported by Ruskin.[12] Lyell, especially, argued for a constant dynamism altering the Earth's appearance. The role of the geologist was to decode the "living language" of nature. Lyell argued against Darwin, noting the absence of fossils in some strata that were sandwiched between layers carrying fossilized remains: "It would be dangerous and irresponsible to argue for a connection between geological phenomena and a linear, progressive development of organic life, for such is not the plan of nature."[13] Ruskin, also suspicious of the fossil record, wrote in 1840, "But although we are found fossil in the rocks now forming, we are *not* in older formations." (1:415) Darwin was at the very epicenter of the debate on fossils. He argued for violent geological changes and main-

tained that "the natural geological record, as a history of the world [has been] imperfectly kept, and written in a changing dialect; of the history we possess the last volume alone."[14] Thomas Huxley, one of Ruskin's enemies in the scientific community, argued in 1908 that eventually the geological record would reveal that Darwin was correct in his assumptions.

Ruskin consistently refused to acknowledge Darwin's theories of evolution. His passionate regard for the Alps, so central to his art and his view of Divine revelation, embroiled him in the heated debate on glaciation. Observations on glaciers form the core of his scientific writings. In the early nineteenth century, pioneering geologists such as Saussure and Charpentier hypothesized that glacial ice was a solid substance. But in 1840 M. le Chanoine Rendu (*Théorie des Glaciers de la Savoie*) proposed that glaciers moved at varying speeds and likened them to river currents, with the center moving at a swifter speed than the rest of the body. Though he did not experiment, he had hit upon a correct assumption through observation. In 1840 and 1841 the Scottish scientist James Forbes visited Unteraar Glacier and noticed its veined structure, which led him to believe that the nature of all glaciers was viscous (Ruskin likened glacial ice to "so much treacle" or "honey"). Forbes proposed in print in 1843 that "a glacier is an imperfect liquid, or a viscous body, which is urged down the slopes of a certain inclination by the mutual pressure of its parts."[15] The publication of Forbes's theories outraged French geologists in particular. While making his observations, Forbes had stayed with a Mr. Agassiz in a stone hut built on the central moraine of the glacier. Agassiz, who had failed to notice what attracted Forbes's interest at that time, was furious, as were his supporters, who argued that Rendu, not Forbes, had originated the theory of glacial movement. Although Forbes was always careful to acknowledge what he owed to Rendu's earlier work, in Britain John Tyndall and Thomas Huxley challenged him and cast aspersions on his character. Huxley was largely responsible for denying Forbes the Copley Prize offered for innovative scientific work by the Royal Society. In 1872 Tyndall published *The Forms of Water in Clouds and Rivers, Ice and Glaciers*, once again attacking Forbes's claims. Ruskin was angry. He did not know Forbes well but considered him an honest man and a victim of jealous rivals. Ruskin penned a scathing, satirical review of Tyndall's book in his letter number 34 of the *Fors Clavigera*, which appeared in October of 1873,[16] and in his Oxford lectures of 1874 he returned to his observations on glaciers and a defense of Forbes. Ruskin found it impossible to accept total dependence upon physical data to support any scientific theory. He was opposed to what he termed "materialistic science." For him, mythology, history, and art were equal to science in revealing Truth to humanity.[17] "In modern days, by substituting analysis for sense in morals, and chemistry for sense in matter, we have literally blinded ourselves to the essential qualities of both matter and morals."[18] For Ruskin, Art, with its attendant handmaiden, Geology, was essential to humankind's quest to understand God.

I've often thought the Heavens high
Another lovely world would be,
And scenes of mighty majesty
Stand ever there for us to see—

Schaffhausen was an important tourist attraction and a favorite subject of sketchers and artists. Ruskin followed Turner there hoping to understand better Turner's way of seeing by comparing his drawings and watercolors with the actual sites depicted in them. Ruskin, and no doubt Turner, knew that the "line of [the] fall is straight and monotonous in reality." Ruskin argued that any artist attempting to draw it must remember that "the first great purpose is to give swing enough to the water," which he exaggerated in this drawing. (7:221) He was able to point out proudly that this drawing was "one of the few, either by other draughtsmen or myself, which I have seen Turner pause at with serious attention." (3:529 n.)

Ruskin described this interpretation of the scene in *Modern Painters 5* as an example of "Turner's fixed principle to collect out of any scene, whatever was characteristic, and put it together just as he liked. . . . Turner wants to get the great concave sweep and rush of the river well felt, in spite of the unbroken form. The column of spray, rocks, mills and bank, all radiate like a plume, sweeping round together in grand curves to the left." (7:222) The swirling motion, repeated through the figures of the soldier and the young lady holding her bandbox, begins "a series of concave lines, which concentrated by the recumbent soldiers, intensify the hollow sweep of the fall." (7:221)

Mountain, and crag, tower and tree,
Terror and peace, and calm and storm;
Yet all before the tempest flee;
From morn to eve, from eve to morn,
Changing their vain and fickle form.[19]

This stanza from a poem written by Ruskin to his father at age sixteen suggests his lifelong obsession with the awesome might of the Alpine peaks, imagined even in the skies. Ruskin's many drawings of the Alps illustrate his perceptive eye and his poetic regard for the scene before him. His *Aiguille Blaitière* (figure 128), drawn with vigorous lines, is a testament to Ruskin's willingness to undergo discomfort to achieve a pictorial truth. He clambered to great heights to get this panoramic view of the sawtooth peaks, which lie behind a great curved sheet of ice and snow. The drawing is inscribed, "Showing finest conchoidal—riband structure J. R. on the spot, 1849." Ruskin argues that, while some might engage in thoughts on the "unknown ages" of such peaks, he did "not care,—and I want you not to care,—how crest or aiguille was lifted, or where its materials came from, or how much bigger it was once. I do care that you should know, and I will endeavor . . . to show you, in what strength and beauty of form it has actually stood since man was man." (26:113) As in so many of Ruskin's drawings, the power of this work is in the aggressive line, line that defines individual elements and makes the viewer aware of the many parts that make up the whole.

From the beginning of his career as an artist and writer, Ruskin attempted to create coherent systems out of fragmented observations. He anguished over the failure of his students at Oxford to appreciate the merit of a simply rendered outline drawing: "Though I have been preaching, crying, shrieking to you that this is the method of all true landscape painting, there is not one of you who sharpens his pencil point, instead of seizing his biggest brush and going dab at the mountains with splashes of colour." (33:532) The animated silhouettes of the peaks are bound up in Ruskin's predilection for assigning anthropomorphic attributes to inanimate nature. "Mountains are to the rest of the body of the earth, what violent muscular action is to the body. The muscles and tendons of its anatomy are, in the mountain brought out with force and convulsive energy."[20] And elsewhere: "The keenness of the artist's eye may almost precisely be tested by the degree in which he perceives the curves that give them [the aiguilles] their strength and grace, and in harmony with which the flakes of granite are bound together, like the bones of the jaw of a saurian." (6:233)

In 1842 Ruskin had seen in the London gallery of Thomas Griffith a set of prepatory watercolors by Turner of Swiss subjects, which were to be worked up into oils upon commission. Ruskin was deeply moved by these "straight impressions," and his 1842 gouache drawing of *The Falls at Schaffhausen* marks his first effort to simulate the spontaneous freedom of Turner. Though it has been suggested that Ruskin's pilgrimages to those sites painted by Turner suggest "the impossible ambition of recovering Turner's sensations before nature,"[21] Ruskin's interest in fact did not exactly mimic that of his mentor.

Ruskin's lively description of the falls accords perfectly with the violent scene he portrays: "Stand for half an hour beside the Fall of Schaffhausen, on the north side where the rapids are long, and watch how the vault of water first bends, unbroken, in pure polished velocity, over the arching rocks at the brow of the cataract, covering them with a dome of crystal twenty feet thick, so swift that its motion is unseen except when a foam-globe from above darts over it like a falling star." (3:529) Ruskin places himself on the north side closest to the rushing torrent, which is wonderfully suggested in the white and blue gouache strokes on the rich creamy paper. As is always the case with Ruskin landscapes, figures are absent. The battle between the mighty, ultimately destructive flow of the water against the boldly silhouetted rocks dwarfs the evidence of human presence. The stone wall at the lower right and the roofs of the village are barely discernible across the foaming onslaught. A view of the falls painted by Turner ten years earlier (figure 126) is taken at the bottom of the cataract. Though the fume of the raging waterfall consumes the central portion of the composition, the violence so central to Ruskin's interpretation has been minimized by the picturesque groupings of peasants and ladies and soldiers picnicking at the river's edge. Turner measures the sublime headlong surge of the water against the small figures who animate the foreground. The eye is carried upward from the lower right through a series of powerful diagonals toward the falls and the sweeping curve of mist that invades the sky. In Ruskin's drawing one is led from the upper right downward in sympathy with the urgent flow of the water. The close-up view of the falls, the emphasis on the physical forces of nature at work, interested Ruskin much as it did in a less spectacular fashion in his *Gneiss Rock, Glenfinlas*. Ruskin once owned the Turner drawing of the scene; what he admired in the work was Turner's ability "to collect out of any scene, whatever was characteristic, and put it together just as he liked," and while every detail could be found at Schaffhausen, "the combinations are wholly arbitrary."[22]

No place on earth excited Ruskin's imagination more than the icy slopes near Chamonix, the Mer de Glace and the proud silhouette of Mont Blanc. Like a magnet, this unspoilt wilderness repeatedly drew Ruskin to it. It was to Chamonix that Ruskin escaped when the shocking news of his annulment was reverberating through London drawing rooms. Here Ruskin saw both the benevolent and apocalyptic powers of the "great Spirit." Writing to a tutor at Oxford in 1842, Ruskin summed up his mixed sensations before the might of the Alpine scene:

> *Nor can you ever forget for an instant either the gentleness or the omnipotence of the ruling Spirit. Though the whole air around you may be undulating with thunder, the rock under which you are sheltered is lighted with stars of strange, pure, unearthly flowers, as if every fissure had had an angel working [there?] all spring; and if the sky be cloudless, and you bury your head in a bank of gentians, and forget for an instant that there is anything round you but gentleness and delight, you are roused by the hollow crash of the advancing glacier, or the long echoing fall of some bounding rock, or the deep prolonged thrilling murmur of a far-off avalanche. (2:223)*

It is this contest of the titanic powers at work that drove Ruskin to create fifty or more drawings of the Chamonix region in 1849 alone. His watercolor *Mer de Glace, Chamonix* (figure 130) focuses on the torn and jagged landscape. The focus is close and, unlike Turner's *Valley of Chamonix* (figure 129), offers little escape from the violent collision of forces that press against the picture plane. Ruskin's drawing avoids the heroic, highly rhetorical suggestions of the sublime inherent in Turner's view or as even more exaggerated in Turner's *The Fifth Plague of Egypt* (figure 133). Nor can Ruskin's drawing be tied to the self-conscious surface pictorial effects of the picturesque tradition, seen in Thomas Creswick's *A Summer's Afternoon* (figure 127), which Ruskin so soundly rejected in his mature years. Ruskin's increasingly metaphorical reading of geology and the landscape was accompanied by drawings in which the view is often from some great height or precipice. As early as the 1840s, a pessimism pervaded both Ruskin's art and poetry.

Figure 127
THOMAS CRESWICK (1811–1869)
A Summer's Afternoon. 1844
Oil on canvas, 40 × 50″
By Courtesy of the Board of Trustees of the Victoria and Albert Museum, London

In contrast to Turner's personal, often abstract vision, Creswick depicted landscape with clear definition of natural form and mass. Ruskin sympathized with Creswick's interest in truth but criticized his color and complained, "Creswick has sweet feeling and tries for the real green too, but from want of science in his shadows, ends in green paint instead of green light." (3:604)

171

Figure 130
JOHN RUSKIN (1819–1900)
Mer de Glace, Chamonix, Switzerland.
1860
Watercolor, body color, and pen and
ink, 16⅝ × 13″
The Whitworth Art Gallery,
University of Manchester, England

Ruskin visited Chamonix, a site also recorded by Turner, frequently between 1840 and 1875. It assumed special geological, artistic, and spiritual significance for Ruskin; as he moved increasingly to topics of social injustice, economy, and politics, he returned to Chamonix to resuscitate his earlier feelings of awe for the wonders of nature. He did this work during his 1860 visit, focusing on the magnitude of the rocky slope and glacial ice.

Opposite, above:
Figure 128
JOHN RUSKIN (1819–1900)
Aiguille Blaitière. 1849
Pencil and pen and ink with watercolor wash on card, 9¾ × 14⅛″
Courtesy of the Syndics of the Fitzwilliam Museum, Cambridge, England

Ruskin was much struck with the curvature of the glacier at the base of these jagged peaks, and he spent hours over the course of several visits exploring its character and situation. In *The Stones of Venice*, he remarked that the glacier was the most perfect of curves, indeed, he used the swelling shape of the glacier as the paradigm for the "leading line" of the powerful, curving organic rhythm that he felt was fundamental in nature and essential in successful drawing.

Opposite, below:
Figure 129
J. M. W. TURNER (1775–1851)
Valley of Chamonix, Mont Blanc in the Distance. 1809
Watercolor and body color with scratching-out, 11 × 15½″
The Whitworth Art Gallery,
University of Manchester, England

This watercolor is based on a sketch from Turner's Saint Gotthard and Mont Blanc sketchbook of 1802. In a lecture to his Oxford students, Ruskin praised Turner's work for its imaginative power: "[Turner's] mountains . . . are the ghosts of eternal mountains, such as have been, and shall be, for evermore." Ruskin argued that Turner added glory to the Alps not by simply copying actual mountains but by infusing them with his own emotions, thus creating a "noble landscape." (22:220)

Figure 131
JOHN RUSKIN (1819–1900)
View of the Valley of Lauterbrunnen.
c. 1866
Pencil, watercolor, and opaque white
on ivory paper, 7 × 10⅛″
The Fogg Art Museum, Harvard
University Art Museums, Gift of
Samuel Sachs

.This late drawing by Ruskin may relate
to an unrealized project to illustrate
Swiss towns, intended in some ways as
a reprise of Samuel Prout's litho-
graphic views of Northern European
cities, which had provided the initial
inspiration for the Ruskin family visit
to the Continent. The little chalet in
the foreground, with its bold lines and
strong contrast of values, is similar to
many Ruskin drawings of this period
dubbed "Düreresque" because of their
affinity with the style of the Northern
Renaissance master whom Ruskin
deeply admired.

Admist the rush of mountain rivers,
He doomed to bear the sound and shock
Of shafts that rend and storms that rock,
The frost that blasts, and flash that shivers;
I am desolate and sunk,
A lifeless wreck—a leafless trunk,
Smitten with plagues, and seared with sin,
And black with rottenness within,
But conscious of the holier will
That saved me long, and strengthens still.[23]

Ruskin's late drawing of the *View of the Valley of Lauterbrunnen*
presents yet again a composition in which the rocky mass is pushed close to
the picture plane. The sketchy scene provides a powerful juxtaposition of
the immeasurable power of nature against man's feeble intrusion in the
form of the small chalet at the base of the mountain wall. If Ruskin failed to
offer human figures, as Turner did, to gauge the magnitude of natural
forms, he introduced architecture for a similar effect. As Ruskin turned to
issues of social criticism and political economy near the end of his active
career, he began to employ what has been termed a Dickensian symbolism.[24] Architecture served as visual allegory for human history, which to
Ruskin seemed increasingly to be a "leprosy of decay [seen] through every
breeze, and every stone." (6:396) The humble timber structure lying at the

174

base of these mighty mountains recalls Ruskin's admiration for the freedom of the Swiss people, their simple life among the mountains. The small but partially drawn building may have for Ruskin echoes of humanity's past and a prophecy of its future. "It is not until a building has assumed this character, till it has been entrusted with the fame, and hallowed by the deeds of men, till its walls have been witnesses of suffering, and its pillars rise out of the shadows of death, that its existence, more lasting as it is than that of the natural objects of the world around it, can be gifted with even so much as these possess, of language and of life." (8:234)

In the 1880s Ruskin held court at his Brantwood estate in the Lake District for his disciples and admirers. Kate Greenaway and Alexander Macdonald, two visitors to Brantwood, produced modest watercolor/gouache studies that reflect the symbiotic relationship Ruskin envisioned between science and art. Alexander Macdonald's *Study of Opal in Ferrugineous Jasper, from New Guinea* (figure 134) was executed at Ruskin's request from a rare specimen in Ruskin's collection of minerals at Brantwood. Ruskin avidly collected examples of unusual crystal formations and minerals from his boyhood days. Near the end of his life he established a number of collections for public display; to his Saint George's Museum near Sheffield he gave more than two thousand specimens. A notable collection went to the British Museum, now the Museum of Natural History, in London. Mac-

Figure 132
ARTHUR SEVERN (1842–1931)
View of Brantwood. 1874
Watercolor, 9½ × 13½"
Educational Trust Ltd., Brantwood, Coniston

In a letter to Thomas Carlyle written on October 23, 1871, Ruskin admitted that he bought the "cottage by Coniston water with a few acres of copse and rock with it . . . without having seen the place." Located in the Lake District, the area reminded him of his beloved Alps, and he described his home's setting as "a bit of steep hillside, facing west, commanding from the brow of it all Coniston lake and the mass of hills of south Cumberland. The slope is half copse, half moor and rock—a pretty field beneath, less steep—a white two-storeyed cottage and a bank of turf in front of it." (37:39) Severn worked as a copyist for Ruskin. He married Ruskin's cousin and caretaker, Joan Agnew, in 1871.

Figure 133
J. M. W. TURNER (1775–1851)
The Fifth Plague of Egypt. Exhibited
1800
Oil on canvas, 49 × 72″
Copyright 1992: Indianapolis
Museum of Art; Gift in Memory of
Evan F. Lilly

The painting actually depicts the Seventh Plague of Egypt, that of hail and fire, rather than the Fifth, of Pestilence, as described by Saint John in Revelation. Ruskin classified this as Turner's first great religious epic in which "his mind was set, so far as natural scenes were concerned, on rendering atmospheric effect . . . so far as emotion was to be expressed, how consistently it was melancholy." Ruskin did not seem to have a high regard for Turner's first, more romantic, works when he wrote *Modern Painters* 1. He described *The Fifth Plague of Egypt* as "a total failure," explaining that "the pyramids look like brick kilns, and the fire running along the ground like the burning of manure." (3:240) However, biblical and mythological themes became increasingly important to Ruskin. By the time he wrote *Modern Painters* 5, he found portentous moral religious meaning in works such as *The Goddess of Discord Choosing the Apple of Contention in the Garden of the Hesperides* (page 33), exhibited in 1806, and other early paintings.

Figure 134
ALEXANDER MACDONALD
(1839–1921)
*Study of Opal in Ferrugineous Jasper,
from New Guinea.* 1884
Watercolor and body color, 6 × 6⅛″
The Ruskin Gallery, Sheffield—The
Collection of the Guild of Saint
George

Macdonald spent the spring of 1884 at
Brantwood making studies of minerals.
He probably executed this minute and
accurate record of the structure, texture, and color of opal held in iron-
bearing jasper while Ruskin cata-
logued the British Museum's collection of minerals.

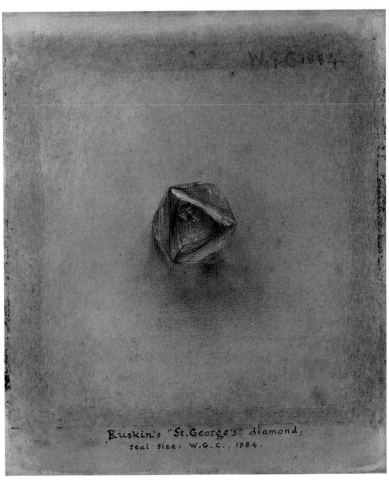

Ruskin's "St. George's" diamond,
real size: W.G.C., 1884.

Figure 135
WILLIAM GERSHOM
COLLINGWOOD (1854–1932)
Ruskin's "Saint George's Diamond."
1884
Watercolor, 4½ × 4½″
Ruskin Galleries, Bembridge School,
Isle of Wight

The natural-history collections of the
British Museum were moved in 1880
to the new Museum of Natural History in South Kensington. Ruskin,
keenly interested in the arrangement
of the minerals, offered advice to his
friend the keeper, Mr. Fletcher. Between 1882 and 1884, Ruskin helped
with the catalogue of the chalcedonies,
a great pleasure for him. He wrote,
"They are such pretty things—such
strange ones, and such *find*able
ones.... A schoolboy can't pick up
diamonds or topazes or rock-crystals
... but every other flint he breaks may
have a bit of chalcedony in it." (26:li)
Ruskin supplemented the collection,
and in 1887 gave the museum what no
schoolboy could pick up, the Saint
George's Diamond, renamed the Col-
enso Diamond. Collingwood recorded
to scale the 130-carat gem for which
Ruskin paid a thousand pounds.

Figure 136
KATE GREENAWAY, (1846–1901)
Study of Rock, Moss, and Ivy. 1885
Watercolor and body color, 7⅜ × 13″
The Ruskin Gallery, Sheffield—The
Collection of the Guild of Saint
George

In the 1880s Ruskin championed female artists such as Helen Allingham, Francesca Alexander, and Kate Greenaway. Although his patronage was generous, it was often overbearing. In a letter to Greenaway in 1884, Ruskin insisted, "The *first thing* you must do is to learn to paint a leaf green, of its full size." (37:488) This drawing was completed at the height of Greenaway's infatuation with Ruskin, an affection that distressed him and which he found impossible to return in kind. Despite Greenaway's feelings, the strength of her personality matched Ruskin's, and she often ignored his attempts to redirect her art. Ruskin's demands and encouragement did yield this drawing, done specifically to satisfy him.

donald, appointed at Ruskin's urging Master of Drawing at the Ruskin Drawing School at Oxford, executed a number of detailed studies to illustrate Ruskin's lectures on geology and crystallography at Oxford. Earlier, seven such renderings had been completed for a paper of Ruskin's read to the membership of the Edinburgh Mineralogical Society in late July 1884.[25] The precise rendering and careful coloring of the uneven facets of the rock, which made the drawings suitable for lecture demonstration, are typical of Macdonald's meticulous style. For clarity, the rock was set against a neutral background.

A similarly unarticulated backdrop is found behind Kate Greenaway's *Study of Rock, Moss, and Ivy*, painted during her stay at Brantwood in mid-April 1885. The delicacy usually associated with Greenaway's more familiar works, images of children and book illustrations such as *The Procession*, is also found here. Late in life Greenaway recalled that, during a ramble through Ruskin's Moorland Garden at Brantwood, he suggested she "do the Piece of Rock." Ruskin selected what he felt were interesting combinations of stone and plant life and brought them into the studio for Greenaway to paint. Ruskin urged Greenaway to execute a number of paintings of flowers and rocks, which he offered to exhibit on her behalf in London, largely in order to counter what he referred to as the "nonsense" to be seen at the annual exhibit of the Royal Academy. Indeed, Ruskin placed great store in Greenaway's acute sense of observation and her

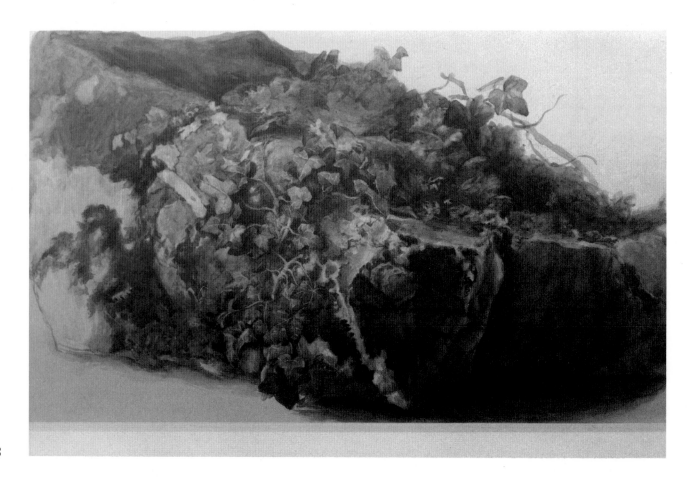

delicate watercolor washes. He predicted great things for her: "I look to you now only for any comfort in English art."[26]

Ruskin's own *Study of Foreground Material* (figure 138) shares with the Greenaway drawing a concern for a skillful notation on what would appear to be incidental, rather commonplace details. But for Ruskin what might have appeared to some as prosaic carried much meaning and worth. The fragile blooms and grasses surrounding and invading the broken surface of the stones focus on the direct, faithful transcription of nature. These careful studies were all suitable for transferring to the print medium for his never-to-be-completed grammars of botany, geology, and zoology planned for young readers.[27]

Ruskin felt it was unnecessary for the British artist to travel to exotic locales to find visual truths: "You all go rushing about the world in search of Cotopaxis and Niagaras, when all the rocks of the Andes and all the river drainages of the two Americas are not worth to you, for real landscape, pathos, and power, this wayward tricklet of a Scottish burn over its shelves of low-levelled sandstone." (33:534)

Admonishing younger artists in 1857 Ruskin wrote: "When a young painter first goes to Nature, he is sure to be charmed by her intricacy in far-away places; and he sets himself to paint what he likes best, not what is best for him. The simpler his choice the better—the door of a cottage, or a rose bush in its garden." (14:138)

The unassuming but accurate transcriptions of the immediate locale found in Greenaway's and Ruskin's sketches have, Ruskin claimed, a grandiose equivalent in the work of Turner: "The foregrounds of Turner

Figure 137
KATE GREENAWAY (1846–1901)
The Procession. October 1, 1884
Watercolor and pencil, 6½ × 11⅜"
Courtesy of the Detroit Public
Library Rare Book Collection

Even while acknowledging, "You do more beautiful things yourself, in their way, than were ever done before," Ruskin cajoled and advised Greenaway on how she might improve her sketches. (37:576) His letters are replete with directives on costume, setting, and color. *The Procession* captures her "minuteness and delicacy of touch," which Ruskin so admired. (32:536) These children, playing at gardening, reflect Ruskin's praise in his lecture "Fairy Land": "Infantine nature in all its naïveté . . . the enchanted smiles of its springtime." (33:343)

are so united in all their parts that the eye cannot take them by divisions, but is guided from stone to stone and bank to bank, discovering truths totally different in aspect according to the direction in which it approaches them, and approaching them in a different direction, and viewing them as part of a new system every time that it begins its course at a new point." (3:492)

Ruskin himself becomes the central element in Frank M. Sutcliffe's photograph of Ruskin (figure 139) taken in 1873. Seated at the base of a wall in his rock garden, Ruskin is surrounded by the tokens of nature he loved so deeply—the winding ivy, weeping ferns, grasses, and broken stones. Intimate associations of place—the garden and lakeside grounds at Brantwood, the rugged Scottish Highlands, the faded and ruined palaces of Venice, and the sublime Alpine terrain of Savoy—possessed Ruskin. His imagination was gripped by the "spirit of a particular place," this poetry of locality produced by an admixture of landscape, history, and memory.[28] There is no place that does not teach the same lesson; speaking of an Alpine valley Ruskin remarked:

> *The village rises again over the forgotten graves, and its church-tower, white through the storm twilight, proclaims a renewed appeal to His protection in whose hand "are all the corners of the earth, and the strength of the hills is His also." There is no loveliness of Alpine valley that does not teach the same lesson. . . . The fairest meadows bloom between the fragments, the clearest rivulets murmur from their crevices among the flowers, and the clustered cottages, each sheltered beneath some strength of mossy stone, now to be removed no more, and with their pastured flocks around them, safe from the eagle's stoop and the wolf's ravin, have written upon their fronts, in simple words, the mountaineers' faith in the ancient promise. . . . "For thou shalt be in league with the Stones of the Field: and the beasts of the field shall be at peace with thee." (6:383–84)*

Ruskin *looked* at nature with the eyes of a poet and amateur scientist; he *envisioned* in his encounters with the simplest and most grandiose rock and stone formations prophecies of humanity's place in the world, and he *saw* Eternal Truths and humankind as powerless against the Divine Spirit's inexorable will to affect that "every valley shall be exalted, and every mountain and hill shall be made low; and the crooked shall be made straight, and the rough places plain."[29]

Figure 138
JOHN RUSKIN (1819–1900)
Study of Foreground Material. n.d.
Watercolor, 7⅝ × 8½″
Ashmolean Museum, Oxford;
Rudimentary Series 133

Ruskin encouraged artists to pay special attention to those tokens of nature closest at hand: "The truths of form in common ground are quite as valuable, quite as beautiful, as any others which nature presents." (3:482) Believing that an honest, devout transcription of nature possessed more merit than most so-called "art," he admonished his students in *The Elements of Drawing*, "If you can draw the stone *rightly*, everything within the reach of art is also within yours." (15:49)

Figure 139
FRANK MEADOW SUTCLIFFE
(1853–1941)
John Ruskin, Seated on a Bank near Brantwood. 1873
Photograph, 5⅜ × 8″
The Ruskin Gallery, Sheffield—The Collection of the Guild of Saint George

Ruskin was fifty-three when he posed for this photograph by Sutcliffe, taken one year after he moved to Brantwood, Coniston, in September 1872. He had suffered a serious breakdown the year before and was fearful that his relationship with Rose La Touche had ended. Nonetheless, he managed to continue his lectures at Oxford and begin his series of letters to the working men of England entitled *Fors Clavigera*. His home at Brantwood provided peace and solitude to him.

NOTES

1. This essay is dedicated to my friend and colleague Donald N. Rabiner (1949–1992).

2. (26: xxvi). Ruskin shared his father's dismay about the inaccuracy of the representation of mountains in earlier art. On September 24, 1854, he wrote: "The grand impression on me in walking through the Louvre often after Switzerland is the utter *coarseness* of painting — especially as regards mountains. No real sense of height or distance — no care, no detail, no affection." (12:472)

3. William Whitaker, "Obituary Notices," *Quarterly Journal of the Geological Society* (London, May 1900) 45, 1x–1xi.

4. Elizabeth Helsinger, *Ruskin and the Art of the Beholder* (Cambridge, Mass., 1982), 3.

5. Herbert Read, *A Concise History of Modern Painting* (New York, 1974), 12–13.

6. Nicholas Penny, *Ruskin Drawings* (London, 1989), 36.

7. Diary entry for July 1, 1849, in John Ruskin, *The Diaries of John Ruskin*, eds. Joan Evans, John H. Whitehouse, vol. 3 (Oxford, 1959), 400.

8. The other scandal is, of course, the famous libel suit brought against Ruskin by James Abbott McNeill Whistler; for discussion see essay by Susan Gordon.

9. (6:368). Found on an adjacent page from this statement is a daguerreotype illustration entitled "Bank of Slaty Crystallines" by J. Armitage, remarkably similar in its effect to the small world revealed in an extract from nature as in Ruskin's drawing *Gneiss Rock, Glenfinlas*.

10. This book not only deals with a wide array of descriptions of crystals, their color and formation, but also digresses into a section on Egyptian antiquities and Greek myth. The lack of a single focus is typical of Ruskin's mind, which leapt from subject to subject with frightening speed. Ruskin had, in fact, published earlier a protracted essay on crystallization, "Compound Crystallines," in *Modern Painters* 4.

11. (26:386). An extended example of Ruskin's habit of posing a series of questions to his listeners after reviewing what his eyes had seen can be found in his address to the Mineralogical Society of Edinburgh in July of 1884, in which he ponders on the nature of colors of certain minerals. (26:374) Ruskin's symbolic association of colors in nature no doubt was dismissed by professional geologists. In the *Deucalion* he argues that the colors of some gems reflect the corruption of contemporary Imperial Britain. (26:192)

12. For a discussion of Ruskin's appraisal of Lyell's theories, see 26:117ff.

13. Charles Lyell, *Principles of Geology, Being an Attempt to Explain the Former Changes in the Earth's Surface, by Reference to Causes Now in Operation* (London, 1830–33), 3:34.

14. Charles Darwin, *The Origin of the Species by Means of Natural Selection, or the Preservation of Favoured Races in the Struggle of Life*, ed. J.W. Burrow (New York, 1982), 316.

15. James Forbes, *Travels through the Alps and Savoy and Other Parts of the Pennine Chain* (London, 1900), 366.

16. Ruskin also was deeply critical of Viollet-le-Duc's glacial theory in *Le Massif du Mont Blanc*. He commented that the author's "quite splendid zeal and industry, had been all wasted." (26:223)

17. In May 1863 Ruskin defended his arguments in the *Deucalion* on the primacy he assigned to myth, allegory, fable, and biblical text over empirical observation. These stories were "incomparably *truer* than the Darwinian — or, I will add, any other conceivable materialistic theory — because they are the instinctive products of the natural human mind, conscious of certain facts relating to its fate and peace; and as unerring in that instinct as all other living creatures are in the discovery of what is necessary for their life." (26:336)

18. (26:115–16). Ruskin was also deeply concerned with the utilization of scientific advances to further the possibilities of war. From a lecture delivered at Oxford on May 9, 1873, he anxiously wrote, "When I spoke, in [my] last lecture, of the vile industries and vicious curiosities of modern science, I spoke of her vile industries, meaning that there is no kind of explosive compound or of machine for the multiplication of death which our *science* is not eagerly and ingeniously producing in perfection." (25:163)

19. From "The World of the Sky," written March 11, 1835. (2:44) For all practical purposes, Ruskin abandoned writing poetry after 1845. In *Praeterita* he acknowledges, "I perceived finally that I could express nothing I had to say, rightly in that manner." As poetry is a form of "self-confession" the poetic works do provide access to what Ruskin was thinking in his early career. Ruskin won the Newdigate Prize for poetry while a student at Oxford in 1839. Collections of Ruskin's poetry were published twice in his lifetime, 1850 and 1891.

20. John Ruskin, *Modern Painters*, abridged version ed. David Barrie (New York, 1987), 114.

21. London Arts Council, *John Ruskin*, introduction by Timothy Hilton (London, 1983), 7.

22. John Ruskin, *Modern Painters* (London, 1860), 5:171–73.

23. From stanza XIII, "The Broken Chain," 1839–42. (2:169).

24. Nick Shrimpton, "Rust and Dust: Ruskin's Pivotal Work", *New Approaches to Ruskin: Thirteen Essays*, ed. Robert Hewison (London, 1981), 61–67.

25. Catherine W. Morley, *John Ruskin: Late Works 1870–1890. The Museum and Guild of Saint George: An Education Experiment* (New York, 1984), 95–96.

26. Rodney Engen, *Kate Greenaway: A Biography*, (New York, 1981), 125.

27. Diana Birch suggests that a careful reading of letter number 67 of *Fors Clavigera* [July 1876], in which Ruskin charts out his scheme to write three *Grammars* that "will embrace as many facts as any ordinary schoolboy or schoolgirl need to be taught" (28.647), demonstrates that Ruskin's moral vision overrode any serious pretensions at accurate scientific observation. Diana Birch, "Ruskin and the Science of *Proserpina*," *New Approaches to Ruskin: Thirteen Essays*, ed. Robert Hewison (London, 1981), 142–43.

28. For a discussion of parallels between Ruskin and Sir Walter Scott's "elective affinity for the poetry of locality," see C. Stephen Findley, "Scott, Ruskin and the Landscape of Autobiography," *Studies in Romanticism* 26 (Winter 1987), 549.

29. *Isaiah*, x1, 4.

"The Germ of a Museum, Arranged First for 'Workers in Iron'": Ruskin's Museological Theories and the Curating of the Saint George's Museum

Susan P. Casteras

At the core of Ruskin's "art of seeing" was a visual system of appreciating objects, which he attempted to codify and apply in his sole museological endeavor, the Saint George's Museum in the working-class city of Sheffield, England. While on many levels Ruskin's formation of the museum's governing organization, the Guild of Saint George, in 1871 was quixotic and doomed to fail, his heartfelt plans for a museum were to some extent realized. An aim of the guild had been to further the issue of education of workers, and the museum, with its teaching collection, was one notable result. Largely funded by Ruskin as well as dominated for the most part by his personality, gifts, and policies, the museum was one of the few aspects of the guild ultimately to survive.[1]

The history and significance of the Saint George's Museum are compelling and play a central role as the culmination of many of Ruskin's theories on art, style, connoisseurship, and museology. In addition to Ruskin's opinions found in other writings, many little-known internal details of this museum, its aims and evolution, are recorded in the unpublished correspondence between Ruskin and Henry Swan, a former student devoted to "the Master," who served as the first curator of the museum. In the 1850s Swan was among the faithful who attended Ruskin's lectures at the Working Men's College; his professional experience included work both as a photographer and as an engraver for Sir Isaac Pitman. An unusual

man (a vegetarian Quaker and spiritualist with a penchant for hobbies such as promoting the use of boomerangs), Swan was hired by Ruskin in 1855 to copy some illuminated manuscripts and engrave a plate for *Modern Painters*.[2] Swan was also directed by Ruskin to give private lessons to the poet and Ruskin protégée Adelaine Anne Procter ("to show her how to lay on gold") and to send a copy of an illuminated manuscript to the famous reformer Octavia Hill.[3] Initially paid forty pounds per annum, Swan served Ruskin tirelessly and actually lived with his family in the cottage, in the Walkley district of Sheffield, that served as the Saint George's Museum. He presided as the curator from his official appointment in January 1876, through Ruskin's bouts of illness and melancholy, until Swan's death in March of 1889.

The idea for the Saint George's Museum seems to have been gestating for some time in Ruskin's mind and was alluded to in his August 1875 letter (number 56) "to the workmen and Labourers of Great Britain" in *Fors Clavigera*. Accordingly, he reported his hope of finding a room in Sheffield, where he proposed "to place some books and minerals, as the germ of a museum arranged first for "workers in iron." (28:395) Even before this, however, Ruskin had confided to Swan the previous month that "the chief point in my own mind . . . is the getting a museum, however small, well explained and clearly and easily seen. . . . Can you get with any

Figure 140
CHARLES FAIRFAX MURRAY
(1849–1919)
Saint George and the Dragon, after
Carpaccio. 1885
Watercolor, 12¼ × 31⅛"
Birmingham Museum and Art
Gallery, England

Ruskin likened his own struggle against the atrocities of industrialized England to Saint George's battle against the evil dragon, and he named his utopian guild after this patron saint of England. Images of Saint George's heroism had, understandably, a special significance to Ruskin. He asked Murray to make this copy of Carpaccio's original, dated 1516, for his Guild Museum but never took possession of it. Murray was a close friend and associate of Rossetti and Burne-Jones, and he ultimately ended his relationship with Ruskin as a guild copyist to pursue an independent career.

Figure 141
JOHN RUSKIN (1819–1900)
Upper part of *Saint George and the Dragon*, after Carpaccio. 1872
Pencil, watercolor, and body color, 13¼ × 19⅛"
The Ruskin Gallery, Sheffield — The Collection of the Guild of Saint George

Ruskin, drawn to the legend of Saint George, found in the battle between the chivalrous knight and the dragon a parallel to the universal struggle between good and evil, vitality and desolution, and his own crusade against modern destruction. Describing Carpaccio's painting in *Saint Mark's Rest* (1877–84) Ruskin wrote, "No dragon that I know of, pictured among mortal worms, no knight I know of, pictured in immortal chivalry, so perfect, each in his kind, as these two." (24:340)

Sheffield help, a room with good light, anywhere accessible to the men who would be likely to come to it? If so, I will send you books and begin with minerals, of considerable variety and interest, with short notes on each specimen, and others of less value, of the same kinds which the men may handle and examine at their end."[4] The two men had evidently debated the matter at some length, as is indicated by Ruskin's reply in the summer of 1875 to his friend. Ruskin said he would ponder the important contents of Swan's (apparently lost) letter and was prepared possibly to "alter my notion of the kind of museum and adopt your friend's plan."[5] If things worked out, he was personally "prepared to meet considerable expense in warming and drying walls, providing I am master of the whole place." In this letter as in others, a practical business side emerged alongside the often tortured, evangelical tones, the stormy emotions, and the desire to control all aspects of the project. (Despite his mental anguish after the 1875 death of his beloved Rose La Touche, Ruskin had the presence of mind to inquire if Swan could locate a solicitor who might work without pay on this endeavor.)[6] His pragmatic interests included sanitation, safety, security, and legal matters.[7] For example, he felt that a "freehold" arrangement for the property was essential and worried about the collection's autonomy and vulnerability to moves or merger due to the interference of politics.[8] With genuine commitment and force he wrote in August 1875, "I am prepared to enter into treaty for the purchase of the . . . detached piece of ground with a building thereon, if it can be bought at a price which I may justify to the members of the Corporation. I will buy nothing for them but on definitely advantageous terms, for any purpose whatsoever; our business is to make things precious when we have got them."[9] Yet, even before the surveyor's report or the deed of sale was ready for the Walkley property (for which Ruskin astutely queried an alleged discrepancy in price of thirty pounds), Ruskin busied himself that fall with packing and elaborately cataloguing his minerals.[10]

From the outset Ruskin seems to have known that the miniscule quarters of the cottage in Walkley would soon prove inadequate. The critics concurred, and ideas to enlarge the space circulated publicly from 1881 on while negotiations were instituted with the Sheffield city council about building a larger museum. Ruskin's ideal edifice was a "two-storied long gallery with skylight on the top story; entered like a barn by external staircase to the top story and well warmed below."[11] He also knew exactly what materials he wanted to use, remarking several months earlier that any brick must be "red, *at least* as dark as a pattern I will have sent. . . . No black, blue, glazed, or yellow brick, nothing but red." Moreover, roofs could not be "leaded or slated," and "no gas or explosive oil" could be utilized anywhere in the structure."[12] He fantasized that his museum might rival the impact of Saint Mark's in Venice, not in size but in effect: "brick with marble casing, so I can get my inner walls built and dry at once, and so at leisure adding panel by panel of decoration."[13] The architect Edward Robson, who was commissioned to design the new edifice, found the project both challenging and frustrating due to Ruskin's suggestions of materials that were unsuitable for the Sheffield climate. Ultimately a combination of legal problems and difficulties with Ruskin ended the realization of a new museum structure, although an extension was built onto the Walkley cottage in 1884.[14] When this additional space was open to the

Letter from John Ruskin to Henry Swan, dated May 6, 1876, illustrating Ruskin's plan for mineral cabinets. The Rosenbach Museum and Library, Philadelphia

public the following year, it contained both a collection of casts and J. W. Bunney's huge canvas entitled *Saint Mark's Venice*.

    With Swan's death in 1889 and Ruskin's worsening mental condition, the trustees and "the Master" voted to accept the offer of the town of Sheffield to borrow all the contents of the Saint George's Museum and place them in a house in Meersbrook Park. As a result, a different institution, with the symbolic name change to the Ruskin Museum, opened in its new quarters in April 1890. This building had several rooms and a professional curator, William White, who created an orderly arrangement and in 1895 wrote *The Principles of Art as Illustrated in the Ruskin Museum*. (That same year the more humble Walkley counterpart, which Ruskin had hoped would remain a storehouse or satellite museum, was sold by the guild and later became a training home for girls, aptly called Ruskin House.)[15]

T he selection of the original site had shocked many people initially, although it was entirely consistent with Ruskin's dream of humanizing and counteracting the woes of industrial capitalism with the power of art and

The Saint George's Museum at Walkley, Sheffield, England

beauty, in this case by choosing a working-class district (where Swan himself already lived) with a large population of working men who could be educated, enlightened, and inspired by the contents of the Saint George's Museum. A commentator for *The Magazine of Art* in 1879 pointed out the incongruity of the unassuming, plain gray building and of Sheffield in general as a backdrop for Ruskin's high purposes, for to him the existence of beauty would be imperiled or destroyed "amid the flame and smoke and sordid ugliness of Steelopolis. . . . The dolorous city . . . would seem to be the grave, rather than the cradle of artistic hopes. Fact—hard, grinding, and repellent—crushes out fancy, beautiful, ennobling and graceful."[16] Understanding the associations of Sheffield as a labor "centre of trade tragedies, the home of trades-union terrorism, the birthplace and inglenook of Broadheadism," he speculated that it was "from the corrupt thraldom of such social heathenism that the religion of Ruskin would deliver us. . . . Mr. Ruskin has placed his museum just where the contrast between town and country, between the work of God and that of man, is seen in most effective contrast." Several years later, in 1888, the same writer reminded readers how paradoxical it was for Mr. Ruskin "to select sunless Sheffield as the casket for his delicate art-treasures." He pointed out how the museum, hidden amid picturesque suburbs and moorland heights, contrasted sharply with the "sordid streets, with buildings suffering from a scrofula of dirt; 'restored churches' . . . noxious vapours, and trees that look like blackened

Ruskin's displays in the museum at Meersbrook Park included intricately worked pictures of architectural facades and decorative details, rendered in watercolor and body color by himself and his hired copyists. Seen in this photograph are Bunney's large portrait of the facade of Saint Mark's Cathedral in Venice (center) and his study of the building's northwest corner. Pictures of the mosaics in Saint Mark's as well as those in Saint Vitale in Ravenna and other sites are also visible. In addition the galleries held casts of sculptural adornments, minerals, shells, and floral specimens.

Figure 142
FRANCESCA ALEXANDER
(1837–1917)
Rispetti. 1881–82
Pen and ink, 15 × 10¾″
Birmingham Museum and Art
Gallery, England

Ruskin met Esther Frances Alexander, whom he called Francesca, in Florence through their mutual friend the American artist Henry Roderick Newman. Ruskin wrote to her mother: "In absolute skill of drawing, and perception of all that is loveliest in human creatures, and in the flowers that live for them, I think these works are in their kind unrivalled, and that they do indeed represent certain elements of feeling and power peculiar to this age." (32:xxi) Ruskin commissioned Alexander's most famous work, *Roadside Songs of Tuscany,* written and illustrated between 1868 and 1882 to preserve traditional Tuscan legends and folksongs. He owned this sheet from the *Songs.*

skeletons. . . . From slag and cinder, from roaring foundries. . . , we come to a pleasant land with fluent air, romantic streams, rocky glens, and ridges of bold moorland, breezy, wild, and undulating." It was a place "just where a painter would have pitched his camp," a meaningful site because it was "at once symbolically instructive and practically sanitary."[17]

The gallery itself was described in a pithy metaphor as "a small room, but probably there is no apartment in the world which crowds together so much that is of unique interest and artistic value in so confined a space. It is a picture-gallery in a portfolio; a panorama in a pill-box. The casket is as commonplace as that which Bassanio selected in the play, but which concealed the real treasure. Mr. Ruskin evidently does not measure beauty by the bulk, or the value of a museum by its immensity; on the contrary, he has been careful to remind his disciples that Saint George's Museum is neither a gasometer, a circulating library, or even the Brighton Aquarium."[18] The effect of this "treasure-box" was corroborated by the

Figure 143
HELEN ALLINGHAM (1848–1926)
Bluebells. c. 1885
Watercolor, 12⅜ × 9⅛″
Harris Museum and Art Gallery,
Preston, England; Haslam Bequest

Bluebells captures two of the qualities
that Ruskin looked for in Allingham's
work: children and rural settings. In
"Fairy Land" Ruskin wrote that Allingham was best suited for "representing the gesture, character and
humor of charming children in country landscapes." (33:341) In addition
to appreciating the charm of Allingham's paintings, Ruskin sympathized with the artist's depiction
of the traditional English terrain and
life that he saw devastated by industrialization.

National Review, whose critic wrote in 1885 that "never did art and culture
find a humbler home than this little room . . . , in which rare stones, fine
engravings, choice pictures, valuable books and manuscripts, are packed so
closely together that one cannot help being reminded of the inside of a box.
Certainly it is a very well-arranged box, and very interesting to trained eyes
and appreciative minds; but to many visitors . . . a continual cause of wonder and perplexity. 'Is that all?' they would say, looking round and round the
tiny room, in which, it must indeed be admitted, there really is NOT air
enough for more than three or 4 people to breathe in comfort."[19]

The Art Journal, on the other hand, in 1882 commented at length
about the significance of the contents, hailing one of the few Verrocchios to
be seen in England as well as two sheets of Mantegna drawings. In the realm
of the fine arts, in addition to some drawings by Turner (owned by Ruskin
himself), the museum was filled with various watercolors by Edward
Burne-Jones, J. W. Bunney, and William Small, copies by Charles Fairfax

Murray and others after works by Vittore Carpaccio, a few early illuminated Bibles, a copy after Hans Holbein, some Dürer engravings, and numerous plates of Turner's *Liber Studiorum*. A supplementary purpose was perceived as collecting "drawings, casts, and photos illustrating the architecture of Saint Mark's Venice." When it was completed, the author hypothesized that this teeming microcosm would offer "a rich mine of wealth to the earnest seeker after knowledge, an ever-fresh oasis of Art and culture amidst the barrenness and gloom of an English manufacturing district."[20]

If the site of the museum occasioned some raised eyebrows, so too, to some extent, did its intended audience. The indigent were not welcome (Ruskin condescendingly stated that museums were not a refuge for "the utterly squalid and ill bred"), nor were the upper classes particularly embraced.[21] Various letters revealed Ruskin's keen interest in the welfare of the workers and even his wish—amid his growing withdrawal from people—to meet some of the men for whom the museum was created. In February 1876 he communicated to Swan, "I should like to meet the men," and in reply to a missive several days later said, "I'm so glad to hear the men are interested."[22] Swan's reports on workers' reactions seemed to whet Ruskin's desire to do things for them, causing him to go into nearly frenzied activity, sending the best frames, minerals, or other *desiderata* to the museum. He cared deeply about the men's reactions to his efforts, material and literary, remarking to Swan in December 1876, "I shall like much to hear what the best men say of [the] next Fors."[23]

In his correspondence, Ruskin typically referred to his audience as "the men," yet most of the principal members or "companions" in the guild's hierarchy were female (in fact, he gave Swan the names of three women in whose names the property, along with all subsequent inheritance conditions, were to be registered).[24] Although he leveled his gaze at "the men," to a limited extent Ruskin also relied upon the "effervescent life and youthfulness" of that "nice creature" Emily Swan, who performed minor curatorial duties in the museum.[25] In speaking of her relationship with him, Ruskin drew the analogy of a "lamb skipping before a broken winded old horse."[26] His reverence for women on one level yet subservient treatment of them on another was characteristic of Ruskin's double-edged attitude toward the women students whom he encouraged and patronized, notably Elizabeth Siddal, Francesca Alexander, and Helen Allingham (figures 142–44).

Whereas the women were cooperative, "the men" did not necessarily conform to Ruskin's high expectations in their motivation and background. As *The Magazine of Art* critic (and others) pointed out, a notice extracted from Ruskin's letter number 59 in *Fors Clavigera* was posted on the garden door to the museum reminding entrants that "a museum is . . . primarily not at all a place of entertainment, but a place of education. And a museum is . . . not a place of elementary education, but that of already far-advanced scholars. And it is by no means the same thing as a parish school, or a Sunday school, or day school, or even—the Brighton Aquarium."[27]

Such caveats notwithstanding, Ruskin did not delude himself by thinking workers would spend a lot of time in his museum; indeed, he

Figure 144
ELIZABETH SIDDAL (1829–1862)
Clerk Saunders. 1857
Watercolor, body color, and colored chalk, 11¼ × 7⅛"
Courtesy of the Syndics of the Fitzwilliam Museum, Cambridge, England

Elizabeth Siddal was influenced by Dante Gabriel Rossetti's early linear, intentionally medieval style. Both artists' fascination with Gothic art, and Ruskin's, was part of a larger, distinctively Victorian interest in and interpretation of that pre-Renaissance period: its piety, romance and chivalry, art, architecture, and literature. In this watercolor, Siddal interpreted Sir Walter Scott's "Minstrelsy of the Scottish Border," a ballad about two ill-fated lovers set in the Middle Ages. The style evokes the poem and its period setting. The gruesome story tells of a young hero, Clerk Saunders, who made love to Margaret May and was then killed by her brothers. In the macabre ending he returned to his love as a ghost. First shown at a Pre-Raphaelite exhibition in 1857, the watercolor was purchased by Ruskin's American friend Charles Eliot Norton. It was subsequently owned by Rossetti, then his brother William Michael Rossetti, and finally by Fairfax Murray.

193

guessed they had perhaps fifteen minutes weekly to devote to such recreation. Accordingly, he felt that focusing on a few objects was far superior to trying to absorb too many things or too much information. He thus advised, "You can no more see twenty things worth seeing in an hour, than you can read twenty books worth reading in a day."[28] This awareness of "object satiation" was quite astute, given the modern application of this term to describe the obsession of some museumgoers with squeezing as much time, culture, and object awareness as possible from a visit, with the concomitant effect of enervating fatigue, if not downright boredom. As quoted in William White's book on "the Master's" museological tenets, Ruskin believed that "the main difficulty which we have to overcome is, not to form plans for a museum, but to find the men leisure to muse."[29] Not only would it be hard to set aside a quarter of an hour weekly to pursue leisure, but also it would be challenging and, in Ruskin's mind, crucial to utilize this time to strike a balance between the daily toll of industrial labor and the restorative enjoyment of the beautiful.

Despite his rather unrealistic hope (as some critics remarked) that his museum would appeal more to advanced connoisseurs/working men than to novices, Ruskin really tried to make the learning atmosphere inviting and stimulating to all. He told a royal visitor that he wanted to provide "pretty things for them to see, and light to read by, and fitting everything close as I do so. And I hope it may be filled by workmen who will join to scientific teaching this study of art and nature, and that it will be felt by the town worth making an effort to fill the rooms with books." (30:313) As such a statement implies, the needs and engagement of the users were uppermost. The library held a pivotal position within this conceptual framework, and books were to be open and available in areas filled with desks and good light. The Saint George's Museum was open daily except Thursdays from nine to nine and by appointment and on Sundays from two to six P.M.; admission was free to students, whose tickets were obtainable on application.[30] Given the flexible, extended hours, including Sunday, it is evident that Ruskin was quite forward-thinking in his efforts to remove numerous barriers of time and access in his appeal to the nonprivileged, nonelite visitor. Moreover, he was aware of the element of comfort for the weary, to which the idyllic setting, study rooms, and availability of food facilities and lodging nearby all contributed.

Ruskin's museological principles and practices were also enlightened and progressive in terms of conservation issues. Especially in his writings on Turner, Ruskin voiced his strong opinions on the subject. Aware of the problem of cracking in the pigments that occasionally disfigured and compromised the surface of some of Turner's pictures, Ruskin was convinced of the expediency of protecting works of art in all mediums under glass. In defending this decision, he argued that such an action would simultaneously prevent injury and preserve the integrity of original hues, regardless of any slight inconvenience caused for spectators by reflections. His consciousness of problems of condition surfaced in his correspondence with Swan, as in a complaint to him in 1879 about how the Verrocchio painting had been transferred from its original panel because of severe peeling and poor varnishing.[31] Ruskin's advocacy of honest objects, unaltered and "unrestored" by other hands or misguided intentions, was surprisingly modern and congruent with his beliefs in other areas.

Besides putting good conservation practices into effect in his museum, Ruskin wanted to create a paragon of installation design. He often criticized institutions for their poor or infelicitous displays of objects, unleashing his invective in scathing prose. With Turner in mind, Ruskin articulated his views on the proper hanging height for paintings, because to him, "The function of a picture, after all . . . is not merely to be bought, but to be seen, it will follow that a picture which . . . deserves a place; and that all paintings which are worth keeping, are worth, also, the rent of so much wall as shall be necessary to show them to the best advantage and in the least fatiguing way for the spectator." Keeping both the work of art and the spectator's line of vision as priorities, Ruskin maintained that large works of art only be lit from above, "because light, from whatever point it enters, must be gradually subdued as it passes further into the room." (13:176) He also believed that "every picture should be hung so as to admit of its horizon being brought on a level with the eye of the spectator, without difficulty, or stooping." Excepting only small pictures under certain conditions, he asserted that "a *model* gallery should have one line only." (13:176–77) This was a somewhat radical suggestion in the mid-nineteenth century, when the typical gallery was a vast, multitiered jumble of works on the walls of the Royal Academy and elsewhere. Ruskin espoused the advanced idea that "some interval [exist or be allowed] between each picture, to prevent the interference of the colours of one piece with those of the rest—a most serious source of deterioration of effect." (13:177) The densely packed, jigsaw effect of many Victorian galleries precluded precisely this kind of individual pictorial autonomy and integrity, yet Ruskin rightly sensed the importance of giving each work sufficient space to generate its own impact, without visual overlap or dissonance from neighboring objects. Generous spacing might affect notice of architectural details and "the gorgeousness of large rooms," and large historical works would benefit from their own special rooms or areas. For example, to achieve ideal viewing conditions for Titian's *Assumption*, "the floor at the further extremity of the room might be raised by the number of steps necessary to give full command of the composition; and a narrow lateral gallery carried from this elevated däis, to its sides." (13:177)

The primacy of the object thus served as a standard for display, and to sustain this Ruskin advised a neutral background. Ruskin's correspondence with Swan confirms that he had the interior gallery spaces at Walkley repainted in white almost immediately (aside from the rooms where Swan and his family resided); he further stipulated, "It is to be as pure white as can be got without poison. Over that I am going to hang curtains fastened down tight,—which can be removed when dirty, and the museum cases are all to be on casters, moveable when the curtains are taken down."[32] This idea of using a plain white background is also amazingly modern, given the preponderance at the time of ornate exhibition rooms with wallpaper, dadoes, knickknacks, and other busy surface ornamentation.

Ruskin also believed that sculpture was the foundation of all painting and should share equal visual status in his installation.[33] He confided to Emily Swan that his aim was for "a small but comfortable gallery for casts of

sculpture, 10′ high, 20′ wide, divided into cells 8′ long, 5′ wide."[34] All this was intended for and integrated with the needs of the visiting student; the sculpture gallery was to be near the reference library and the casts were always to be lit from the left, with "desks below for students to draw on." In an 1885 letter, Ruskin directed his curator to have the catalogues readily at hand and to keep the drawers open for students to inspect specimens, additional affirmations of the high priority he accorded the concept of open and easy availability and usage.[35]

Even seemingly inconspicuous details were thoughtfully conceived and executed. *The Magazine of Art* commented in 1879 on the effective way that precious stones were displayed, "placed upon such silken texture as is best suited to bring out their delicate lustre. This attention to minute detail, indeed, strikes the intelligent observer in all the arrangements of the room."[36] Whether it was the huge Bunney canvas or a rock fragment, Ruskin lent his energies to their optimal display. His creative approaches ranged from putting opals ("best seen in water") under a magnifying glass to inventing an "entirely new Alphabet of mineral arrangement" to appeal to viewers.[37]

As his peevish tone in an 1883 letter to Swan indicated, Ruskin was annoyed by the way other museums exhibited objects and vowed to reform this situation in his own institution. "They have made such an accursed mess of the Natural History British Museum at Kensington that I'm piqued to show what can be done with proper light and illustrations at Sheffield."[38]

Cast and Mineral Gallery, Ruskin Museum, Meersbrook Park, Sheffield, England

Not long thereafter he complained that "the Bird Gallery in the British Museum is a *total* failure in the new building wholly the Architect's fault, and I hope to get the help of the head of the Zoological Department Dr. Gunther to help me in arranging one in our New Museum as it should be."[39] Improvements would include doing away with "weeds or decorative stuff" and using instead *"pure wood* for block support."[40] Once again, these insights were distinctly un-Victorian in feeling; in lieu of the expected clutter and visual or decorative excess, the values of plain, honest viewing of the real thing were openly extolled and at least partially realized in the more

Letter from John Ruskin to Henry Swan, dated May 6, 1876, illustrating Ruskin's plan for mineral cabinets. The Rosenbach Museum and Library, Philadelphia

Figure 145
JOHN WHARLTON BUNNEY
(1827–1882)
The Northwest Portico of Saint Mark's.
c. 1872
Watercolor, 46⅜ × 27½"
The Ruskin Gallery, Sheffield—The
Collection of the Guild of Saint
George

Ruskin met Bunney at the Working
Men's College and employed him as a
copyist from 1859 until the early
1880s. Ruskin commissioned him to
add to his "memorial studies" with this
watercolor of Saint Mark's northwest
portico. The rapid deterioration of architecture on the Continent was a major concern of Ruskin's. He wrote in
1849, "Nominal restoration has . . .
hopelessly destroyed what time, and
storm, and anarchy, and impiety had
spared. The picturesque material of a
lower kind is fast departing. . . .There
is not . . . one city scene in central Europe which has not suffered from some
jarring point of modernisation."
(12:314)

spacious galleries devoted to pictures, minerals, prints, and reading in the
Ruskin Museum.

In organizing the different kinds of art objects for his museum,
Ruskin tried to retain coherence for the viewer as a prominent goal. In
Deucalion he stated, "In all museums intended for popular teaching, there
are two great evils to be avoided. The first is, superabundance; the second,
disorder."[41] At least theoretically (in photographs his museum interiors
still appear crowded to modern eyes), in lieu of excess and chaos, his own

museum was supposed to symbolize a selective microcosm of the real world, synthesizing many fields but doing so with legibility and taste. To attain this clarity with paintings, Ruskin recommended that "the works of each master should be kept together." (13:177) This unity could generate a singular, sustained effect, because to him "the contrast of works by different masters never brings out their merits but their defects." Indeed, he was perspicacious in noticing that mixing artists or styles can sometimes prove visually unnerving or confusing to a spectator, causing one "to throw his mind into their various tempers, [which] materially increases his fatigue." Even if his "evolutionary" or progress-oriented concept of art and artists was by modern standards naive, the desired unity of effect was intended to profit both the object and its viewer, providing a clear advantage "in peace of mind and power of understanding" and enabling a spectator to move without inpediment from the "progress" of one artist's intellect and style to the next. Ruskin also had foresight in suggesting that governments cooperate with "a little reciprocal courtesy" in order to obtain preliminary sketches and studies for notable paintings, collecting these "at any sacrifice" to teach about process and technique. The final disposition of objects should be orchestrated "in the centre of the room in which the picture itself is placed" and supplemented by any relevant engravings. (13:178) He instructed that Bunney's painting of Saint Mark's cathedral (figure 145) which, according to correspondence with Swan, was bought with the museum in mind—be put in a recess at the end of a small room. Complementing this was an army of drawings, studies, photographs, and casts of Saint Mark's and its architecture. The impact, according to an 1888 *Magazine of Art* commentator, was palpable: "Next to the personality of Mr. Ruskin, Venice pervades the place."[42]

In the eternal conflict, then as now, between the so-called container and the objects contained within a museum environment, Ruskin generally advocated minimizing strong architectural qualities or the personality of a room. Avoiding "bold architectural effects" was important so that the individual beauty of the rooms was secondary, not primary, and "by decoration so arranged as not to interfere with the colour of the pictures." Aware that this notion "involved externally, as well as internally, the sacrifices of the ordinary elements of architectural splendor," Ruskin again preferred simplicity and clarity, two words not often associated with Victorian museum interiors. His specific architectural preference was for an arcade configuration within a loggia, with long spaces that could double back viewers by creating outer walls to protect objects from light and to contain niches for sculpture. While a museum was arguably secular, its inspiration, compared by Ruskin to the Baptistery of Pisa, was divine. Everything was aimed at legibility or readability of form and intention in order "to save the visitor from the trouble of hunting for his field of study through the length of the labyrinth; and the smaller chambers appropriated to separate pictures should branch out into these courts from the main body of the building." (13:179) As he reiterated to Swan, "Put everything away but what people can see easily and keep the rest clear and comfortable in the little room."[43]

Despite the emphasis on lucid architectural layout and fields of vision, moralism also invaded the walls of Ruskin's museum both in content and mood. Citing in "Discrimination in Art Teaching" the negative example of the Crystal Palace, Ruskin demonstrated the dangers of indiscriminate juxtapositions, remarking how the placement of the Soho bazaar and Surrey pantomine near Greek statues had proved disastrously unfair to the latter and made viewers who were "abused" by the "indecent" lower art less responsive to the sculpture. (29:560) This error was perpetuated even more seriously at Kensington, "for there fragments of really true and previous art are buried and polluted amidst a mass of loathsome modern mechanisms, finery, and fatuity, and have the souls trodden out of them, and the lustre polluted on them, till they are but as a few sullied pearls in a troughful of rotten pease, at which the foul English public snout grunts in an amazed manner, finding them wholly flavorless." To him, curators had a sacred responsibility as well as absolute authority to exercise their judgment in weeding out anything inappropriate, acknowledging that "even the best Greek vases (perhaps due to sometimes erotic content) must always be entirely unintelligible and useless to the British public." Instead he proposed—and entrusted his own institution to embody—the overriding superiority of "good art, and chiefly of a quality which the British public can understand, or may in time come to understand." (29:560) Longing for an ideal environment "perfect in stateliness, durability, and comfort . . . beautiful to the utmost point consistent with due subordination to the objects displayed," (34:249) Ruskin wanted to counteract the idea that "a great museum in the present state of the public mind is simply an exhibition of the possible modes of doing wrong in art, and an accumulation of uselessly multiplied ugliness in misunderstood nature." (30:305)

As such statements underscore, the power of selection was paramount, and Ruskin himself did not shy away from his own admonitions in this regard. In one of the *Fors Clavigera* letters he expounded upon this "principle of selection . . . only, like all practical matters, the work must be done by one man, sufficiently qualified for it; and not by a council." (28:407) In the case of the Saint George's Museum, it was he who singlehandedly exercised the taste and selection process, personally and almost exclusively superintending its installation during his lifetime. Unafraid to pronounce judgments on what was "good," "bad," or otherwise, as prime mover of his museum Ruskin placed his taste and standards as supreme and handily banned topics like "rogues" and "races." (34:259) To him goodness in art connoted both quality and impact, for objects that inspired were superior to those that were exciting to look at but empty of real worth. Not surprisingly, his goal was to select things that affirmed "the beauty and life of all things and creatures in their perfectness," abjuring skeletons or eviscerated specimens, as well as things which reinforced violent, emotionally brutal, or repulsive values. (34:252)

Was Ruskin's judgment about objects in museums as reliable as he espoused? Certainly he conveyed some radical ideas, for example, in his lack of emphasis on so-called masterpieces and their significance to a museum or its visitors. Yet the Saint George's Museum was ultimately a monument to his own way of seeing and thinking, arranged more according to his personal beliefs, intellect, and imagination than by externally imposed historical or chronological principles. Ironically, he was in some ways liberated by both his idiosyncrasies and his convictions, remaining curi-

PONIFICES · CLERVS · PPLS · DVX MTE S G ɞ ENS

Figure 146
THOMAS MATTHEW ROOKE
(1842–1942)
*The Doge, Clergy, and People of Venice,
Eastern End, South Side of the Choir,
Saint Mark's.* 1892
Watercolor and gold over tracing
mounted on card, 20 × 15½"
The Ruskin Gallery, Sheffield — The
Collection of the Guild of Saint
George

Rooke's first assignment from Ruskin
was an urgent one: to record the walls
of Saint Mark's Cathedral before they
were "restored." Rooke began immediately on the mosaics, including *The
Doge, Clergy, and People of Venice,* that
Ruskin had discovered only two years
earlier, a find particularly significant
for its inscription referring to harmony
between sacred and secular government. Ruskin later called the mosaic
"the most precious historical picture
. . . of any in worldly gallery, or un-
worldly cloister. (24:296) Rooke's first
version was destroyed by fire in 1879,
this replacement was done in 1892 for
the Ruskin Museum.

ously unfettered by some of the more traditional historical, stylistic, and
chronological standards used to classify and display objects.

Ruskin's desire to control and mold the museum environment
extended even to the fabrication of special museum furniture. For example,
he designed wooden frames with special mounts, asking that fifty be
fabricated "to slide into portable boxes."[44] He also designed mineral cabinets and ingeniously fitted them with numerous compartments, lined
interiors (to keep stones from chipping), and outside straps for por-
tability.[45] His chests on wheels (initially made for Whitelands College)
functioned essentially as "hands-on" minimuseums, suitcase versions of the
collection that could travel to branch divisions in schools and elsewhere.
Even these unorthodox museum furnishings and fittings fit into Ruskin's
scheme for the museum as a rational, educational means to encourage
visual and aesthetic experience. Everything, from the walls to the objects
themselves, was chosen for its beauty, quality, and inherent value and was to
be coordinated in an intelligible, sensitive, and harmonious manner.

The accessibility conveyed by the museum and its contents all reflected Ruskin's credos of art education and his hope that they would be realized by the guild and its membership.[46] His instincts were characteristically over-ambitious; in an 1875 letter in *Fors Clavigera*, Ruskin promised he would compose a book list for guild members, including a system of art instruction, and a list of "purchaseable works of art, which it will be desirable to place in the national schools and museums of the company" along with a master list of worthy objects of study in European museums. (28:407) In addition, he suggested a list of suitable library holdings for each household, and indicated that members could borrow books or small reproductive works of art for their homes. The latter was a reassertion of his endorsement of art for the masses, mainly affordable reproductions that brought pleasure as well as inspiration to its purchasers, because to him books and works of art were life-affirming sources of sustenance after food, shelter, clothing, and other necessities.

Within his educational program, the very emphasis on both adult and children as museum audiences was rather modern and liberal. He counseled the inclusion of four key works as a cornerstone for the guild museum curriculum, upholding their innate qualities as sufficient to stimulate the highest and best responses from viewers. In addition to his lists of recommended books and works of art for self-improvement, Ruskin planned a small children's school with its own garden and library in connection with the museum, although he stopped short of agreeing to a playground, asking Swan, "Where are your wits, my dear fellow, do you fancy a library and Museum can be confused with a skittleground?"[47] Perhaps he believed that not only could a new generation of the visually "illiterate" be educated according to his own principles, but also that the "innocent eye" of childhood might be preserved in the perception of works of art if the art instruction were properly organized and administered. At one point he also contemplated adding a possible ironwork school, needlework room, and metal workshop, although he rather testily wrote to Swan, "I have no intention of confusing museum with workshops or studios. I *may* establish both. But not in connection with the Museum *on principle.*"[48]

For viewers of all ages he felt proper cataloguing and labeling were crucial learning aids, and he believed that his mineral catalogues "will make people open their eyes a bit, or I'm mistaken."[49] Whereas his obsession with producing "grammars" as guides to his mineral and other collections bordered on a desire to control aesthetic experience totally, it was perfectly in keeping with his taxonomic fixation evident from *Modern Painters* onward. "Reading" a work of art was both perceptual and literal, and through text Ruskin expanded his own symbolic approach to language and art into the realm of the institutional, ever hopeful that "the men" and others would see how and what he personally saw.[50] The text, like the principles of instruction it served, nonetheless required a considerable amount of self-motivation from artisans, iron workers, and others. Individual learning was the key to success and advancement as a connoisseur, but this necessitated self-discipline, earnestness, commitment, and an implied—almost personal—social contract with Ruskin himself.

Besides the innovations embodied in many of the previous examples, Ruskin showed remarkable foresight in anticipating current museum

Figure 147
HENRY RODERICK NEWMAN
(1843–1917)
View of Santa Maria Novella. 1879
Watercolor on paper, 18¼ × 22¼"
Maier Museum of Art, Randolph-Macon Woman's College,
Lynchburg, Virginia

Trained as a physician, Newman became an ardent disciple of Ruskin after reading *Modern Painters*. He left America for Europe in 1869, settled in Florence, and began a career as a watercolorist. Ruskin commissioned Newman to paint historic buildings in Florence, including Santa Maria Novella, with its marble facade designed by Leon Battista Alberti between 1458–70. The purpose of these commissions was to record for posterity the appearance of beautiful but threatened monuments of historical significance. Many such artistic documents entered Ruskin's Saint George's Museum for the edification of visitors who would never see the originals.

practice in other areas. Beyond his educational imperatives—art, books, and objects on wheels prefiguring branch museums, "lesson photos" (of works by Fra Filippo Lippi, Diego Velázquez, Titian, plus a bas relief) for individualized rates of learning, and the merger of the library with the museum—Ruskin's suggestion that "less is more" for viewers was also decidedly farsighted. The underlying assumption that the educational value gained from scrutinizing a few objects could be greater than exposure to a display of grander size or conception prefigures our own era's reassessment of the small, "in-house" show as an antidote to the unwieldy "blockbuster." Moreover, his emphasis on nonmasterpieces, especially for local museums (national collections might house them instead), is refreshing in spirit. Similarly, Ruskin's attitude to the reproductive work of art was also innovative. He employed various copyists on salary to the guild to work from originals in Europe, and displayed some of their work at the Saint George's Museum. Copying art was consistent with Ruskin's way of learning to see, and his antihierarchical approach indeed suggested that a good

Figure 148
FRANK RANDAL (c. 1858–1901)
Saint Luke, North Side of Choir, Saint Vitale, Ravenna. May 1884
Watercolor, 13⅝ × 5⅛″
The Ruskin Gallery, Sheffield — The Collection of the Guild of Saint George

Reproductions, such as these of mosaics in the church of Saint Vitale (c. 547), were a vital part of Ruskin's program for historic preservation and art education. He wrote, "I am training and employing various artists (one, Mr. Randal, at a fixed salary of £160 a year, others by consistent purchase of their successful work), in obtaining such record as I think most desirable of the beautiful buildings or pictures on which this century occupies itself mainly in completing the destruction wrought during the last six." (30:72)

copy was authentic, creative, and unstigmatized, and to him certainly superior to a mediocre painting. Studying or producing drawings was an important step in appreciating art, and Ruskin wanted his collection of elementary examples to be lent out for students to copy.[51] Watercolors also ranked high in his estimation as a means to appreciate technique and quality, and Ruskin accepted and collected photographs as educational aids in the museum and the classroom.

Throughout Ruskin's pronouncements on museological issues there is the implication that the aesthetics of seeing and the process of

Figure 149
FRANK RANDAL (c. 1858–1901)
Apostle Medallions, Choir Arch, Saint Vitale, Ravenna. April–May 1884
Watercolor and body color,
11⅞ × 7¼″
The Ruskin Gallery, Sheffield — The Collection of the Guild of Saint George

Ruskin fully recognized the importance of the Byzantine mosaics adorning the walls of Ravenna. He sent Randal there in the spring of 1884 to make copies in preparation for a study of the city's art and history. This careful reproduction of the technique, color, and style of the mosaics depicting Saint Bartholomew and Saint Matthew in the church of Saint Vitale was in the collection of the Saint George's Museum.

Figure 150
FRANK RANDAL (c. 1858–1901)
Pescate from Pescarenico, near Lecco.
Spring 1885
Watercolor and body color, $6 \times 9⅝''$
The Ruskin Gallery, Sheffield—The
Collection of the Guild of Saint
George

Frank Randal shared the role of guild copyist with many artists but only Thomas Matthew Rooke can be compared for his prolificacy. Randal worked for Ruskin from 1881 to 1886, submitting to criticism and technical instruction while enjoying Ruskin's support. Ruskin's cajoling nature is suggested in a letter to Randal dated December 27, 1884. The artist had complained about the weather while on holiday and was told, "You grumble at a wet day and don't know what to do with yourself! For shame! What do you think *I* would give to be your age, and able to draw like that! and to be free at Lecco!" (30:1xv)

gaining this insight were more important than the object itself. By extending the traditional boundaries of fine art to embrace the applied arts, copies, and other fields such as natural history, botany, and geology, Ruskin was also radically reinventing the act of seeing in museums. For him it was normal that the natural world be blended with that of the fine arts; thus, zoological specimens could and should be seen and compared with engravings and paintings. The museum was, in effect, a learning laboratory where illuminated manuscripts, paintings, prints, minerals, casts, photographs, and other objects all enjoyed some parity and could equally be available and suitable for study. Ruskin also anticipated some modern precepts of installation in his display, for example, of birds posed in mid-flight, not merely stuffed and static or immured under a glass bell jar. (34:254) His very consciousness of the nonaesthetic ways of experiencing a museum were prescient, too, ranging from his sensitivity to visitor fatigue resulting from object satiation and poor design, his disdain for traditional Victorian interiors in preference for white walls (anticipating the modern high regard for "the white cube"), to his incorporation of study rooms, a garden, and a projected coffee room into the museum. Even his arrangement of works of art was innovative, rejecting traditional hierarchies and chronology to mix various aspects of nature with art in an interdisciplinary, participatory fashion.

As this brief analysis of the Saint George's Museum has implied, Ruskin expected a serious moral and aesthetic obligation—almost a holy covenant—from visitors (whether artisans or aristocrats) to his museum. While it was ultimately impossible for Ruskin to force passion for art or a visual "epiphany" to develop, in his museum he attempted to provide the "raw data" to encourage such revelations and to empower museum visitors with this experience and with the ability to improve themselves, their society, and even their nation. The focus on details, on comparing forms in art with those in nature, could engender both intensity and a sense of discovery in viewers. Indeed, stimulation and discovery through good books, art, and natural specimens were all essential to the process of "the art of seeing."

In the end, the little room at the Saint George's Museum was neither a purely populist chamber nor an elitist "palace of art." Despite its limited size and the fact that Ruskin was not able to realize all of his written goals in this museum, a great deal was accomplished by this "panorama in a pill-box." With a mixture of brilliance, romantic naïveté, realism, and evangelicalism, Ruskin commanded a unique mélange of artistic theory, architectural design, educational programming, moral teaching, and economic policy, all coexisting in the tiny cottage.

In the face of the failure of the guild as an agricultural community as well as other disappointments, Ruskin seemed at times to channel his energies almost fanatically into this utopian project. Although often contradictory in his writings, he was rarely neutral in his pronouncements about objects or the relationship of spectators to them, and in this respect

Figure 151
ARTHUR SEVERN (1842–1931)
Ruskin's Bedroom at Brantwood. 1900
Pencil and watercolor, 11 × 15¾"
Santa Barbara Museum of Art,
Collection of the Estate of Ina T.
Campbell

This painting of Ruskin's bedroom is revealing: It documents the works Ruskin treasured up to his death, including, over the fireplace, a drawing by his father, *Conway Castle*, and a still life, *Grapes and Peaches*, by William Henry Hunt. The remaining works are by Turner. On the upper right wall hangs *Devonport and Dockyard, Devonshire* (figure 44). Though Ruskin argued for the necessity of protecting watercolors from direct sunlight, temperature changes, and filth in his Saint George's Museum, in his own home he chose to ignore these precautions.

his museum might be viewed with late twentieth-century hindsight more as a battleground for social and aesthetic change than as a tame encyclopedic repository. As an experiment in the provinces, the museum perhaps did not fully accord with a contemporary description of its having "nothing crowded, nothing unnecessary, nothing puzzling"; nonetheless, it undoubtedly served as an important personal and institutional response to industrial capitalism and as a prototype for several key modern museological concepts, highlighting for audiences in the nineteenth century as well as the twentieth the talents of Ruskin as prophet, pragmatist, and museological proselytizer. (34:247)

NOTES

1. The Guild of Saint George was Ruskin's attempt to put his ideas and his ideals of humane social organization to practical application. With himself as Master of a strictly ruled, morally sound society, Ruskin planned to develop a model for life outside of the cities by acquiring land and working it for the benefit of the group: "We will try to take some small piece of English ground, beautiful, peaceful and fruitful. We will have no steam-engines upon it, and no railroads; we will have no untended or unthought-of creatures on it; none wretched, but the sick; none idle but the dead." (27:96) It was to be supported by the physical labor of Guild Laborers, Marshalls, Landlords, and, last of all, Companions, whose assistance was financial. Ruskin himself expended considerable energy and money on the guild. Education was an integral part of the overall scheme.

2. These and other useful details on Swan are found in the typescript notes by William S. Allen (son and executor of the estate of George Allen, Ruskin's publisher) accompanying the unpublished collection of letters in the Rosenbach Museum and Library in Philadelphia.

3. These instructions are recorded in Ruskin's letters to Swan dated December 10, 1855, and May 27, 1865, respectively. These letters and all others cited in this essay belong to the collection of "Unpublished Letters from John Ruskin to Henry and Emily Swan, 1855–1876" in the Rosenbach Museum and Library.

4. July 13, 1875, letter from Ruskin to Swan.

5. July 23, 1875, letter from Ruskin to Swan.

6. March 17, 1875, letter from Ruskin to Swan.

7. For example, he wrote to Swan on July 17, 1880, about insurance arrangements, pointing out that "for a lump sum of £3000 if the Alliance will take pictures, books, drawings, and stones in a lump." On the issue of building inspectors, he penned with some exasperation to Swan on May 25, 1882, "You may state to all Sanitary Authorities that I mean my Museum to be as Sanitary as Pisa Cathedral and no Sanitarier!" He referred shortly thereafter (June 5, 1882) to building "an iron, temporary room . . . for our things . . . [that] would be fireproof and warm."

8. As expressed in a July 23, 1875, letter from Ruskin to Swan and also a March 19, 1883, letter to Emily Swan.

9. August 18, 1875, letter from Ruskin to Swan.

10. October 14, 1875, letter from Ruskin to Swan.

11. *Ibid.*

12. March 25, 1877, letter from Ruskin to Swan.

13. February 15, 1879, letter from Ruskin to Swan.

14. A useful modern overview of the Saint George's Museum and its successor is Janet Barnes, *Ruskin in Sheffield: The Ruskin Gallery, Guild of Saint George Collection* (Sheffield, England, 1991).

15. Although many private and public collections in Great Britain hold important works by Ruskin, special mention must be made of four. The Ruskin Gallery in Sheffield maintains and displays works owned by the Guild of Saint George in an integrated manner that reflects Ruskin's own aims. The Ruskin Galleries located at Bembridge

School, Isle of Wight, hold a very rich collection of papers and drawings by Ruskin as well as his followers. It is administered by its curator, James Dearden, who is also responsible for the works in the Education Trust Ltd., displayed at Ruskin's home at Brantwood, Coniston. Current plans are to move the contents of both of these collections to a Ruskin Library at Lancaster University in the near future. The Ruskin Museum, Coniston, is located near Ruskin's home at Brantwood and contains works of art, memorabilia, and a wealth of minerals, shells, etc.

16. Edward Bradbury, "A Visit to Ruskin's Museum," *The Magazine of Art* 3 (1879), 57.

17. Edward Bradbury, "Mr. Ruskin's Museum at Sheffield," *The Magazine of Art* 11 (1888), 346.

18. *Ibid.*

19. E. S. P., "Mr. Ruskin's Museum at Sheffield," *National Review* (1885), 404–5.

20. William C. Ward, "Saint George's Museum, Sheffield," *The Art Journal* (1882), 242.

21. Ruskin also banned "the idle or disgraced." (34:250) Moreover, Ruskin admonished a young lady, "The Saint George's Museum is for working men, not little girls and you must not waste Mr. Swan's time. Go to the National Gallery. That is *your* place for study." As quoted in Catherine W. Morley, *John Ruskin: Late Work 1870–1890. The Museum and Guild of Saint George: An Educational Experiment* (New York, 1984), 57.

22. February 1 and February 14, 1876, letters, respectively.

23. December 24, 1876, letter from Ruskin to Swan. Despite his early enthusiasm, however, later Ruskin glumly wrote to Swan on August 29, 1878, "My ill health will not admit of my making any more experiments, or allowing myself to be involved in the plans and hopes of the British workman in his present state of semiknowledge and diluted morals."

24. On March 17, 1876, Ruskin gave Swan the names of Miss Livesey, Miss Taylor, and Mrs. Talbot and on March 31 instructed his lawyer to transfer property to them. A letter of April 2, 1876, dealt with the specific issues of inheritance, marriage, and property rights thereafter.

25. March 13, 1876, letter from Ruskin to Emily Swan. In a November 10, 1877, letter to her husband, he said of a box of "exquisite flint fossils" he was sending that "Emily must handle them with her best and daintiest care."

26. March 13, 1876, letter from Ruskin to Emily Swan.

27. As quoted in Bradbury, "Mr. Ruskin's Museum at Sheffield," 346.

28. As quoted in Bradbury, "A Visit to Ruskin's Museum," 58.

29. See the introduction by William White in *The Principles of Art as Illustrated by Examples in the Ruskin Museum at Sheffield With Passages, By Permission, from the Writings of John Ruskin Compiled by William White* (London, 1895).

30. These details are noted in Bradbury, "A Visit to Mr. Ruskin's Museum," 60.

31. February 15, 1879, letter from Ruskin to Swan.

32. November 3, 1875, letter from Ruskin to Swan.

33. Ruskin maintained that "painting, if first studied, prevents, or at least disturbs, the understanding of the qualities of Sculpture. . . . The Sculpture Gallery of the Walkley Museum will . . . be arranged on the Master's strong conviction and frequent assertion that a Yorkshire market-maid or milk-maid is better worth looking at than any quantity of Venus de Milos. . . . The Sheffield Art Gallery . . . will show only such examples of the art of Sculpture as may best teach the ordinary workman the use of his chisel, and his wits, under such calls as are likely to occur either in the course of his daily occupations." (30:55–57)

34. January 5, 1877, letter from Ruskin to Emily Swan.

35. July 2, 1875, letter from Ruskin to Swan.

36. Bradbury, "A Visit to Ruskin's Museum," 58.

37. A letter from Ruskin to Swan received August 14, 1876, also suggested that some stones be "enthroned" upon "little separate velvet squares, in gold thread, by my lady friends"; the reference to a minerals alphabet appeared in a letter from Ruskin that Swan apparently received slightly later, on August 29, 1876.

38. November 15, 1883, letter from Ruskin to Swan.

39. December 10, 1883, letter from Ruskin to Swan.

40. December 13, 1883, letter from Ruskin to Swan.

41. As quoted in Bradbury, "A Visit to Ruskin's Museum," 58.

42. Bradbury, "Mr. Ruskin's Museum in Sheffield," 347.

43. May 13, 1885, letter from Ruskin to Swan.

44. March 13, 1876, letter from Ruskin to Swan.

45. He stipulated in a May 6, 1876, letter that "each cabinet was to lock all its drawers in each compartment at once—but by some simple and solid wooden bar—no springs or jacknape patent things."

46. For fuller details and examination of this subject, see Morley, *John Ruskin, passim.*

47. July 19, 1879, letter from Ruskin to Swan.

48. August 20, 1876, letter from Ruskin to Swan.

49. June 17, 1876, letter from Ruskin to Swan.

50. An excellent example of modern scholarship that analyzes the multiple dimensions of Ruskin's use of text as symbolic language and vision is Elizabeth Helsinger, *Ruskin and the Art of the Beholder* (Cambridge, Mass., 1982).

51. May 5, 1882, letter from Ruskin to Swan.

Figure 152
FREDERICK HOLLYER
(1837–1933)
John Ruskin. 1894
Cool platinum print, 7¼ × 8¼″
The Ruskin Gallery, Sheffield — The
Collection of the Guild of Saint
George

In the fall of 1894, Hollyer photographed Ruskin at age seventy-five, no longer active but still revered by many. Referring to Hollyer's image, Canon Scott Holland wrote in *The Commonwealth*, "He lifted his voice . . . in praise of high and noble things through an evil and dark day, and now he sits there, silent and at peace, waiting for the word that will release him and open to him a world where he may gaze on the vision of Perfect Beauty unhindered and unashamed." (35:lxxvi)

1819   John Ruskin, only son of James John and Margaret Cox Ruskin, born on February 8.

1830   First poem, "On Skiddaw and Derwent Water," published in *Spiritual Times*.

1832   Receives birthday gift of Samuel Rogers's *Italy* with engraved vignettes by J. M. W. Turner.

1833   First tour of Continent (France, Switzerland, and Italy) with parents.

1834   Publishes first prose essay on geology in *Magazine of Natural History*.

1835   Second tour of Europe with parents.

1836   Writes defense of Turner in response to a critical review in *Blackwood's Magazine*, unpublished at Turner's request.

1837   Enters Christ Church College, Oxford, as a gentleman-commoner.

1838   Publishes articles entitled *The Poetry of Architecture*, serialized in the *Architectural Magazine*. Tours Lake District and Scotland.

1839   Begins to collect works of Turner. Wins Newdigate Prize for Poetry at Oxford. Meets William Wordsworth.

1840   Meets Turner. Falls ill and makes a ten-month tour of Italy. Becomes Fellow of Royal Geological Society.

1842   Takes B.A. at Oxford.

1843   Publishes *Modern Painters* 1, discussing truth in landscape painting.

1844   Reads A. F. Rio's *La Poésie de l'art Chrétienne*. Acquires Turner's *The Slave Ship*.

1845   First trip abroad without parents.

1846   Publishes *Modern Painters* 2 on theories of beauty and imagination.

1847   *Modern Painters* inspires the work of William Holman Hunt, John Everett Millais, and Dante Gabriel Rossetti.

1848   Marries distant cousin Euphemia (Effie) Chalmers Gray. Tours Normandy studying architecture.

1849   Publishes *The Seven Lamps of Architecture*. Studies architecture of Venice and its history. Joins Arundel Society, an organization for print collectors and graphic-art students.

1851   Death of Turner. Friendship with Thomas Carlyle begins. Publishes *The Stones of Venice* 1. Defends Pre-Raphaelites in letters to the *Times* and his pamphlet *Pre-Raphaelitism*.

1853   Millais on holiday with Ruskin and Effie at Glenfinlas in summer. Publishes *The Stones of Venice* 2 and 3. Formulates his ideas for the Oxford Museum of Natural History. First lectures in Edinburgh.

1854   Marriage annulled on grounds of nonconsummation. Travels to French and Swiss Alps with parents. Publishes *Lectures of Architecture and Painting*. Begins teaching at Working Men's College. Friendship with Rossetti and Siddal begins.

1855   Begins *Academy Notes* on annual Royal Academy exhibitions (1855–59, 1875). Meets Alfred, Lord Tennyson. Effie marries Millais.

1856   Publishes *Modern Painters* 3 and 4, defining great art and artists, the rise of landscape painting as a modern development, mountain form and its influence on human life. Meets Charles Eliot Norton, American admirer and lifelong friend.

1857   Catalogues Turner drawings bequest to nation; delivers in Manchester series of lectures, *The Political Economy of Art*. *Elements of Drawing* published.

1858   Meets and falls in love with Rose La Touche, thirty years his junior. Abandons Anglican faith during an "unconversion" in Turin.

1860   Completes *Modern Painters* 5 in which he equates good composition in art with social help or cooperation, thus signaling a shift from problems of art to those of society. *Unto This Last*, an attack on inhuman economic systems, serialized in *Cornhill Magazine*.

1861   Gives his collection of Turner drawings to colleges at Oxford and Cambridge; travels to France. Deep depression and religious crisis.

1862   Travels in Italy with Edward Burne-Jones and his wife, Georgiana. Publishes *Essays in Political Economy* in *Fraser's Magazine*.

1864   Death of father; cousin Joan Agnew comes to live with family. Writes *Sesame and Lilies*, one of his major essays advocating social reform (published the following year).

1866   Proposes unsuccessfully to Rose La Touche; composes *Ethics in the Dust*. Revisits France and Switzerland.

1867   Publishes thoughts on ideal commonwealth, *Time and Tide*.

1869   Elected Slade Professor of Art at Oxford. Publishes *The Queen of the Air*, a study of Greek mythology.

1870   Establishes his Drawing School and publishes first lectures at Oxford. Tours Switzerland and Italy.

1871   Death of mother. Experiences mental and physical illness. Purchases Brantwood estate on Lake Coniston. Begins *Fors Clavigera: Letters to the Workmen and Labourers of Great Britain*. Continues to lecture at Oxford; publishes *Lectures on Landscape*. Initiates social projects: road mending, tea shop, street sweeping.

1872   Lectures at Oxford through 1875; tours Tuscany and the Veneto and publishes *The Eagle's Nest* and *The Relation between Michelangelo and Tintoret* and *Ariadne Florentina*. George Allen, a carpenter and a Ruskin disciple, becomes Ruskin's sole publisher. Moves to Brantwood.

1875   Rose La Touche dies insane. Ruskin publishes *Deucalion* and *Proserpina*.

1876   Plagued by delirious visions; founds Saint George's Farm at Totley. Winters in Venice.

1878   Attack of mental illness, the exact nature of which is unknown (probably some form of acute depression); each subsequent attack will become more severe. Suspends *Fors*. Whistler versus Ruskin trial begins. Saint George's Guild established and museum opened at Walkley.

1879   Resigns from Slade professorship. Publishes *Notes by Mr. Ruskin on Samuel Prout and William [Henry] Hunt*.

1880   Resumes *Fors* after recovery from mental illness. Visits northern France. Begins *Bible of Amiens*, a study of Northern Gothic architecture (completed 1885).

1881   Second attack of mental illness.

1882   Tours Continent.

1883   Resumes Slade professorship; publishes *The Art of England*. Suffers third attack of mental illness.

1884   Publishes Oxford lectures as *The Storm-Cloud of the Nineteenth Century* and *The Pleasures of England*.

1885   Fourth attack of mental illness. Forced to step down from Slade professorship. Begins his uncompleted autobiography, *Praeterita*.

1887   Left helpless by fifth attack of mental illness.

1888   Proposes, without success, to art student and disciple Kathleen Olander. Last trip to Continent.

1889   Active career ends. Under the care of Joan Agnew Severn at Brantwood, Coniston.

1890   Ruskin Museum at Meersbrook, Sheffield, opens.

1900   Dies of influenza on January 20 at Brantwood.

BIBLIOGRAPHY

Abrams, M. H. *The Mirror and the Lamp: Romantic Poetry and the Critical Tradition.* New York, 1953.

Arts Council of Great Britain. *John Ruskin.* Exhibition catalogue. London, 1983.

Barnes, Janet. *Ruskin in Sheffield: The Ruskin Gallery, Guild of St. George Collection.* Sheffield, England, 1991.

Birch, Dinah. "Ruskin and the Sciences of *Proserpina.*" In *New Approaches to Ruskin: Thirteen Essays*, edited by Robert Hewison. London, 1981.

Boyce, George Price. *The Diaries of George Price Boyce.* Edited by Virginia Surtees. Norwich, 1980.

Bradbury, Edward. "A Visit to Ruskin's Museum." *Magazine of Art* 3 (1879): 57.

——. "Mr. Ruskin's Museum at Sheffield." *Magazine of Art* 11 (1888): 346.

Bradley, J. L. *Ruskin: The Critical Heritage.* London, 1984.

Burd, Van Akin. "Ruskin's Quest for a Theory of Imagination." *Modern Language Quarterly* 17 (1956): 60–72.

——. *Christmas Story: John Ruskin's Venetian Letters of 1876–1877.* Cranbury, New Jersey, 1990.

Butlin, Martin, and Evelyn Joll. *The Paintings of J. M. W. Turner.* 2 vols. New Haven and London, 1984.

Clark, Kenneth. *Ruskin Today.* London, 1964.

Cook, E. T. *The Life of John Ruskin.* London, 1911.

Darwin, Charles. *The Origins of the Species by Means of Natural Selection, or the Preservation of Favoured Races in the Struggle of Life.* Edited by J. W. Burrow. New York, 1982.

Engen, Rodney. *Kate Greenaway.* New York, 1981.

Findley, C. Stephen. "Scott, Ruskin and the Landscape of Autobiography." *Studies in Romanticism* 26 (Winter 1987): 549.

Flaxman, Rhoda L. *Victorian Word Painting and Narrative: Toward the Blending of Genres.* Ann Arbor, 1987.

Forbes, James. *Travels through the Alps and Savoy and Other Parts of the Pennine Chain.* London, 1900.

Gombrich, Ernst H. *Art and Illusion: A Study in the Psychology of Pictorial Representation.* 2d ed. New York, 1961.

Helsinger, Elizabeth K. *Ruskin and the Art of the Beholder.* Cambridge, England, 1982.

Hewison, Robert. *John Ruskin: The Argument of the Eye*. Princeton, 1976.

————. *Ruskin and Venice*. Exhibition catalogue. The J. B. Speed Art Museum, Louisville, 1978.

Hilton, Timothy. *John Ruskin: The Early Years*. New Haven, 1985.

Holloway, John. *The Victorian Sage: Studies in Argument*. London, 1953.

Houghtons, Walter E. *The Victorian Frame of Mind, 1830–1870*. New Haven, 1957.

Johnson, E. D. H. *The Alien Vision of Victorian Poetry: Sources of the Poetic Imagination in Tennyson, Browning, and Arnold*. Princeton, 1952.

La Bossière, Camille R. *The Victorian "Fol Sage": Comparative Readings on Carlyle, Emerson, Melville, and Conrad*. Lewisburg, 1989.

Landow, George P. "J. D. Harding and John Ruskin on Nature's Infinite Variety." *Journal of Aesthetics and Art Criticism* 28 (1970): 369–80.

————. *The Aesthetic and Critical Theories of John Ruskin*. Princeton, 1971.

————. "There Began to Be a Great Talking about the Fine Arts." In *The Mind and Art of Victorian England*, edited by Josef L. Altholz. Minneapolis, 1976.

————. "Your Good Influence on Me: The Correspondence of John Ruskin and William Holman Hunt." *Bulletin of the John Rylands University Library of Manchester* 59 (1976–1977): 96–126, 367–396.

————. *William Holman Hunt and Topological Symbolism*. New Haven and London, 1979.

————. *Elegant Jeremiahs: The Sage from Carlyle to Mailer*. Ithaca, 1986.

Leon, Derrick. *Ruskin: The Great Victorian*. London, 1949.

Lyell, Charles. *Principles of Geology, Being an Attempt to Explain the Former Changes in the Earth's Surface, by Reference to Causes Now in Operation*. 3 vols. London, 1830–33.

Merrill, Linda. *A Pot of Paint: Aesthetics on Trial in Whistler v. Ruskin*. Washington and London, 1992.

Morley, Catherine W. *John Ruskin: Late Works 1870–1890. The Museum and Guild of St. George: An Education Experiment*. New York, 1984.

Norton, Charles Eliot. *Letters of Charles Eliot Norton*. Boston, 1913.

P., E. S. "Mr. Ruskin's Museum at Sheffield." *National Review* (1885): 404–405.

Penny, Nicholas. *Ruskin Drawings*. London, 1989.

Read, Herbert. *A Concise History of Modern Painting*. New York, 1974.

Rhodes, Robert, and Del Ivan Janik, eds. *Studies in Ruskin: Essays in Honor of Van Akin Burd*. Athens, Ohio, 1982.

Rosenberg, John D. *The Darkening Glass*. London, 1963.

Ruskin, John. *Modern Painters*. 5 vols. London, 1860.

————. *Library Edition of the Collected Works of John Ruskin*. Edited by E. T. Cook and A. Wedderburn. 39 vols. London, 1903–12.

———. *The Diaries of John Ruskin.* Edited by Joan Evans and John H. Whitehouse III. Oxford, 1959.

———. *Ruskin in Italy, Letters to His Parents, 1845.* Edited by H. I. Shapiro. Oxford, 1972.

———. *Modern Painters.* Abridged version, edited by David Barrie. New York, 1987.

———. Unpublished letters from John Ruskin to Henry and Emily Swan, 1855–1876. Rosenbach Museum and Library, Philadelphia.

Shrimpton, Nick. "Rust and Dust: Ruskin's Pivotal Work." In *New Approaches to Ruskin: Thirteen Essays*, edited by Robert Hewison. London, 1981.

Sumner, Ann. *Ruskin and the English Watercolour from Turner to the Pre-Raphaelites.* The Whitworth Art Gallery, University of Manchester, 1989.

Sussman, Herbert L. *Fact into Figure: Typology in Carlyle, Ruskin, and the Pre-Raphaelite Brotherhood.* Columbus, 1979.

Tate Gallery. *The Pre-Raphaelites.* Exhibition catalogue. London, 1984.

Viljoen, Helen Gill. *Ruskin's Scottish Heritage.* Urbana, 1956.

———. *The Brantwood Diary of John Ruskin.* New Haven, 1971.

Walton, Paul H. *The Drawings of John Ruskin.* London, 1972.

Ward, William. "St. George's Museum, Sheffield." *The Art Journal* (1882): 242.

Whistler, James Abbott McNeill. *The Gentle Art of Making Enemies.* Rev. ed. New York, 1967.

Whitaker, William. "Obituary Notices." *Quarterly Journal of the Geological Society* 45 (May 1990): lx–lxi.

White, William. *The Principles of Art as Illustrated by Examples in the Ruskin Museum at Sheffield with Passages, By Permission, from the Writings of John Ruskin Compiled by William White.* London, 1895.

Index

Photograph and Illustration Credits

The Phoenix Art Museum and Harry N. Abrams, Inc., thank the lenders to the exhibition *The Art of Seeing: John Ruskin and the Victorian Eye*, named in the illustration captions, for providing photographs for publication. Additional photograph credits are given below:

Alinari/Art Resource, New York: 33, 39, 40, 43, 48, 50, 71
David Briggs Arps: 27
The Bridgeman Art Library: 130
Prudence Cuming Associated, Limited, London: 42, 87–91
Copyright President and Fellows, Harvard College, Harvard University Art Museums: 14, 62, 102, 174
Hawkley Studio Associates, Surrey: 20 (top)
Antonio de Jesus: 21, 61, 145
Courtesy The Leger Galleries: 156
John Mayers, Ltd., Swinton: 105 (top)
John Mills Photography, Ltd., Liverpool: 144
Otto E. Nelson, New York: 17, 58, 132, 140
Godfrey New Photographics, Kent, England; copyright, Guildhall Art Gallery, Corporation of London: 60, 77
Copyright Royal Academy of Arts; courtesy MacConnal-Mason Fine Paintings, London: 66
Frank Taylor, Newport: 15, 41, 67
John Taylor: 177 (bottom)
John Webb: 72, 153 (bottom)

Note: The works of art, primary documents, and photographs on the following pages are reproduced as reference photographs only and were not included in the exhibition *The Art of Seeing: John Ruskin and the Victorian Eye*: 33, 39, 40, 43, 45, 48, 50, 64, 66, 71, 120, 160, 187, 188, 196, 197